YOUR VICTORIAN WEDDING
A MODERN GUIDE FOR THE ROMANTIC BRIDE

GEORGENE MULLER LOCKWOOD

WITH PHOTOGRAPHS BY TOM ECKERLE

Prentice Hall

New York   London   Toronto   Sydney   Tokyo   Singapore

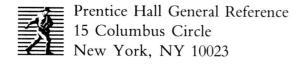 Prentice Hall General Reference
15 Columbus Circle
New York, NY 10023

Library of Congress Cataloging-in-Publication Data

Lockwood, Georgene Muller.
    Your Victorian wedding : a modern guide for the romantic bride /
Georgene Muller Lockwood : with photographs by Tom Eckerle.
        p.   cm.
    Includes bibliographical references and index.
    ISBN 0-13-932724-X : $40.00
    1. Weddings—Planning.   2. Wedding etiquette.   I. Title.
II. Title: Victorian wedding.
    HQ746.L63   1992
    395'.22—dc20   91-43022
                                                              CIP

Tom Eckerle photos © Tom Eckerle

Design by Frederick J. Latasa

Manufactured in the United States of America

10 9 8 7 6 5 4 3 2 1

First Edition

ACKNOWLEDGMENTS

So many people helped me retain my sanity, find sources, and generally keep on track, but there are a few who added that extra something. My special thanks to all the brides who shared their personal Victorian wedding experiences with me; to my husband, who read every word, no matter when I asked; to Amanda and Rachel, who never failed to ask, "How's the book coming, Mom?"; to June Hansen just for being who she is; to my stepsons, Jim and Jon, and their wives for allowing me to be a part of their wedding days; to Janet Burgess, Kari Geiger, Debbie Cole, Scot Fritz, Fred and Jessie Storms, and Josie Nigro for their practical advice, information, and encouragement; and to the late Arnold Brackman, who was there at the beginning.

CONTENTS

Overleaf: Photo by Tom Eckerle.

To my husband, Jim Lockwood, the world's most original romantic; and to my children, whose energy and love have always been my inspiration.

INTRODUCTION

This book was written to help those of you with an interest in the Victorian era and style create a wedding with as much or as little period detail as you desire. It's intended as a sourcebook of ideas and resources for every aspect of your Victorian wedding—from the most exquisite wedding gown you can imagine to flowers that symbolize your love for each other and food people will remember for years to come. Hopefully, it may serve some additional purposes as well.

For those who are not specifically creating a Victorian wedding, but have an interest in the past, I hope this book will serve as a model for becoming immersed in any time period and re-creating it for modern events. Many of the sources I've listed here, particularly books and other print sources, cover historic periods besides the nineteenth century.

I also hope that *Your Victorian Wedding* will be a book you'll turn to again and again. I've planned each individual chapter as a springboard for future interests—perhaps you'll be inspired to become an avid gardener or wildflower enthusiast, a Victorian epicure or vintage dancer, an antique jewelry collector or a calligrapher—in your new life together. Or you may come away with a yen to learn more about your Victorian ancestors and bring elements of that more gracious time into your own. All this would be an added bonus, and nothing could please me more.

The ideas gathered here come from the personal experiences of brides and bridal professionals all over the country, some of whom created Victorian weddings and others of whom re-created another period for their special event. Sources were assembled from recommendations, both from individuals and from other publications. Whenever possible, resources were personally evaluated.

There are many ways for you to use this book, and it's designed to be flexible. It's not at all my intention to dictate how your wedding *should* be, but instead to suggest ways for you to personalize and make it perfect for you.

So, welcome to *Your Victorian Wedding*! May your day fulfill all your hopes and dreams.

Overleaf: Photo by Tom Eckerle.

PART I

PRELUDE

TO

HAPPINESS

There is only one happiness in life, to love and be loved.

GEORGE SAND

CHAPTER ONE

COURTSHIP, PROPOSAL, AND ENGAGEMENT

And on her lover's arm she leant,
And round her waist she felt it fold,
And far across the hills they went
In that new world which is the old.

Tennyson

So, you're engaged. Or about to be engaged. Or wishing you were engaged and fantasizing about your dream wedding. Whatever state you might be in, a Victorian wedding is something you're pondering.

Well, let's get into the spirit right from the start. Why don't we peer back in time and see what a woman contemplating marriage in, say, the 1850s might be concerned with? How might she select a husband? How would she symbolize her acceptance of his proposal? Once engaged, how would her life change and what kinds of activities might she be busy with?

Did you ever think of keeping a journal or diary of your courtship? Many young nineteenth-century women did just that, and they were filled with the same joys and trepidations that modern brides experience.

Although we're not usually separated by the distances that many Victorian couples were, maybe you and your love can rediscover the art of writing love letters; so what if the lovers live in the same house? Some of the greatest romantic correspondences we know evolved during the Victorian period.

Or maybe the sentimental tokens of affection exchanged during a Victorian courtship would be fun to give now: a locket, an antique coin, a portrait, or perhaps your own sketch of your beloved.

Today, there are no strict rules to be followed and few are slave to custom, but by choosing to revive some of these romantic ideas from a more innocent age, we might just add some art and beauty to events as old as history—falling in love and getting married.

OTHERWISE ENGAGED

In Victorian times, deciding to marry effected many changes in a couple's life. A successful courtship ended with a proposal, its acceptance, and plans to be wed.

Early in the nineteenth century, young men and women got to know each other in a casual way. But by the end of the century, strict rules and customs, especially for those in wealthy society, governed this aspect of life (as it did all others). Playing parlor games at home (under Mother's watchful eye), sitting on the front porch swing, and taking a walk (chaperoned, of course) gave couples little opportunity to be alone.

Then, with the advent of the bicycle and a new abundance of public entertainment (many a couple discovered the new intimacy of the darkened theater), courtship slipped away from the vigilant parental eye and was conducted under new self-imposed pressures and detailed codes of behavior.

For a fascinating study of how ideas and customs surrounding courtship and marriage evolved throughout the century, you might enjoy reading Ellen Rothman's book

There is no happiness comparable to that of the first hand-clasp, when one asks "Do you love me?" and the other replies "Yes."

Guy de Maupassant

Hands and Hearts: A History of Courtship in America (see appendix). Her research is largely based on the diaries, letters, and journals of both men and women winding their way down the road to romance. Reading them may give you some ideas for your own romantic journal or correspondence.

One thing is certain: the engagement period had one fundamental purpose—to serve as a transition from single to married life. It was, and still is, a private journey toward a publicly symbolized rite of passage. Yes, it included the usual wedding preparations and flurry of activity to get the new home ready, but it really wasn't until late in the century that weddings were such terribly elaborate affairs. The emphasis was on getting to know one another and preparing for the future.

For the young Victorian couple, marriage meant moving into separate spheres. Although a woman may have had a job before marriage, once married she was to devote herself to creating a home—that stronghold of values and source of all happiness. Many a prospective bride felt ill-prepared for the heavy responsibilities of being moral guardian of her family and manager of a large home with servants and longed to preserve her "girlhood." The man, on the other hand, was to become more involved "out in the world," if he were to be successful and provide for his family. That's why this transition period was so important; there were entirely new roles that had to be assumed once the marriage vows were exchanged.

The courting couple would spend evenings at the woman's home, playing games, reading aloud, making fudge, singing, and playing the spinet or pump organ. They attended parties, dances, church socials, and musical events.

Today, our mobility, changes in the workplace, and the vast array of entertainment available to us create entirely different circumstances for courtship. Many couples live together before marriage. Women expect to continue their careers and men are expected to take an active part in building and maintaining a home. Yet the engagement period is still one of transition. Once the decision to be married has been made, many couples say they experience a shift in the relationship. A new sense of commitment is present.

Still, some of the innocent pleasures of courtship from a bygone era are perhaps worth rediscovering. On one of our earliest meetings, after other company had departed, my future husband sat beside me at the piano and we sang old love songs from the thirties and forties. In those few hours at the Steinway I'm convinced we fell in love. The traditional twentieth-century date of dinner and a movie could never rival our musical "date" in my mind.

There's also a trend toward creating the home as a retreat from the cares of the world, much the way the Victorians did. Comfort, beauty, a melding of tastes and interests—the home was a place for renewal and sustenance.

Our interest in Victorian decorating and lifestyles may very well reflect a renewed sense of home and hearth as a refuge from a hurried and troubled present, what modern social observers are calling "cocooning." In a world where high technology leaves us longing for a more intimate, "high-touch" atmosphere, it's no wonder there's a resurgence of interest in periods during which attention to physical, emotional, and spiritual details mattered.

Although women today seem to know that to be powerful is to be female and don't want to go back to the social repression of the Victorian era, they still want to express the feminine side of their nature much the way women did then. They know they can be strong *and* gentle, and their homes reflect this.

A book on alternative ways to wed written in the early 1970s proposes, wisely I think, that there are six basic values underlying a wedding ceremony: celebration, expression of uniqueness, symbolic beginning, honesty, participation, and respect. It seems to me that if you keep these things at the forefront as you enter this period of engagement, it will be a time that only deepens the bonds of love. With these values as the foundation of your relationship and the goals of your wedding ceremony, you can't possibly go wrong.

You're not only planning a wedding, you're telling

the world your sentiments. Together you're embarking on an adventure. It can be either an ordeal or an opportunity to create grace and meaning. It can keep you apart with separate activities or it can be a process in which you discover one another. I am honored that you've chosen to take me along!

For some of us, this is not the first time. But this time should be the only time. This marriage is unique and stands on its own.

This book is designed to show you how to make your Victorian wedding a truly creative enterprise—how to not only plan a day but to evoke an era, perhaps even define a lifestyle. Its aim is to show you how to avoid the slick, packaged, factory-style wedding and invent an experience that will light your way into the future. *Your Victorian Wedding* will help you have the wedding of your dreams— whether you're on a tight budget or have lots of money set aside, whether you've got plenty of help or are doing everything yourself.

Throughout, I'll encourage you to learn more about this fascinating time you've chosen as a frame for your present-day wedding celebration. I'll send you to galleries and museums, to bookstores and libraries. I'll also pose questions . . . questions to ask yourself that will help you decide just how far you want to go with your theme. Do you want a thoroughly accurate recreation of an 1850s wedding, for example, or would you rather observe the occasion in a more modern fashion with a few Victorian touches for elegance and romance? You decide; I'll be your guide.

As with most things, the more energy, concentration, and love you put in, the more you will receive in return. If you dive in and immerse yourself in another time, you might just find yourself with one foot in the past century and the other about to enter the next! But above all, your experience should be fun, both for you and for everyone celebrating with you.

✢　✢　✢

Communicating Your Love

So, here we are, present-day Victorians. We have telephones with answering machines, faxes, and overnight delivery services—instant communication. Yet we long to hear the words of love. We send more greeting cards than ever before. Romance novelists abound. And love songs still sound as sweet.

To the Victorians, the written word was the window to the heart (and sometimes saved them from embarrassment). Gentlemen could have small cards printed that politely asked a lady whether he could walk her home. She might answer by resting her fan (if she were carrying one) on her right cheek (which meant yes), or she could hand back the card with the appropriate corner turned up—one meaning "yes" and the other, "no," as indicated by symbols conveniently printed on opposite sides.

Victorians were prolific letter writers. I still believe the letter is one of the most underrated forms of communication, and I think we should reinstate it as an art, if only motivated by its cost-effectiveness.

Although my husband and I have rarely been separated for any length of time, I've been wishing for little bundles of ardent missives I can tie with a ribbon and keep in a box in the attic. As we grow old together I'll take them out and reminisce. . . . He promises me he'll oblige.

What a wonderful surprise to receive a scented love letter in the mail, filled with words thought of in solitude that one might forget to say in the hectic bustle of day-to-day living! Or you can leave them on a pillow, in a briefcase, on a dresser, or at the breakfast table (if you happen to leave first). Just be careful they don't get into the wrong hands!

If you think romantic thoughts and can get them onto paper, you'll have written the best kind of letter. But if you're stumped for words, you can read some of the best poets—the Brownings, the Rosettis, Keats, and Shelley, as well as Shakespeare's sonnets and those of John Donne (some of my all-time favorites)—and letter writers. I've given you a list of some places to look in the appendix.

There is only one situation I can think of in which men and women make an effort to read better than they usually do. When they are in love and reading a love letter, they read for all they are worth. They read every word three ways; they read between the lines and in the margins. . . . They may even take the punctuation into account. Then, if never before or after, they read.

Mortimer Adler

And speaking of poetry . . . why not try your hand at some? Oh, come on, it's not really *that* difficult! Victorians loved to write poems and essays commemorating important occasions; why not you? If they needed some help, say, to write a Valentine verse, there were little booklets called "Valentine Writers" (see appendix), from which they could select phrases to express their thoughts.

I ran across an absolutely delightful book in the library, a sort of modern-day "Valentine Writer." It's called *Pearls of Love: How to Write Love Letters and Love Poems* by Ara John Movsesian. Movsesian, a licensed architect and award-winning published poet, has produced a practical guide that's like having your own personal friend named Cyrano to help you get those *mots d'amour* down on paper.

The following, the book's inscription, gives you some idea of its spirit:

Words *that fit your heart's intent;*
Words that seem so Heaven sent;
Words that flow with feelings true,
Are found within to be used by you.

These letters, poems, quotes and such,
Are here for you to add your touch.
Transform them well to suit your needs;
These words of love will do good deeds.

So when the words are hard to find,
And you have really wracked your mind;
Use these "Pearls of Love" to say,
"I love you" in a special way.

Not "serious" poetry, but then, who said love had to be serious?

The Proposal

Words that shouldn't be overlooked are those contained in the proposal of marriage. It may not seem terribly important now, but in years to come those words will resonate in your memories.

You might drop a hint when the two of you are talking of marriage that you'd like the proposal to be a special event and that the setting is important to you. You can recount a story of a famous proposal or one made by someone you know. Once, at a dinner party we gave, the conversation drifted to matters of the heart. Each couple recalled how they met and how one or the other actually proposed marriage. It was one of the most misty-eyed evenings I'd spent in a long time.

I actually proposed to my husband (all right, I forgot my Victorian manners, but I was in love—and besides, Queen Victoria did it!), and there's a funny story that leads up to it that we both tell, adding new embellishments each time.

These stories, the romantic history each couple develops, can take on almost mythic proportions as years go by. Don't follow any script . . . be creative, but *do* make it count. These are the details that warm the heart on a cold winter's eve. Remember, what leads you to your wedding day is a proposal, however put, whenever spoken. It asks a question and begs an answer—the answer is "yes." Make lots of proposals to each other: "Would you like to take a quiet walk?" "Would you like me to rub your back?" Proposals are, quite simply, opportunities to say "yes."

Symbolizing Betrothal

Victorian men and women exchanged rings or other love tokens to symbolize their intent to marry. They felt the ring was an especially appropriate symbol because its endless circle stands for constancy and eternity, deeply held Victorian values. The wedding ring was even called a heavenly circle in some religions, because it is without beginning or end.

I've come to bring this little ring,

I'll put it, sweetheart, on your hand,

The days will pass and soon m'lass,

Before the altar we will stand.

Popular Victorian verse

Alternatives to a ring might have been hair combs, a bracelet, a locket, several small trinkets, a fan, a pair of beautifully made gloves, or a jeweled clasp for a woman. Studs, cuff links, a watch, or a key chain might be given to a man. Either could be given a silver Bible case or special box.

Rings associated with engagement became common in the 1840s. Rings with gems set in a row, the first letter of the gem's names together spelling out a word, were very popular. For example, a **r**uby, **e**merald, **g**arnet, **a**methyst, **r**uby, and **d**iamond would say "regard."

A hand and heart together or clasped hands that when pulled apart reveal a hidden heart were also favored. Tied bows or buckles, symbols of fidelity, were fashioned into wedding bands and sometimes worn by both husband and wife. Multicolored bands of white, pink, and yellow gold, sometimes in flower motifs and set with small gems, were also used as wedding bands.

A popular motif, since it was Queen Victoria's favorite and was used for her engagement ring, was the coiled snake, which wrapped around the finger several times and might have jewels for eyes. This could be used as an engagement ring or wedding band if the tiny reptile suited the taste of the wearer. It might also be an interesting choice for a man, even though these were more commonly worn by women.

There are many beautiful rings from the Victorian period that, although perhaps not intended then to symbolize betrothal, may be used as engagement rings today. There are lovely filigree ones with diamonds or other gems. Or you could use a birthstone ring.

Garnets were extremely popular and varied greatly in color and treatment. These are quite reasonably priced today and are more readily available than some other gems (although even these are disappearing, as antique jewelry collectors are born every year). You can choose from different hues—from the more purple "almandine" garnet to wine red ones, often combined with pearls (and these were real pearls, mind you, because cultured pearls were not yet used in the nineteenth century).

Symbolic jewelry, such as these reproductions of a "hidden heart" ring, were popular love tokens. *Photo courtesy of Abigail's Heirlooms, Newport, Rhode Island.*

Some other popular styles of the period were cluster rings (having a stone in the middle with smaller stones set around it), the crossover style (displaying a kind of an S with gems set at either end), and the half-loop (the lower half of the circle is a simple narrow band; the upper half is set with gems of the same size in a row).

Whether you choose an antique, reproduction, or modern ring, I'd like to suggest letting your beau make a selection of several in his price range. He could then have them put aside for you to see. You'd choose a few favorites and he could make the final choice on his own. I think this is a great way to bring him into the picture right from the beginning, and his choices (which, by the way, probably reflect his vision of you) might be quite revealing.

Another unusual type of ring you might want to consider is the gimmal. It dates back to Elizabethan times, but was used long after. A set of three interlocking rings that comes apart, one was worn by the groom, one by the bride, and one by a witness during the engagement period. On the wedding day, all would be joined on the bride's finger.

There are two-piece rings available that might be used the same way for just the bride and groom, especially if the groom doesn't intend to wear a wedding band. Or two such rings could be purchased and each of you wear half of your own ring and half of your partner's. At the ceremony you each would receive your half back. Although an old ring of this type is a rare find, there are reproductions available or they can be made up for you.

An antique ring has the advantage of being unusual (you're certainly less likely to see one just like it on someone else's finger) and it often offers greater value in terms of materials and craftsmanship than a new one. Remember, during the Victorian era some of the most accomplished craftsmen were emigrating from Europe, bringing their techniques for making exquisite handcrafted jewelry with them from the Old World.

To locate an antique ring, look for sales of estate and antique jewelry in local newspapers and antiques weeklies, check with area jewelers and ask whether they sell estate and vintage rings, and consult your local yellow pages for antiques dealers who may either specialize in old jewelry or know who does.

Be advised, however, that *estate* doesn't necessarily mean "antique." The term simply means that someone has died and that person's belongings are being sold to settle his or her estate. Much of what you'll find there will be modern, but then there's always the occasional antique family piece that makes these sales worthwhile.

If you're thinking of buying an antique ring, here are just a few things to keep in mind before you buy:

- ✧ Are you buying from a reputable dealer? Consider how long dealers have been in business and their reputation.

- ✧ Ask to have an independent appraisal. You should get another opinion as to the quality of the gems and the setting, the ring's authenticity, and whether the price is reasonable. If the dealer is reluctant to let you get a ring appraised, don't buy it. *Warning*: It was extremely common in the Victorian era to use paste (leaded glass) gems in precious metal settings. An amateur would be hard put to tell the difference. That's why a jeweler's appraisal is essential.

- ✧ Is the dealer offering any kind of warranty? How long does it last and what does it cover? Make sure you get the warranty in writing.

- ✧ Can the ring be enlarged or made smaller without compromising its design or durability? If the ring is enameled (often true of Victorian antiques), it can't be sized.

- ✧ Bring a ten-power jeweler's loupe (like a magnifying glass) and check for scratches, imperfections, and poorly done repairs.

- ✧ You should definitely have a jeweler check the settings to make sure none of the stones is

With a little research and patience, you can find lovely antiques suitable for engagement rings and wedding bands, as well as gifts for the groom-to-be. *Photo courtesy of Abigail's Heirlooms, Newport, Rhode Island.*

loose, especially if you are buying from an antiques dealer rather than a jeweler.

✣ If the ring has *sterling* or *14K* stamped on it, it's not Victorian; these marks were used after the turn of the century.

✣ Educate yourself about gem cuts. Methods for cutting diamonds in the nineteenth century were less advanced, and simpler cuts like rose and old mine cuts were used. Silver was more often used with diamonds than gold (platinum and white gold weren't in use until the turn of the century), because craftsmen of the period believed it showed off the simpler gem cuts better.

I think the custom of using an ancestor's ring is a wonderful one, too. Had my grandmother's engagement ring not been taken in a burglary, I might be wearing it as my own. Instead, my husband and I found an early twentieth-century filigree ring like none I've ever seen before in an antiques store. I delight in wearing it and fancy it once belonged to someone as wonderful as my grandmother.

If your fiancé-to-be hasn't suggested it, you might ask whether there's an engagement ring in the family he'd like to use. If there is but it doesn't quite suit your taste, you might consider having the stones reset in an antique-style setting you do like. This may be an acceptable compromise, depending on the feelings of the ring's current owner. As always, be delicate, be considerate, and use good judgment.

There are more and more good nineteenth-century reproductions cropping up, not only in jewelry but in china, silver, and linens. Familiarize yourself with the styles of the period, so you know the design elements you like. Then check into some new rings created from old designs. I've included sources for you in the appendix. You can also show your ideas to some creative jewelers who make pieces to order. They'll work with you to duplicate the ring you want.

Rings given to men as engagement gifts or love tokens were not uncommon. I once gave my husband a handsome silver ring with a malachite stone for his birthday, which he wears every day in addition to his wedding ring. Something similar could easily serve as a man's engagement ring, as could a classic signet ring.

Although you might find a "set" of both engagement and wedding rings designed to match, this won't necessarily be the case. The majority of Victorian women wore a plain gold band and men often wore no wedding ring at all. You can be looking for a band at the same time, however, and find something quite compatible. You also might want to consider wearing your engagement ring on your right hand, a common practice of the period, if finding a band that looks good with it proves to be difficult. Or, once you've chosen your ring, you can design a band to complement your choice and have it made to order.

Before you actually head off to Forty-seventh Street in Manhattan (the jewelry district) or your local antique-jewelry dealer, here is a selection of books you might consult

The Meaning of Gems

Emerald. Domestic bliss and success in love

Ruby. Warm flame; legend has it that the ruby, a popular engagement ring, will darken if love is not true; also assigned the power to ward off evil spirits and prevent bad dreams

Amethyst. Perfection, faithfulness, and sincerity; believed to ensure a husband's love

Sapphire. Truth and faithfulness; good health and good fortune

Garnet. Constancy and true friendship; something of a love charm in folklore, having the power to influence someone to love the giver

Diamond. Matrimonial happiness; courage; protection from evil spirits; innocence

Aquamarine. Helps wearer read another's thoughts; endows wearer with courage and intelligence

that are readily available through your interlibrary-loan system:

+ *All About Jewelry*, by Rose Lieman Goldemburg (Arbor House, 1983)

+ *The Diamond Ring Buying Guide: How to Spot Value and Avoid Ripoffs*, by Renee Newman (International Jewelry Publications, 1989)

+ *Engagement and Wedding Rings: The Definitive Buying Guide for People in Love*, by Antoinette L. Matlins, Antonio C. Bonanno, and Jane Crystal (GemStone Press, 1990)

+ *Buying Jewelry/Everything You Need to Know Before You Buy*, by Anne Bingham (McGraw-Hill, 1989)

+ *Buying Antique Jewelry/Skipping the Mistakes*, by Karen Lorene (Lorene Publications, 1987)

✤ *Answers to Questions About Old Jewelry 1840–1950*, by Jeanene Bell (Books Americana Inc., 1985)

If you have any trouble locating these books through your own library, most can be purchased from the Gemological Institute of America, listed in the appendix.

If the ring's design allows (even the thinnest band usually can be engraved), you might want to consider adding a personal inscription.

It's always fun to look inside antique rings for an inscription (don't forget to bring a jeweler's loupe). If the ring you've chosen already has one, you may decide it adds a special charm and want to leave it be. Or you can have it buffed out and put on your own inscription.

ANNOUNCING THE ENGAGEMENT

For the Victorian bride-to-be, an announcement of engagement might have been as simple as having the gentleman in question sit with her in her family's pew at church. Or a few words may have been said from the pulpit. The bride would then write personal notes to her circle of friends and the groom to his, telling of their impending wedding. Announcements could be made in the newspaper, as they often are today, and sometimes formal printed announcements were sent out.

Somehow the idea of sending out formal engagement announcements seems outdated and not worthy of being revived. They always appeared to me to be an appeal for gifts, but you certainly can specify that no gifts be sent if you are truly set on formal announcements.

Announcing your engagement might be a wonderful excuse for a party! If it also employs the Victorian theme, it can easily be used to set the tone for the whole wedding and get people participating right from the start. How about a tea or Victorian Valentine party (if that's appropriate to your date) or a *fête champêtre*? (See chapter 7 for menus and other suggestions for each of these and more.) Or you could all gather for an outdoor croquet party.

To add to the fun, you might want to refrain from mentioning the purpose of the gathering and announce your engagement then and there (which could be made by the bride's father, the two of you, or a close friend). Then, with glasses raised, all those present can salute the happy couple with a toast.

Engagement signals the start of a busy time of planning and arranging. But before you both get caught up in the hectic whirl, answering the obvious questions of when, where, and how, there are important questions to ask.

What, exactly, does your wedding day mean to each of you? It wouldn't be a bad idea to go off separately and put this on paper in your own words—creating individual "wedding wish lists." You may discover that you each have very different expectations for your wedding day and you'll want to make every effort to plan the day you've *both* imagined.

Think, too, about what you want the people who participate in your wedding, either as attendants or guests, to come away with. Visualize their faces, peer into their hearts, and see if this special day for you could be of even greater value. Focus out on the needs and enjoyment of others and you will be blessed manyfold with a most spectacular day.

What about the "feel" of your wedding? Do you want an atmosphere of grandeur and opulence or one of homey intimacy? What do you want to create for yourselves and everyone present? The Victorian theme is easily adaptable to just about any effect you can envision. It can be serious or lighthearted, grand or simple. You decide, and don't lose sight of these desires. They will guide you through the entire planning process and beyond.

Getting Help

In times past, when extended families lived near one another and childhood friends stayed their whole lives in the same town, planning a wedding was almost a community activity. Mom, sisters, aunts, cousins, and girlfriends were there for support and to provide the many hands needed to get things done.

Love should run out to meet love with open arms. Indeed, the ideal story is that of two people who go into love step for step, with a fluttered consciousness, like a pair of children venturing together into a dark room.

Robert Louis Stevenson

Today, the bride may live far away from her parents and other relatives. Even her closest friends may live in distant cities or towns. She may have a demanding career and be taking extra classes, as well as keeping her own apartment or house. If these are your circumstances, a professional bridal consultant may help.

Using a wedding consultant has both advantages and disadvantages, as there are always differences when someone other than you interprets your ideas and implements them. But whether you use this book to do it yourself or to help you communicate to a bridal consultant exactly what you want, you can still have your Victorian wedding made to order.

If you choose to use a wedding consultant, first, be sure to find someone who understands and is sensitive to your values and dreams, someone who is capable of translating them into reality and won't impose his or hers. Make it clear that you are doing a Victorian-theme wedding and that you want to work with someone who has done similar specialty weddings. I've given you the name of professional associations of bridal consultants that will refer you to people in your area with just the specialty you seek (see appendix).

The wedding consultant can manage your wedding. He or she can save you some of the legwork and time you might spend looking for local sources. Because consultants plans many weddings, they know all the vendors in your community and can sometimes save you money or keep you from making the wrong choice.

A wedding consultant should be familiar with etiquette, both modern and Victorian; with the customs and history of the period; with sources for Victorian flowers, food, and specialty photography; and with authentic or Victorian-style locations and their availability. The consultant should help you plan, budget, organize, and implement. He or she should make you aware of options, provide creative ideas, and help you make decisions. You're paying the consultant a fee to take over the details you would otherwise handle yourself.

You should meet with your consultant once you've

set the date. There might be a fixed fee for the initial planning/budgeting session, then an hourly rate, a package price, or a percentage of the cost of the wedding. Find out about fee arrangements before you go.

You may want to consider doing most of the arrangements yourself and using a consultant only for certain things. You may decide that you want very much to tend to the details and that one planning/budgeting session to get you organized is all you need. Make sure you inquire whether this is an option with each consultant you interview.

Maybe what you want is not a wedding consultant per se, but a historical consultant—someone associated with a historical society or small local museum that knows a lot about your subject and would be willing to guide you. In appreciation, you can make a donation to the organization or museum he or she is associated with or offer to pay an hourly rate.

The disadvantages of using a consultant fall more into the intangible category. As I said earlier, to me planning one's wedding is part of the coming together of two people. It's an opportunity to unite friends and families. If time and temperaments allow and your family situation is conducive to such an arrangement, there's a lot to be said for doing it yourself and recruiting other people to get involved in the fun. Only you know what will work best and what your personal limits are.

I might prefer to scale down the size and scope of the wedding so I could manage it myself, asking for help from my fiancé, family, and close friends so I could oversee each facet and learn in the process. However, if a large wedding is what you have planned, and your schedule is nothing short of a nightmare, a wedding consultant could be your saving grace.

Another wise idea, I think, is to at least discuss some form of premarital counseling with your fiancé, something that wasn't available to couples in the nineteenth century. (However, there was plenty of advice both written and spoken, especially for the bride-to-be. I have a copy of a book titled *Pastor's Wedding Gift*, published in 1858 and given by ministers to the couples they married. With chapters like "Duties of the Conjugal Relation," you can guess how useful such advice would be today!)

Meeting with a counselor or one's minister can help define goals and identify trouble spots. Check counseling centers, therapists, and churches, or ask other couples to make recommendations based on their experiences.

There are several books on the market to help couples share their vision of the future, beliefs, values, and even sexual fantasies. These are basically fill-in-the-blanks journals that, when approached with an earnest desire to learn more about each other and appreciate the person you're about to marry, can be a real aid to communication and can help guide the wedding planning process with openness and understanding.

THE TROUSSEAU

The typical Victorian trousseau consisted of lingerie, gloves, handkerchiefs, boots and slippers, sachets, a simple wardrobe, plus a "traveling suit." The bride sewed a complete set of linens for her new home, embellished with embroidery, tatting, or crochet, and carefully laundered them and tucked them away.

I was lucky enough to meet a man who hangs onto everything. He had saved his mother's and grandmother's linens, china, and silver, to which I added some passed on to me by my grandmothers and mother. You can now see me at tag sales, thrift shops, and flea markets, rummaging through tables of old linens looking for more to add to my collection. Although I hate to iron, these fine handmade things almost make the chore bearable!

Today we often buy lingerie and linens for ourselves or we receive them as gifts for any number of occasions. But there's still something special about some new feminine things to be worn or used only after the wedding.

Even though I was being married a second time and just a little shy of forty, my mother gave me a wedding ensemble, which I wore on my wedding night. Every time

The trousseau was traditionally hand sewn by the bride herself. You can do the same, or choose from the many lines of fine lingerie available in stores and boutiques. *Photo courtesy of Léron, New York, New York.*

I look at it I think of that special time and the significance of her blessing, and I save it to wear only on special occasions.

Did you know you can have a Victorian trousseau? And if you really want to be authentic, you can sew it yourself, just as a young nineteenth-century woman would have done. If you refer to the appendix, I have listed sources for patterns to create an authentic wedding dress. Some of these also offer patterns for undergarments. One of the prettiest is available from Folkwear Patterns, and the same pattern can be reused later to make a feminine dress in a pretty cotton print for street wear.

I have also listed several mail-order companies that offer ready-made Victorian and Edwardian underthings. You can even order a ribbon corset or bloomers, if you've a mind to!

FLOURISHES

✦ Get a pair of beautiful bound books to keep your journals in—his and hers. Share their contents only if you want. Never, *never* read another's journal without permission!

✦ Give your fiancé some fine stationery and a handsome pen—so he can start writing you those wonderful love letters.

✦ If your fiancé, or some member of your family, is handy, maybe you can coax him into making you a hope chest. Or perhaps there's an old family chest or trunk that's yours for the asking. (A source for trunk restoration materials is listed in the appendix, as are sources for ready-made hope chests.)

✦ Sew some sachets for your trousseau. Sew or buy some luxurious lingerie bags to keep your pretty underthings in. Use antique ribbons and laces and scraps of material found at flea markets and vintage clothing shops to decorate them.

Overleaf: Family heirlooms, such as a grandmother's jewelry or an ornate hand mirror, can add a special touch to your trousseau. *Photo by Tom Eckerle.*

A hope chest becomes a treasured heirloom used to hold sentimental keepsakes. *Chest by MAB Woodworks, Poughkeepsie, New York. Photo (c) Victorian Sampler.*

- Give your fiancé a book of Victorian love poetry to get him in the mood to write some to you. Encourage him in your inscription by telling him what you love about *him*.

- Look for Victorian whimsy boxes at antiques stores. These little boxes, used for keepsakes, would make a perfect box for presenting an engagement ring or present (and it just might be the beginning of a collection).

- Start a photo album of your "love story" that includes only pictures of the two of you. Automatic focus cameras make it possible for almost any bystander to add to your personal romantic chronicle. You may want to include old photos of yourselves when you were children, too.

- If your intended is traveling, arrange to have a card or letter there when he arrives at his hotel. Make sure it's been sprinkled with his favorite perfume.

- In your correspondence, pay attention to the little things. Scent your paper with some of your signature perfume. Seal the envelope with a small sticker that says "Forget Me Not" or an impression from your special rubber stamp. (Sources for both are in the appendix.)

- Make an old-fashioned scrapbook, and fill it with everything from cocktail napkins and matchbooks to ribbons from important packages. Add your own sketches, photos, and handwritten comments.

- There's a lovely book available in bookstores called *I Marry You Because . . . .* Such a simple idea—it pairs statements on the right-hand page, such as "I marry you because you are the nicest thing I could ever do for myself," with famous quotations on the same theme on the left-hand page. Read it together and then get a blank book and write your own!

A wedding consultant may save you time and money and should be able to direct you to sources for everything you need. *Photo courtesy of Abigail's Heirlooms, Newport, Rhode Island.*

COURTSHIP, PROPOSAL,
AND ENGAGEMENT

CHAPTER TWO

SAY IT IN WRITING

*Only on paper has humanity yet achieved glory,
beauty, truth, knowledge, virtue and abiding
love.*

George Bernard Shaw

The written word is the exclusive province of the human race. Through it we conduct
business, mark important occasions, remind, rebuke, describe, record, question, and
answer. Although the romance of the written word was discussed briefly in chapter 1,
the focus was on the personal correspondence between lovers and the ways couples
used journal keeping as part of the courtship process. In this chapter, we'll explore the
more formal words that will be a part of your wedding: invitations, wedding ceremony
and vows, marriage certificates, toasts, thank-you notes, and letters.

But first, a word about dates. You may have already selected your wedding
date, and your choice quite naturally may be based on availability of location, work
and family obligations, or some family custom or sentiment, but you may still have
time to consider some dates pertinent to your Victorian theme.

Although May and June have become popular months to tie the knot, Victorians earlier in their century actually favored Easter week. If you examine documents,
such as old invitations and marriage certificates, dates are all over the lot, influenced
by events of the day and personal convenience. (Remember, America was at war from

1846 to 1848, from 1861 to 1865, and in 1898, and was experiencing a westward expansion that spanned the entire Victorian period.)

Frontier brides sometimes married immediately on arriving at their destination. Rural brides sometimes had to wait until the circuit minister rode into the settlement. There were even cases where the father of the bride "married" the couple and a proper wedding was held when there was benefit of clergy or magistrate. No one seemed to mind.

Queen Victoria was married on February 10, 1840, a rainy Monday, at 1:00 P.M. Mary Todd and Abraham Lincoln were married hurriedly on November 4, 1842, in Springfield, Illinois, with three bridesmaids standing up for Mary and no one for Mr. Lincoln (which, admittedly, caused some comment).

Although there were superstitions surrounding days of the week (Wednesday was considered the "best day of all") and months of the year (September and December were favored; May was considered an unlucky month, bringing "rue for aye"; and, by the latter part of the century, June was thought fortuitous), in actuality, dates varied widely based on personal circumstances and regional differences. Just be open to alternative dates that may contribute even further to your theme or add a seasonal touch that will help pull all the decorative elements of your wedding together.

If you choose a winter wedding, for example, the rich golds, greens, and reds of the season and its built-in festivity would make an ideal setting for a warm, cozy celebration or an ornate, extravagant one. There's no more Victorian holiday than Christmas, with so many of the symbols and rituals we still observe having their origins in the nineteenth century.

Each of the seasons held its own activities, attire, foods, and customs for the Victorians, and you might consider researching some of these as a framework for your wedding. Or how about a holiday dear to the Victorians, such as Queen Victoria's birthday (May 24), May Day (May 1), Guy Fawkes Day (November 5), or Valentine's Day?

Let all thy joys be as the month of May,

And all thy days be as a marriage day:

Let sorrow, sickness, and a troubled mind

Be stranger to thee.

Francis Quarles, "To a Bride"

Choosing any of these dates might add yet another layer of meaning to your day and might certainly be explained to guests with an enclosure in the invitation and in the wedding program.

INVITATION TO THE FUTURE

Traditionally, Victorian couples mailed invitations about two weeks before the wedding (or had them hand delivered) and sometimes even closer to the date. These were often a simple handwritten note, the bride writing to her family and friends, the groom to his. Or the invitations were engraved, plain black ink on white satin-finish paper with a separate reception card. Formats of the time were often larger in size than standard invitations today, and the type was usually a fancy Gothic or copperplate script, with no border to distract from the written message.

One engraved 1876 invitation reads:

Mr. & Mrs. G. W. Pierson

request the pleasure of your presence at the

Marriage of their Daughter,

Wednesday, June 14th, 1876

At their Residence,

Clifton Springs, N.Y.

Ceremony at Seven, P.M.

Austin C. Bagley   *Minnie C. Pierson*

(from the personal collection
of Linda Otto Lipset)

If the wedding was to be held in a church, the invitation most likely would read, "request the honour of your presence," and a separate reception card would be enclosed.

Today, much more time is needed to book a location, entertainment, a caterer, and a photographer. Even getting invitations engraved or printed can take some time. Of

Traditional invitations were engraved and relatively simple in design. *"Perfection" invitations courtesy of Elaine of Bedford Park, Illinois.*

course, the simpler and more intimate the wedding, especially if held at home (as the Victorians many times did), the less advance preparation needed.

The important thing to remember is that the invitation is often the first official news your guests have of your impending marriage, and it sets the tone for what is to come. It can intrigue and excite, move the recipient to a tear of joy, or elicit a smile. Visualize your guests' faces as they open your invitation. What would you like to see on their faces? What would you like to hear them say? And how can you tell them that Victorian is your theme?

Usually the bride's family announces the upcoming marriage and sends out the invitations. A custom today, although not traditional, is to include the groom's parents on the invitation as well. Printers' sample books have examples of traditional wording and more contemporary styles, as do conventional bridal guides and etiquette books available in bookstores and libraries.

However, many couples may, in fact, be living together and may be planning and paying for their own wedding (or a large share of it). They are inviting their friends and family to join with them in their celebration. Or perhaps there have been divorces and remarriages among parents of the bride and/or groom, or a parent may be widowed. Or maybe alternative wording simply feels "right" to everyone involved—you may just want to extend your invitation in words that seem more natural to you and the occasion.

A short verse or phrase from a poem along with the pertinent information about time and place might be all that's needed. Pick a poet of the time or one likely to be read by the Victorians. A passage I especially like is Poe's famous line from "Tamerlane" (written in 1827):

O, *human love! thou spirit*
given,
On Earth, of all we hope
in Heaven!

How about making your own invitations, which could take a completely different form from the conventional invitation? They could be printed on a single sheet of paper, rolled up and tied with a lacy ribbon, and mailed in a tube along with a preserved rose or paper fan. You could explain the nature of your Victorian wedding and why you chose it as your theme and suggest ways for guests to participate. Or you could include this information in a separate enclosure.

Sure, this breaks with strict tradition, but then so does using a theme for your wedding, so why not create your own methods, as long as you don't sacrifice clarity, joy, and good manners for the unconventional? Don't forget, however, to remind your guests to RSVP!

To make your own invitations, don't overlook sources for coypright-free graphics such as Dover's large, reasonably priced collection of "clip art" books and typographic catalogs (see appendix). Especially workable are those titled *Borders, Frames and Decorative Motifs from the 1862 Derriey Typographic Catalog; Victorian Borders*; and *Victorian Pictorial Borders* (wonderfully ornate or excessive, depending on your personal taste—this is my favorite!). Artwork from these combined with an appropriate typeface or original calligraphy can produce an unlimited number of unique invitations appropriate to your theme or themes.

The same process can be used for any other printed materials you might want to have for your guests—wedding programs, directions, instructions, and sources for Victorian paraphernalia (if you're encouraging guests to come in Victorian dress).

One couple I know even held a workshop before their theme wedding so guests could either adapt existing clothing to the theme's style or create their own from scratch. Some of the guests rented authentic costumes to join in the fun. All the necessary information was included in their wedding invitation packet.

If you're not the artistic type, you might have a friend who's a graphic artist design your invitation for you or consider hiring a free-lance designer. You may find that printing costs for your one-of-a-kind invitations will be lower than the thermographed ready-mades available from the big companies in your printer's sample books or through mail-order catalogs, so you can afford to hire a professional to create your special design.

If you have a personal computer, one of the desktop publishing programs now available, and a laser printer (and some artistic talent), you can create the type and basic layout for your invitation yourself. With the addition of some vintage artwork (remember those copyright-free sources I mentioned before?), you can produce a finished piece ready for printing.

Another possibility is to take a stock invitation that has a Victorian feel or design element and add some personal artwork. One couple who had their wedding in a castlelike mansion asked an artistic family member to do a sketch of the unusual structure, which was reproduced on the invitation.

If you've decided to use conventional sources for your invitations, look for design elements that suggest Victoriana, such as fans, roses, and parasols, and those with a

Pretty pressed flower invitations are especially romantic. *Photo courtesy of Imagem Corporation, Salt Lake City, Utah.*

lacy look. Use a flowing, classic type style, rather than a contemporary one.

Some stationery companies and museum shops (see appendix) offer cards with Victorian-era paintings reproduced on the outside that are blank on the inside. I've seen several with bridal scenes or romantic couples that would be very appropriate. You can then take them to your local printer, who would finish the job by printing your information on the inside and help you select reply cards and envelopes that would complement your choice. Or, of course, you could use these cards for very authentic handwritten invitations.

There are three methods you can use to print your invitations professionally: engraving, thermography, and offset. Engraving, although period, is quite expensive. Thermography creates that raised type of lettering you most often see and usually needs to be sent out. Offset is the least expensive method and can even be done by a competent local "quick" printer with very little lead time.

Invitations with fine art reproductions from the Victorian period are a fitting way to announce your theme. *"Wedding Morning" invitations courtesy of Elaine of Bedford Park, Illinois.*

Janet Burgess, who operates a mail-order business for nineteenth-century re-creation, found some fancy multicolor bordered notecards at a fine stationer's for her wedding invitations. The paper lining the envelopes and small reception cards matched, and all were handwritten in complementary-colored ink in the formal style, adapted, she says, to "the mature age of the couple."

Another idea for personalizing any invitation is to enclose a tangible object relating to your theme. How about some rose petals, a tiny bow stapled to the corner (staples come in colors, or you can use glue), or a ribbon rose (instructions for these are available in many craft books and magazines—check with your local craft or fabric store; I've also given you some sources in the appendix)?

If you're really pressed for time and money, consider a postcard invitation, perfectly appropriate if the wedding is truly informal. There are lots of Victorian reproduction postcards available, or you can buy some actual unused antiques if the number of guests is small. The recipient would have an authentic keepsake, as well as an invitation to your wedding.

A word about handwriting: If yours is less than legible, a handwritten invitation should be avoided, and you might even want to consider letting someone else address the envelopes for you. If, however, your handwriting is lovely and easy to read or if you happen to know calligraphy, then by all means, do it yourself. Try your skill at copperplate (imported from Europe to the colonies and the "hand" the Declaration of Independence and Constitution were written in) or the later derivative Spencerian style, a more streamlined version that was used throughout the nineteenth century.

If you don't consider yourself expert enough and would like to have your invitation hand lettered and then printed, professional calligraphers are available in most areas of the country and often advertise in the yellow pages, leave their names with printers and graphic-design agencies, or show their work at craft shows. If you want to locate one and haven't had any luck in your area, you might want to contact a professional organization for cal-

A traditional hand-lettered wedding scroll is a beautiful addition to your home when professionally mounted and framed. *Wedding scroll by Pendragon, Ink, Whitinsville, Massachusetts. Photo courtesy of Nash Studio, Inc.*

ligraphers (see appendix) or try your local college art department.

Some calligraphers will design custom invitations and most do envelope addressing at a cost ranging from $2 to $4 per envelope. Make sure you tell them that your theme is Victorian, as there are several "hands" a calligrapher might know and all may not be appropriate to your time period. The ones I would most recommend are chancery (also known as italic), copperplate, and Spencerian, but be sure to look at samples before you make your decision.

Also, check with your wedding party—you might have a calligrapher in your midst! If one would be willing, maybe as a wedding present, he or she might be persuaded to do your handlettering for you. Once it's done, you can organize an invitation work party for stuffing envelopes and licking stamps. Have plenty of tea and scones or old-fashioned lemonade on hand to make it thematic!

Wedding Programs

Wedding programs are very helpful at any historical theme wedding, especially if you've planned some activities that are out of the ordinary or need to give your guests some special instructions to guide them through the events of the day. It's something they can refer to periodically so they'll know what's going on and can be prepared. This can be done in the form of a booklet or a scroll and can be fashioned using the same methods I outlined in the previous section on invitations.

Ushers and greeters can hand out your programs as guests enter the church, hall, or home entrance. It's also a good idea to have extras in a decorated basket or on a silver tray so guests can take their own if they've been missed somehow. These become mementos for both yourselves and your friends. If there are separate locations for the ceremony and reception and explanations are needed for both, you may end up with two printed pieces.

One good format is the question and answer. What is high tea? What is the history and origin of the wedding breakfast? Is there any significance to the date you've chosen? Are there any historical facts that would add to an understanding of what will follow? What will be the order of events?

It's here that you can anticipate any areas of confusion and provide information. You might want to tell guests about some of the decorations, the bride's dress (especially if it's an authentic reproduction or vintage dress), or the music and entertainment. Is there any special behavior or deportment (how *do* you use all that silverware?) appropriate to the meal? When will the dancing begin, and will there be any instruction for those who don't know how to waltz?

CEREMONY AND VOWS

In 1848, according to the etiquette set forth by *The Art of Good Behavior*, the then-popular version of Miss Manners,

> The wedding party, consisting of the happy couple, with the bridesmaids and groomsmen, walk into the room arm in arm; the groomsmen each attending the bridesmaids, preceding the bride and bridegroom, and take their position at the head of the room, which is usually the end farthest from the entrance; the bride standing facing the assembly on the right of the bridegroom—the bridesmaids taking their position at her right, and the groomsmen at the left of the bridegroom.

Other sources, including descriptions of actual weddings, describe the bridal couple entering the church or hall together first in line, with the wedding party following. The

How forcible are right words!

The Book of Job

custom of the bride's father, or close relative, giving the bride away was not common.

Personally, because giving away the bride reflects the historical concept of women as property, I favor either of the aforementioned arrangements over the traditional American wedding of today. And there's another side benefit—if the bride's parents are divorced, a lot of awkwardness can be eliminated. The advice columns are filled with tales from brides about hurt feelings and angry exchanges before the wedding. A bride may feel closer to her stepfather than to her biological father, or she may have spent most of her life being raised by her mother, with little contact from dad. If changes in the usual are explained in the wedding program as having a historical precedent, guests should welcome them and not be unsettled.

Of course, if you're having a religious ceremony, there will be rituals and traditions that must be observed, although in some faiths there's quite a bit of leeway for adding personal words to the ceremony, either in the form of quotations or in vows written by the couple. If certain elements are cast in stone and are an issue, there may be a way around them. For example, one clever response to the "who-gives-this-bride-away" question came from a father who said, "With her mother's and my blessing, she gives herself."

Poetry and readings from literature of the period might be a way of orienting the wedding ceremony to the nineteenth century. Think of writers of the period or earlier that were likely to be read by the educated nineteenth-century couple.

There's Shakespeare, especially the sonnets—try Sonnet 116, for example:

Let me not to the marriage of true minds
Admit impediments. Love is not love
Which alters when it alteration finds,
Or bends with the remover to remove:
O, no! it is an ever-fixed mark,

That looks on tempests and is never shaken;

It is the star to every wandering bark,

Whose worth's unknown, although his height be taken.

Love's not Time's fool, though rosy lips and cheeks

Within his bending sickle's compass come;

Love alters not with his brief hours and weeks,

But bears it out even to the edge of doom.

If this be error, and upon me proved,

I never writ, nor man ever loved.

or excerpts from *A Midsummer Night's Dream*:

So *we grew together,*

Like to a double cherry, seeming parted,

But yet an union in partition;

Two lovely berries molded on one stem.

A personal favorite of mine are the sonnets of John Donne, my own ideal of the devoted husband.

Of course, there are the romantics, such as Keats and Shelley, or the love poems of Elizabeth Barrett and Robert Browning or Christina and Dante Gabriel Rossetti. Get out your old literature textbooks or check in the library for collections and read them together. You forgot how beautiful they are, right? Or you could write your own poem (or take a favorite from those love poems you exchanged after you read chapter 1)!

My husband and I wrote our own vows. Following the exchange of rings and the first kiss, my father read a passage from Kahlil Gibran (I know it's not period, but he liked it!) and a gorgeously spare and simple Native American prayer (*definitely* period!)

Wedding vows can take any form the couple desires and the marriage will still be legal—as long as the bride and groom have purchased a marriage license, had the blood test required by their state, are married by an officiant recognized by the state, and have a marriage certificate signed by two witnesses affirming that the wedding took place.

So, again, let your imaginations loose and brainstorm with your intended. This is just one more way you'll get to know even more about your partner! The two most important things to keep in mind are that what is said is worthy of the occasion and that it honestly reflects your feelings for each other.

Before you begin putting together your ceremony, you might want to take a look at the wedding traditions of religions or cultures other than your own. Sometimes they can call attention to certain concepts otherwise overlooked. One wedding ceremony I've always liked is the Quaker wedding. Here, too, no one gives the bride away, because, Quakers believe, only God makes the sacred union of marriage.

The Quaker couple repeats these words in turn:

"In the presence of God and these our friends, I take thee, ——, to be my wife (husband), promising with Divine assistance to be unto thee a loving and faithful husband (wife) as long as we both shall live."

Finally, the married couple signs the marriage certificate followed by all those present. Sometimes prayers are offered or a brief statement is made by one or two Friends. This brief ceremony hasn't changed appreciably in more than 200 years.

If you aren't going to be reading your vows or the passages you've chosen, make sure you give copies of everything to your officiant and that he or she knows what's expected.

Even if you aren't having a religious ceremony, you might want to include a prayer, sometimes used to open and close the ceremony, sometimes said just after the declaration of marriage. The important thing is that you both are satisfied that the words spoken for all to hear are what you believe and feel in your heart. At each anniversary imagine yourself repeating those words to each other, still ringing true.

Just to throw one more fly in the ointment, I want to make a case for using the traditional marriage ceremony ("Dearly beloved," etc.), perhaps making a few minor changes in the "obey" category. It's likely that these words were used by the majority of couples in your wedding company, and their familiarity makes them emotionally potent. They've been repeated by couples throughout history and have a strong ritualistic connection in our consciousness. There's something to be said for using them again, but if you choose to do so, do it with a renewed sense of feeling—a thoughtful, deliberate repetition that conjures up both the continuity of marriage and the uniqueness of yours.

MARRIAGE CERTIFICATES

The official marriage certificate issued by the state would probably not be something you'd like to mount and frame. This is not true of those from the nineteenth century. Some are lavishly illustrated and colored—with delicate flower sprays, charming cherubs and angels, biblical scenes, or country churches—and most are ornately lettered. The floral ones can be fun to interpret in light of the Victorian "language of flowers," which I'll be talking about in chapter 7.

In Jewish wedding tradition, the marriage certificate was a work of art commissioned by the family and signed by the rabbi and two witnesses. The Quaker wedding service closes with its signing, and there's a spot set aside for all those in attendance to write their names. The document is later presented to the couple by a close family member or friend.

There are several companies listed for you in the appendix that offer antique reproduction certificates. Some will custom letter your marital information and will mat and frame the certificate. Why not tell your maid/matron of honor that if someone asks what you'd like for a wedding gift, this would be a good choice? You could supply her with all the facts the giver needs to place the order and let her take it from there.

If you prefer, of course, you can order one for yourself. And, while you're at it, isn't there a couple close to you celebrating an important wedding anniversary? Such a gift would be a unique recognition of their enduring love.

Toasts

A toast to love and laughter,
and happily ever after.

Popular wedding toast

Toasting, whether at the rehearsal dinner or after the wedding-day food has been consumed, usually accompanies the serving of an alcoholic beverage, such as champagne or wine. However, nonalcoholic beverages, such as a punch or sparkling grape juice or cider, can easily be substituted.

The word *toast* comes from the sixteenth-century French, when a piece of toast was placed at the bottom of a goblet of wine when toasting one of the ladies, and the goblet was passed around. The last one to receive it was the honored lady, who got to eat the wine-soaked toast and bask in everyone's compliments.

In Victorian times, only men made a toast in mixed company. The round of wedding toasts began with the toast to the bride and was usually made by a member of the family, a family friend, or the best man.

Today, the toast is most often made by the best man to the bride and groom. The groom can respond by making his own toast to his bride and then complimenting the wedding party and thanking both sets of parents. He can speak for both himself and the bride, or she can make her own separate toast echoing his, or they can stand together and share in a toast, taking turns.

Allow some time for any wedding guests who feel

the urge to express their feelings about the couple and their union (unless, of course, you anticipate this might cause some problems). In the case of a remarriage, older children might also want to participate. Just feel them out and make it clear they don't have to unless they *want* to.

A toast can be spontaneous if you're good at that sort of extemporaneous speaking, but you may want to write down some key phrases and encourage others to do the same. It can be a lighthearted poem or a compliment, or it can recall an incident that reveals personal knowledge of the one being toasted (without, of course, ever causing embarrassment).

Toasting, done well, adds another dimension to the wedding drink that involves all the senses, and the words said with glasses raised bring the company closer together. At most of the modern weddings I've attended, toasting has been a somewhat lackluster part of the party. With a little thought and planning, it can be a real high point of the day. Is there someone in your families who has a way with words? By all means, ask him or her to make a toast!

KEEPING IN TOUCH

Victorians were great letter writers. In the sprawling American frontier, mail was the lifeline of business and relationships (lost letters even ended some). Much of what we know about courtship and other social phenomena has come to us through the long correspondences between separated lovers, friends, and families.

Today, we pick up the phone when we have something to say, but we lose the preciousness of thoughts gathered in solitude, apart from the rush of life. We deprive ourselves of the time taken to compose a letter. I'm reminded of what Alexandra Stoddard says in her book *Gift of a Letter*:

More than any other medium, letters provide an uninhibited view of everyday life—the most accurate

The happiness of life is made up of minute fractions—little soon forgotten charities of a kiss or smile, a kind look, a heartfelt compliment and the countless infinitesimals of pleasurable and genial feeling.

Samuel Taylor Coleridge

and natural form of autobiography. Like an intimate conversation between friends, they record immediate circumstances, events, news, gossip and feelings. They are detailed; they act as a zoom lens into specific moments, experiences and emotions.

When you sit down to write those thank-you notes, think of them more as personal letters, telling the givers what you cherish about them, as well as what pleased you about their gifts. Thank them for being able to celebrate with you if they were at the wedding and tell them specifically how their presence made the day special.

A friend of mine, who had someone with a video camera come to each table and record each guest's message for the bride and groom, obviously reviewed the tape just before she wrote our note. She recalled our words and her reactions, and noted moments when we were caught smooching on the dance floor. We felt appreciated, more for who we are than for the gift we gave.

Whenever you can, write a letter, even a short one. Make it from your heart. Keep supplies within easy reach—pens, paper, envelopes, stamps. Make the paper nice to touch, the colors inviting to put words next to, the pens a delight to hold.

If writing a letter really isn't in your schedule right now, don't lose touch—write a postcard. When chosen for the person you're writing to and sent off with a thoughtful message, it can be just the thing.

I collect Victorian reproduction art and advertising postcards (some great ones are available from museums and galleries or through Dover) and then embellish them with a tiny sticker to add yet more color. Even a few words, expressive of true emotion, are better than none at all!

FLOURISHES

✢ Arrange your invitation in a shadow box that hangs on the wall with other keepsakes from your Victorian wedding—maybe a lace fan, some preserved flowers from your bouquet, a crocheted glove, or some faux pearls. Or frame it, encircled by pressed flowers from your bridal bouquet (more on this in chapter 7).

✤ Have your name, address, and phone number printed on antique-reproduction calling cards from Victorian Papers or Bronwen Ross. These are helpful to leave with tradespeople or whomever you please. And it helps get them (and you) in the romantic spirit.

✤ Instead of the usual gift wrapping for attendants' gifts, put your small token in a delicate lacquered bag from The Gifted Line or Victorian Papers. Or make your own wrappings from fabric scraps and pretty ribbons.

✤ Save your fiancé's love letters, notes, and little meaningful scraps of paper in an envelope or a decorated folder or box. I've been doing this for years with cards, artwork, and newspaper items from my children. These keepsake boxes make for some wonderful rereading when you're missing your loved ones or if things get a bit stormy and you need to remind yourself how wonderful they really are.

✤ You might want to consider "at home" announcements, especially if you wish to make it clear that the bride is keeping her maiden name. This simply says "At Home" followed by the names of the bride and groom, your address (especially helpful if you've also moved after marrying), and the date after which you'll be back from your honeymoon and will be ready to begin socializing. By the way, keeping one's maiden name after marriage is not a new idea. Victorian women's rights activist Lucy Stone and her husband agreed she should keep her maiden name after they were married, and that was in 1855!

❖ A wedding guest book is a nice idea, and there are some Victorian-style ones you can order by mail (see appendix). You can ask younger members of the wedding to take it around for signing or just put it in a prominent place.

❖ If you're having a multiday wedding or have planned prewedding or postwedding activities for out-of-town guests, make sure to put together something in writing to inform them. This will prepare them and help create excitement. You may want to leave some things as a surprise, but at least let them know surprises await them. Besides, knowing something is going to happen, but not knowing what it is, makes the anticipation that much more intense!

❖ Use special stamps, such as "love" stamps or a pretty floral, available from the post office. Ask next time you go.

❖ The addition of stickers (some with vintage artwork are available from sources mentioned in the appendix) or a rubber stamp (I have some Victorian houses and a wonderfully elaborate angel from two sources also in the appendix) makes your mailings even more special.

❖ Another great possibility for a tangible enclosure is a small white paper doily (the kind you used as a kid to make homemade valentines). It could be folded to enclose a handwritten message, your menu, or a small amount of scented potpourri. Keep these in mind again when wrapping attendants' gifts; they make lovely box liners or wrapping paper.

❖ When thinking of invitations (especially if your guest list is short), think three-dimensional. Send a box filled with a single bonbon or a ribbon rose with the invitation attached. You're limited only by your imagination!

✤ To make letter writing or writing out invitations a treat, buy a pretty pen with colored ink cartridges (the fountain type), a nice letter opener, and a stamp holder. Keep them along with your stationery in a beautiful box or beribboned basket.

✤ How about a lap desk so you can move your writing things wherever you like—outdoors on a patio or in bed on a lazy weekend morning?

Overleaf: Photo by Tom Eckerle.

PART II

THREADS

*I chose my wife, as she did
her wedding gown, not for a
fine glossy surface, but
such qualities as would
wear well.*

OLIVER GOLDSMITH

CHAPTER THREE

HER BEST DRESS

There has never been a woman born, a real woman, who did not honestly and truly love a bride, who did not want to touch and look at all her pretty gowns and belongings and who did not find a great pleasure in going to see the ceremony and crying for very joy.

The Ladies' Home Journal,
November 1890

When twenty-year-old Queen Victoria married her beloved Prince Albert on February 10, 1840, in the Chapel Royal at St. James's Palace, the day began in wind and rain. But "the Queen's weather" triumphed, and after the ceremony the sun broke through. She rejected the traditional queen's wedding garb of richly colored brocades, velvet, and fur and, in her own words, wore "a white satin gown with a very deep flounce of Honiton lace" (see *Queen Victoria*, in appendix).

Two hundred people worked for nine months to make the one-of-a-kind dress, which included a court train of white satin with orange-blossom sprays around the edges. Victoria had twelve young trainbearers who wore dresses in the same material as her gown, trimmed with white roses. She wore a wreath of orange blossoms in her hair, a diamond necklace and earrings, and Prince Albert's wedding gift, a sapphire brooch.

Of course, not everyone had the resources of Queen Victoria and neither do we! The average bride of the 1800s made her own dress, even though the superstitious might have said it was bad luck. Sometimes it was simply her "Sunday best" and was later worn to church and on other special occasions. Often it wasn't white, but that didn't cast any aspersions on the chastity of the bride. Various colors had meanings and superstitions attached to them, and, in the case of a recent death, an elaborate system of mourning sometimes dictated that the bride wear gray, purple, or even black.

This chapter will give you the information you need to create your perfect Victorian wedding dress, whether it be handmade, an actual antique, or a ready-made dress with a Victorian look. We've already explored a lot of the preliminary decisions you'll be making for your wedding, but the bridal attire is in many ways the centerpiece of the occasion and will influence some of the other choices you ultimately make in regard to flowers, music, transportation, invitations, and the ceremony itself.

The appendix will give you a long list of sources. As you begin your quest for the perfect dress for your special day, you're sure to find even more. Be sure to give yourself time to fantasize. If you could have exactly the dress you want, what would it look like? Actually fulfilling your dress fantasy may be less expensive and easier than you might imagine.

Researching ideas for your wedding dress can also be a wonderful way to learn about the Victorian era, because the history of costume encompasses so many things: custom and superstition, ideals of beauty and chastity, pastimes and occupations, family and friendship.

Enjoy your journey into the past and feel free to follow wherever it leads. Try to put aside the modern concepts you may have about what a wedding dress should be and share with the women of another era the unique ways they had of creating their own "best dress."

A vintage Victorian gown, handed down through the family or discovered in a boutique, can make a stunning twentieth-century wedding dress. *Photo courtesy of the State Historical Society of Wisconsin.*

Customs and costumes make not only many times the history of the world, but the history of the heart.

The Ladies' Home Journal,
November 1890

TEACHING THE EYE

Start by going to your local library and looking for costume books that include the Victorian period. After checking the card catalog under "Victorian," "costume," "clothing," and "fashion," feel free to ask your reference librarian for additional help. Be sure to tell him or her what you're trying to do. You may find you'll have a valuable assistant throughout the planning stages of your Victorian wedding. Don't forget to check the rare books section, too.

Be aware that, although similar in many respects, Victorian fashion differed between England and America—and throughout Europe, for that matter. I would recommend looking at everything you can to get ideas. No decisions have to be made yet.

One great source of books on period costume is Dover Publishing, Inc. I've listed their information in the appendix. I've also given you a brief list of books on Victorian costume, dressmaking, and needlework available from other sources in the appendix. I've tried to concentrate on books that either are readily obtainable in libraries or can be ordered in reasonably priced softcover editions through mail-order houses.

Probably the single volume I would most suggest you purchase is *Bridal Fashions: Victorian Era* from Hobby House Press. In addition to fashion plates from the popular ladies' magazines that include millinery, trousseau items, and other accessories, it includes the original descriptions that accompanied them, articles describing the customs of the day, fascinating ads, a glossary, and a bridal dress pattern for a doll, complete with instructions—all for under fifteen dollars!

Don't neglect facsimile editions of mail-order catalogs of the period. One of my favorites is Dover's edition of Montgomery & Ward & Co.'s *Catalogue and Buyers' Guide from the Spring and Summer of 1895* (1969). By looking at such headings as "Dress Goods," "Dress Bones," "Steels and Stays," and "Dress and Cloak Ornaments and Trimmings," you can become familiar with some of the details that accompanied dressmaking of the day.

Facsimiles of period ladies' magazines, such as *Godey's Lady's Book* and *Harpers Bazaar*, are also available. *Godey's* was published in Philadelphia from 1830 to 1898 and was one of the most influential magazines of the nineteenth century. I have the facsimile for January 1861, which includes a fold-out fashion plate of ball gowns and some woodcuts of children's clothing, complete with embroidery motifs. There are stories; sheet music; recipes; menus; and descriptions of books, art, and accessories that could be ordered. There's even a gossip column!

If you're lucky, sometimes you can find actual copies of these magazines floating around in someone's attic or in a used or antiquarian bookstore. Grab them if they're not priced too high.

Next, order some of the pattern catalogs I have listed in the appendix. The one put together by Amazon Drygoods is especially good, because it combines patterns from several different companies and spans the entire nineteenth century.

You can make a mid-1860s skirt with either a fitted or gathered bodice, which could be adapted as a wedding gown through the use of certain fabrics and trims, or an actual wedding gown from the year 1885, complete with cathedral train. A princess gown from the turn of the century, originally intended as a dinner or reception gown, would make a magnificent wedding gown. (All of these are from Past Patterns.)

Some patterns make suggestions for fabrics and trims, and even tell you where to get them. There are also patterns for chemises, petticoats, corsets, and drawers, if you decide you want to go authentic inside and out.

For many people, it's easier to visualize a dress when they can see actual examples. If you're fortunate enough to have a Victorian house or costume museum nearby, the curator and museum assistants may be able to help you. I called a small museum near my home in Connecticut to inquire if an exhibit on Victorian white dresses included any bridal gowns. The curator said it didn't, but offered to give me a private showing of a collection of wedding dresses stored in the museum attic! You never know where your investigations may lead or what nice people you'll find along the way.

You also might want to consider becoming a member of your area's historical society. Members can often provide information and aid you in your research. Let them know what you're doing and ask whether any members have a specific interest in the Victorian period. I found a vintage clothing expert through my local historical society, and she's proven invaluable. She shared her knowledge of preservation and conservation techniques and told me how to get out the most peculiar stains from delicate fabrics. She's also the owner of a large collection of spectacular vintage pieces, some from the Victorian and Edwardian eras, which I was fortunate enough to view.

The Victorian Society in America is a national society strictly devoted to the period. As a member, you will receive a quarterly magazine about a wide variety of nineteenth-century topics and have access to 2,800 Victorian enthusiasts who may be able to share information. There are also regional chapters that plan activities and can put you on to local sources you might need.

Another useful source of information is *Vintage Fashions* magazine. Although not strictly devoted to Victorian costume, it covers various topics from sewing techniques for re-creating period pieces to collecting and preserving antique garments. Order an index issue and see if any back issues might have articles you can use.

Now that you've requested catalogs of patterns and have a pile of books and magazines, sit down with a cup of tea and look through them. Get a feel for which dresses seem the most "you" and jot down what dates correspond. Imagine how you'll look walking down the aisle, greeting guests, dancing with your groom. (This is the fun part!)

When I was researching my dress, I started a "wedding wish book," which was just a spiral notebook covered with pretty paper. In it I kept scraps of paper, pattern numbers, sketches, ideas, and cutouts from magazines. A picture of what I really wanted began to emerge almost like magic and the book has become a treasured keepsake.

Remember, fashion changed a great deal from the early Victorian period of the 1830s and 1840s to the late 1800s and early 1900s and into the Edwardian era. Some dresses had bustles; some had hoops or crinolines. Some had high necks; others had quite revealing necklines. And there are many different accessories and types of detailing to consider. Also remember that evening or formal wear was often quite different from day wear. For wedding gowns, try to find examples of actual bridal dresses or look at evening or dinner gowns.

As you glance through the pages and begin to notice differences and similarities, you'll see that styles seem to fall roughly into decade-long trends. This isn't exactly true (history is rarely that tidy, even the history of costume), but it will at least give you a reference point.

These are some of the trends to look for:

+ 1840s. Shoulder capes, high-set sleeves, longer bell-shaped skirt, many petticoats, the pelisse (a mantle, usually fur lined and fur trimmed).

+ 1850s. Crinoline took the place of petticoats (a crinoline is a bell-shaped petticoat stiffened from waist to hem by horizontally placed bands of steel or whalebone), very full skirts, skirts in tiers or a series of flounces, overdress, full coats or capes.

+ 1860s. Bodice had downward pointing lines from the shoulder to the center of the waist, low décolletage for evening, sleeves set a little below the shoulder, plain sleeve or bell sleeve with bishop sleeve beneath, and fullness of skirt (especially at back).

+ 1870s. Bustle began to appear (sometimes as an overskirt bunched up at back), bodice had a short point in front or a rounded base, begin-

Overleaf: A wedding gown does not have to be an authentic Victorian reproduction to capture the romantic spirit of the age. Photo courtesy of Lambert Photographs, Columbus, Ohio.

ning of the cuirass bodice (fitted to the figure and covering the hips), skirt began to narrow toward the end of the 1870s.

- ÷ 1880s. Narrower skirt, cuirass bodice, bustles grew in size in early decade—got smaller at the end, sleeves slightly raised and sometimes three-quarter length.

- ÷ 1890s. Slimmer skirts, leg-o'-mutton sleeves, high collar, bustle began to disappear.

You may decide that certain dresses not intended for formal occasions in their time (a summer white Victorian dress or a Gibson Girl blouse and skirt, for example) would do very nicely for your dream wedding. What was more casual then may appear quite formal enough to your twentieth-century eye.

Take notes and, if you can, make sketches of what features you like. Be honest about your own figure's pluses and minuses (and we all have them). I chose a princess-style waist for my own dress to minimize my somewhat ample hips and a scalloped lace neckline to emphasize my neck, which I've been told is long and graceful (at least, that's what my sweetheart says).

Keep in mind how various styles and undergarments might restrict movement. If you decide to go with a hoop or bustle, there are places to get those undergarments (see appendix), but they take some practice wearing if you've never dressed up in period costume before.

Also keep in mind that some of the illustrations you're looking at reflect the ideal of the time, much as today's fashion magazines depict clothing that seems to flatter only tall, underfed models. The Victorian figure adored by the painters of the time (just look at the Pre-Raphaelites or Sargent, Monet, or Renoir) shows a different ideal. That's why I like photographic sources so much. These record real women with different body types, not the hourglass figure of some Victorian-period models, which was far easier to sketch than to *have*.

Two sources I found especially charming were *To*

Love and to Cherish: Brides Remembered, by Linda Otto Lipsett, and Alison Gernsheim's *Victorian and Edwardian Fashion: A Photographic Survey* (see appendix). Lipsett's book is a wonderful and poignant portrait of women across America who courted and were married during the nineteenth century. It's filled with stories, anecdotes, and descriptions of many of the day's bridal traditions, often from the letters and diaries of women representing a variety of nationalities and economic backgrounds. It would make a delightful gift for any prospective bride, including yourself. Both books have wedding portraits that show quite a lot of detail that can give you inspiration for your own.

Another photo source not to be overlooked is that of your own family or your prospective groom's. If you happen to have a family member that's the "keeper of the archives," he or she might have actual photographs of Great-Grandma Sophie in her wedding dress. They provide a great way to delve into your family history or get closer to your fiancé's family, and these photographic records might actually suggest a dress you'd like to copy. Someone may even have kept Great-Grandma's wedding dress. It never hurts to ask.

Actual gowns preserved in museums are generally simpler than those represented in fashion plates—they reflect real life and real people in their infinite variety and individual flair. Even better than photographs, you can see them for yourself and gain a firsthand appreciation of their design and workmanship.

The costume collection in the Metropolitan Museum of Art in New York City, for example, is world renowned and well worth a trip if you live nearby or happen to be in the area. Check to see what fashion treasures museums in your community might hold, and don't overlook smaller museums and collections—they're often little gems.

While you're museum hopping, don't forget to take a minute to glance at the works of artists of the period. As I mentioned before, their paintings were often of real people with figures we may recognize as resembling more closely our own. They also supply a record of the garb of the period.

Now when you look through some of the bridal magazines you'll see ready-made bridal dresses with a new set of eyes. You'll recognize elements of style from your costume research and see how modern designers have adapted and combined them with today's fabrics and trims. You may yet opt for a commercially made gown, but now you'll be choosing one that helps fulfill your desire to bring a touch of the Victorian style to your wedding.

Before you decide to go "modern," though, let's examine what might be involved in having a period gown. We'll start with some of the methods for creating a hand-made dress. It can be one inspired by the period, but not necessarily authentic, or a reproduction made from an actual pattern of the era. Then I'll talk about the viability of wearing an antique gown. And finally, I'll discuss some companies that sell ready-made dresses specifically designed to capture the period.

THE HANDMADE WEDDING DRESS

At this point, you probably have some idea of just how far you want to go with authenticity. The choices for a hand-made dress range all the way from an exact copy of a vintage dress to a conventional dress pattern that reflects some of the Victorian style elements you like. My own dress fell into the latter category. I ended up adapting the neckline more to my liking and adding a two-tiered hem to allow the dress to be shortened to tea length so I could wear it again, but otherwise it had a Victorian feeling.

Sometimes you can combine two commercial patterns or simply alter one existing pattern to get the lines you want. You can make the bodice and sleeves in scrap cloth first, to be sure your design changes are going to work before you cut into your final fabric.

There's a pattern company in Nevada called Bridal Elegance (see appendix) that offers patterns for parts of dresses. You can combine one sleeve pattern with another bodice and skirt pattern (all sold separately) and put the elements together in pieces. The company also offers design guides for making dresses, slips, hats, and veils.

Making your own wedding dress allows you to create exactly the dress you want and invests the gown with special meaning. *Photo by Tom Eckerle.*

Before you decide to take on the project of sewing a true reproduction Victorian wedding dress, you might want to ask yourself some very important questions. These are not meant to scare you away, only to let you know what could be involved and some possible challenges you might face relative to your own sewing ability and interest or that of people available to do the work for you.

✤ Are you willing to do further research about the wedding fashions of the era? Would you enjoy it? (Of course, if you already know exactly what dress you want and have a picture of it and a pattern, you're all set!)

✤ Do you want an authentic copy of a historic dress or pattern, or do you want to create something uniquely your own that's interpretive of the period you've chosen?

✤ Are you willing to track down the necessary materials, which might involve some serious legwork and time?

✤ Do you have the time to devote to the sewing and handwork involved, or do you have the resources to pay someone else to do it (or a magnificent friend or relative who'll consider doing it as a wedding present)?

✤ Do you have the skills to do fine tailoring and detailed handwork? Are you willing to take the time to learn these skills as you go along? If you have some skills, but will need help with others, do you have someone dependable who can assist you?

✤ Are you willing to wear undergarments that might be cumbersome—or uncomfortable—to have a truly authentic look, or are you willing to adapt your design and compromise authenticity for comfort?

In order to create an authentic Victorian wedding dress, some of the sewing skills you might need are

- Tailoring
- Working with fabric that may be difficult to handle, fragile, and sometimes expensive
- Hand sewing, embroidery, and appliquéing
- Creating a new pattern from an existing one or working with a vintage pattern

You may need to work with tricky materials, such as tulle, satin, *peau de soie*, taffeta, organdy, silk, lace, and possibly even velvets or brocades if it's a winter wedding. Before cutting out the final pattern pieces, experienced sewers make a mock-up of the garment to see how it fits together and if any alterations need to be made.

Vintage patterns may not include your size, and you might have to downsize or upsize patterns to your measurements. (*Note*: Be sure to go by measurements, not traditional dress sizes, because some pattern size numbers don't correspond to those you may be used to.) Some patterns, called "Brown Paper Copies for Seamstresses and Tailors," are in one size only, obviously necessitating reducing or enlarging. Occasionally, a pattern will be presented doll-size and have to be enlarged. However, there are systems to accomplish this, and it's not as difficult as it may sound.

The "Patterns of History" series from the State Historical Society of Wisconsin are "adjusted to fit modern women without corsets." Decide whether or not you want to wear period undergarments *before* you cut out your pattern; you'll need to make adjustments accordingly.

You may find after your research that a dress in a costume book or photograph is more to your liking than something you've found in a pattern book. You will then need to be able to create your own pattern from one that resembles it, adding the details you want included.

One bride in California decided she preferred the ball gowns of the mid-nineteenth century to the somewhat

heavier wedding dresses of the period. She found a ball-gown pattern, lengthened the train, embellished the silk bodice with lace and pearls, and added antique silk ribbon and a veil of her own design to fashion an exquisite wedding gown that embodied her fantasy—a light, floating confection of a dress that a princess could dance in!

LETTING SOMEONE ELSE DO IT

Now that you've decided the direction you'd like to take, perhaps you've also decided you aren't prepared to sew it yourself. If that's the case, how do you find someone to make your dress for you?

There are several ways to find a seamstress, but finding one who can do the kind of detailed work you want may take a little searching. You can start with the yellow pages or get referrals from sewing centers or fabric stores, but, although these people might be quite competent, they may never have done the kind of fine tailoring and handwork you'll need if you're doing a reproduction dress.

Sometimes bridal salons use good seamstresses to do alterations on ready-made gowns. You might call and ask if they'll give you a referral, explaining the kind of work you're looking for.

Another place to check is your local community theater group or commercial theater, if there's one in town. Usually, there's someone associated with the group who does costuming and has some background in period garment construction and sewing techniques. But a word of caution here. Costumers learn "fast-sew" techniques, which look splendid at a distance but don't hold up under closer scrutiny. You want to be sure that the person you hire can perform the work you need. In any case, ask to see what he or she has done and examine the workmanship.

Still another source is the local chapter of a historic re-creation group (see appendix). One of the largest is the Society for Creative Anachronism (SCA), a medieval re-creation group, which has some very competent craftspeople as members. Find out who is considered to be the ultimate garb maker in the group. As always, though, ask to see what they've made, because experience and skill in these groups varies widely.

You also might try a Colonial, Revolutionary War, Civil War, or Sherlock Holmes group. Or there may be a country or vintage dance society in your area that teaches Victorian dance. There's a dance group that stages Victorian balls in a town near my home. Some of the members sew Victorian clothing for these events and others collect vintage garb.

Although the group you locate may not be reproducing costume of your period of interest, many of the techniques involved in sewing clothing for other periods are similar. Again, ask to see the work of the person referred to you, and show her or him (yes, some men are excellent costume makers) what you've garnered from your research. Together you might be able to create the dress you've been dreaming about. Of course, make sure you agree on a fee and that everyone understands exactly what work is being contracted for.

You also might try perusing the letters column in *Vintage Fashions* magazine or reading the ads. There are people who advertise themselves as makers of custom period garb. If they happen to be near you, great. If not, working at a distance might be difficult, but they may know of someone in your general area.

My wedding dress was made by a former theatrical costume designer and member of the SCA who is also a good friend. I had seen her work and admired it, and she had also won several regional competitions for making period clothing. Her expertise was specifically in the Italian Renaissance period, but she made Tudor clothes for an entire wedding party for a bridal celebration I was privileged to attend. Her level of skill and experience were ample for the most ambitious sewing project. Her mother is also a skilled hand sewer and needleworker.

My seamstress friend and I went through costume books together and I showed her my "wedding wish book." We sketched out the design and found a commercial pattern we could adapt. Together we found a pale peach satin and an overlay of imported French reembroidered lace in two flounces. The entire process took about six months and cost approximately $800. She and her mother donated their labor of love and friendship as a wedding gift.

My bridal gown turned out exactly as I had envisioned it. One sunny September morning not very long ago, I walked out onto the veranda of a turn-of-the-century Connecticut country inn wearing the dress of my dreams. I will treasure the moment and the dress forever.

Fabric and Other Materials

Fabrics available in the Victorian era were quite different from those we see commonly today. In some ways they were of higher quality, woven in the finest mills. Laces, ribbons, silk, and other materials had a quality and delicateness difficult to reproduce. On the other hand, some of our twentieth-century synthetic blends are more durable, easier to care for, and more comfortable to wear. They don't crease as quickly and are less fragile. In period dressmaking, uncomfortable boning sewn into the seams stretched the fabric to keep it from creasing. Aren't we lucky we don't have to do it that way!

Fabrics closely akin to those of the era are obtainable, but they can be prohibitively expensive. Reproduction silks, for example, are rare but do exist. However, they can cost as much as $150 a yard! Most modern silks are too lightweight.

You need to decide here, again, how faithful to the original you want to attempt to be and what your priorities are. If you're interested in creating an heirloom that someday might be worn by a granddaughter with a twenty-first-century interest in the nineteenth, durability is certainly an issue, and preserving your dress after the wedding is a special consideration. (I'll discuss preservation techniques later on in this chapter.)

Make friends with your local fabric-store owner or manager. If you find someone who really knows fabric, tell that person what you're attempting and the final results you're seeking. If they don't have what you need in stock, the store may have swatch books for you to look at for special order. Be sure to check the phone book and call ahead. Ask whether the store carries fabric for bridal gowns, such as satin, organdy, taffeta, or moire as well as damask and brocades.

If you can't find what you want in local fabric stores, you might check with a good interior designer. People in this field have access to the heavyweight imported damasks and brocades used for drapery and upholstery that might be just the right thing for your period and season.

Another source for fabric close to that found in the period is Amazon Drygoods. You'll notice I mention them a lot—that's because they're a great source for just about everything Victorian. The company's full name is Amazon Vinegar & Pickling Works Drygoods, Ltd., but don't let that scare you. This is one catalog you should have, regardless of how deeply into the period you want your wedding to go. Self-billed as a "Purveyor of Items for the 19th Century Impression," this strictly mail-order business is run by Janet Burgess, a former clothing designer, theatrical producer, and free-lance artist. She has an extensive background in historic costume and is an accomplished seamstress.

Through her catalog, Janet offers fabrics for making historic eighteenth- and nineteenth-century costumes. She's available by phone and fax, and even lists her home phone number and encourages questions.

Yardgoods available from Amazon Drygoods include slipper satin, taffeta, king moire, cotton, nainsook, English cotton net, and pure silk illusion. It's also one of the few places I know where you can get custom-made and ready-made corsets, corset kits, and nineteen different kinds of hoopskirts.

Although it was in vogue (the trend was set by Victoria herself) and touted in the ladies' magazines of the day, white was not always worn. It was considered wasteful to make a dress to be worn only once and white was just impractical otherwise. During the Civil War in the South,

Above all, the heart should be in harmony with the whiteness of the gown. It should be unmarred by any thoughts save those that are good and noble and be like a book of vellum on which is written in letters of gold a promise to God to be faithful, loving and true to the man chosen from all the world. It should be free from all thoughts of envy or uncharitableness; the sacred name of "love" should be its help in time of trouble.

The Delineator,
February 1889

HER BEST DRESS

when there were shortages of just about everything, white was simply unobtainable. Scarlett O'Hara's dress made of drapery material in *Gone with the Wind* reflected reality, and many a Southern bride did the same for her wedding dress.

There are plenty of preserved dresses that were made of colored materials, including prints. As previously noted, mourning customs had an impact on color selection, as did various superstitions. Take, for instance, this little poem popular at the time:

Married in white,

You have chosen all right.

Married in gray,

You will go far away.

Married in black,

You will wish yourself back.

Married in red,

You'd be better dead.

Married in green,

Ashamed to be seen.

Married in blue,

You'll always be true.

Married in pearl,

You'll live in a whirl.

Married in yellow,

Ashamed of the fellow.

Married in brown,

You'll live out of town.

Married in pink,

Your spirit will sink.

I'd definitely avoid being wed in red, green, yellow, black, or pink, wouldn't you?

A Word on Laces and Trims

This is another case where synthetic is usually best. Look for delicateness and fine quality—often polyester and nylon laces are the most beautiful. Today's cotton lace is too coarse to be usable.

You can use modern trims with an antique look or search for antique trims. Sometimes a vintage garment can't be salvaged as a whole, but trims can be taken off and used. However, be careful to match trims with fabric. If you're using washable cotton fabric, use cotton trim that can be washed, too. The same goes for matching dry-cleanables.

Many trims were handmade in the Victorian era—crocheted, tatted, or knitted. There was a kind of piping used called rouleau, which actually dates back to medieval times. The Victorians also used fringes, tasseled trims, grosgrain ribbon, braids, piping, scallops, and cording.

A word about today's ribbons: Don't try to use silk ribbon; it just isn't worth working with. There's a new kind of French ribbon that has a nearly invisible wired edge, so it can be molded to fit any shape. Although a synthetic blend, it looks like antique silk and can be found at florist shops, florist supply stores, or craft shops. It's also available in an unwired version.

In my area there's actually a trim warehouse, open one day a week only, selling a spectacular variety of trims and laces at discount prices. In your travels, you may find a similar place. That's the fun of doing period dress—it becomes an adventure where an unusual button or trim shop becomes a precious find!

Accessories

To add to the splendor and authenticity of your wedding garb, you might want to consider shoes, headpieces, veils, hats (Victorian brides often wore bridal bonnets rather than veils), bags, and capes or cloaks.

Bonnet forms, capes, and cloaks can be ordered from catalogs. Several pattern sources listed in the appendix offer patterns for wraps and capes. Corset kits (which in-

Quillings and Ruches of ribbon, net, and tarlatan, Plaitings of any material for dresses, fringes, spangles, beads, gimps, and braids of every colour, or mixture of colours, in cotton, silk, and worsted, and every description of lace, are all to be included under the Trimmings. They may also be had in strips of fur of all kinds, and in arrangements of flowers and feathers.

Encyclopedia of Victorian Needlework (originally published in 1887 as The Dictionary of Needlework)

Overleaf: Hats, bonnets, and flower circlets are lovely alternatives to a veil. This Victorian hat complements the antique linen blouse perfectly. *Photo courtesy of Michelle's, Nantucket, Massachusetts.*

clude all parts, pattern, fabric, and trim) and patterns for undergarments are also available.

I've found antique handkerchiefs, bags, and undergarments at vintage clothing shows and shops. Expect to pay dearly for them, however, unless you happen on an unusual auction or sale. I've included sources for modern-day versions in the appendix.

Victorian women were seldom without gloves, indoors or out. Gloves were made of silk or kid or were crocheted. The crocheted cotton kind are available from several sources—or maybe you're fortunate enough to know who can crochet you a pair.

For footwear, women wore low, square-toed slippers with wedding garb. High-laced and high-button shoes were considered less formal, but to us, they seem more so. The high-laced kid leather boot from Amazon Drygoods is fashioned after the Balmoral boot, which was designed by Albert for Queen Victoria. It's available in black and in some colors and can be custom ordered in any color you want. The selection in high-button shoes is a little smaller, but the catalog suggests you ask about variations. The ones with the scalloped edge look especially dressy.

Victorian purses were often referred to as "reticules" and were made of tapestry, embroidered cloth, or jeweled satin and set on a frame. However, after the 1850s, bags were less common and small pockets sewn under or in the seams of skirts were used to carry a small purse and handkerchief. In the later Victorian period, ladies sometimes used a chatelaine (a fancy hook with a bunch of chains worn at the waist for holding small accessories).

The fan was another important accessory and had an elaborate language of its own (by fanning slowly, you're signaling to everyone that you're married). There were two varieties—folding and rigid—and they were most often made of silk, feathers, or paper.

Jeweled pins and combs for the hair, long drop earrings, lockets, and cameos were all worn, some with semiprecious stones, as well as precious stones for the wealthy. Look for period fakes, which are becoming increasingly popular and are reasonably priced.

My daughters attended me as bridesmaids, and each wore a borrowed matching antique cameo suspended on a black velvet ribbon. You may find relatives or friends who have similar heirlooms they'd be willing to lend. This can easily be your "something borrowed," which echos the superstition that the happiness of another couple blissfully wed will rub off on the newlyweds. So make sure what you borrow comes from the right source!

A Final Word on Authentic Dress

In your research, you may have found a dress from a period other than Victorian that you thought was simply "you." Or maybe there were various parts of different dresses you liked. You don't have to be authentic if you don't want to. It's not for everybody, although you may surprise yourself once you get into it. This should be fun, and if it's not . . . don't do it!

If you like, you can create your own fantasy dress by combining several style elements that seem to go together well. Look for basic compatibility of lines and balance. Make your dress the way *you* want it. In my opinion, if you want to combine the Empire-waist dress of the early nineteenth century with later period decorations, music, and foods, then do it. Whatever "pleasures" you is what's important.

Antique Dresses

When discussing the actual wearing of vintage garments, we are immediately faced with a conflict. Although clothing was obviously made to be used, at what point does it become a historic artifact that should be preserved and not worn?

Although the Costume Society of America takes a strong stand against wearing antique dresses, vintage clothing enthusiasts take a more moderate position. Unless articles are of interest to a museum (and only a few pieces actually are), most feel these items should be worn and enjoyed.

Before you decide to wear an antique dress, you need to use good judgment. If it's something that's been in the family, of course, technically it's yours to do with as you wish. If you purchased it at an estate sale, a vintage clothing show, or a shop, the same holds true. However, what you *don't* want to do is ruin an especially rare, old, or fragile garment, when it should be preserved instead.

So, if there's any doubt, I would advise taking it to an expert for identification. The information you obtain will be valuable and fun to have anyway. Just be forewarned that the person you may consult could try to discourage you from wearing it. Again, local museums and historical societies can be a good source for identification.

Here are some guidelines to follow when wearing vintage clothing:

✢ First, make sure the fit is loose, never snug. Victorian styles tended to be close-fitting, but too tight a fit puts stress on the garment, and it's likely to tear (and not always in a way that's repairable). A waist tape sewn into skirts and dresses can ease the strain.

✢ Consider the fabric. Some fabrics are more durable and stronger than others. Certain silks, organdy, and other very light, delicate fabrics should probably be avoided.

✢ Take special care to keep body oils and perspiration, as well as food and drink, from coming into contact with the dress. I would recommend wearing it for the ceremony only and changing into something less fragile for the reception, where you'll be eating and dancing. This is period, by the way. Several etiquette books of the era instruct brides to change after the "bridal tour" and before the reception.

✢ Some vintage clothing experts suggest wearing a body suit or a muslin liner under the dress to serve as a barrier between natural body oils and delicate fabrics. This just seems to make good sense. Dress shields and a good antiperspirant are other important precautionary measures.

This Swiss batiste gown, with its delicate Battenburg lace on the points and bodice, was crafted using vintage fabrics. *Photo courtesy of Michelle's, Nantucket, Massachusetts.*

Shopping for vintage fashions can be both exciting and exhausting (to mind, body, and pocketbook). But if you decide to give it a try, there are a few things you should know. Eileen MacIntosh, author of the book *Sewing and Collecting Vintage Fashions*, offers these tips:

+ Have two important measurements at your fingertips—from shoulder tip to shoulder tip and your waist.

+ If you're attending a show or an estate sale, get there *early!*

+ Hold the item up against yourself to get a rough idea of the fit, then measure. You probably won't have an opportunity to try it on, so be as sure as you can that it will fit properly.

+ Hold it up to the light to look for holes, tears, or signs of wear.

+ Spread the garment out to look for fading or stains.

+ If you find damage, consider the possibilities of hiding or fixing it and what this will take.

READY-MADE DRESSES

What if you've done all your research, weighed the pros and cons of a handmade gown or a vintage dress, and decided you'd rather just buy something ready-made—but you still want it to *look* Victorian?

Despair not! There's at least one company that makes lovely dresses with a Victorian or Edwardian look, and many others have individual styles in the same vein.

Dresses and coordinated headpieces by Susan Lane's Country Elegance may be just what you had in mind. Located in California (see appendix), the Country Elegance line is available at stores throughout the country. You can write for the store nearest you and a color brochure. Jessica McClintock Bridal, a division of the well-known dress manufacturer, also has dresses with a Victorian—or at least romantic—look that might suit you.

With the background research you've done, you can look through bridal magazines and catalogs with a new perspective. You'll find many bridal-wear manufacturers have added Victorian-style dresses to their lines, some with bustles and high necks, others with even earlier details.

When you go to your local bridal salon, tell the person helping you exactly what style elements you're looking for. He or she should have a good idea of what's available in a variety of price ranges.

A bride I know wanted a Victorian-inspired wedding and longed for a simple dress with an old-fashioned look. She chose a ready-made gown from a well-known bridal manufacturer with spare, graceful princess-style lines that made the most of her diminutive size (she's barely over five feet tall). The dress was of antique satin and lace with a minimum of beading. She used the location (a nineteenth-century church in Westchester County, New York), flowers, and decorations for a romantic atmosphere and put her ring bearer and flower girl in Victorian garb.

CLEANING AND PRESERVATION

Whether you're restoring an antique dress for the big day or want to ensure that your dress will become an heirloom, knowing something about cleaning and storing fine garments will be helpful.

With a vintage garment, the first thing you need to know is what type of fabric you're dealing with and whether it can be subjected to soap and water or whether it would be better to have it dry cleaned. If you're unsure of the fabric, you may need an expert to help you identify it before you can proceed.

How to Wash Vintage Garments

If it's washable (you can spot test on a seam allowance or hem), prepare a solution of all-fabric bleach (Terry McCormick, editor of *The Vintage Clothing Newsletter*, recommends Clorox 2) and water—about one-quarter cup of bleach to two quarts of tepid (preferably distilled) water. Leave the garment soaking for about thirty minutes and rinse thoroughly.

If there's a stain that hasn't rinsed out, and because you can never really be sure of the origin of the stain, try working on the spot directly, always pretesting on some hidden part of the garment. Spots on white cotton or linen sometimes respond to a paste of lemon juice and salt. Apply it to the spot, tamp it with a soft brush, and leave to dry. Rinse thoroughly.

Dipping in a bath of soap flakes and distilled water can perk up a garment and remove superficial dirt. Just make sure to rinse well, until water is clear. A solution of one tablespoon of baking soda to one quart of distilled water is another effective solution.

For cottons and linens only, Terry recommends boiling in clear, distilled water for fifteen minutes or so (yes, boiling!). Stir carefully with a smooth wooden spoon and rinse with water of equal temperature (or else dirt doesn't come out completely, Terry warns). She says an enzyme presoak such as Biz is sometimes effective on cotton and linen, but should never be used on silk or wool.

Any of these methods may need to be repeated more than once. If it seems to be working, try the process again. Better to repeat several times than leave something in a solution too long and damage it.

Brown or yellow age stains are often impossible to remove. Certain stains, such as rust, mildew starch, and some foods, chemically alter and weaken the fabric, making it too fragile to clean without causing damage. You can judge whether the overall fabric is in good condition. If it appears to be weak or has small separations or tears, leave it alone.

Dry Clean Only

Finding a good dry cleaner who can handle vintage clothing can be like finding a glass of water in a desert. Most people new to the business simply don't have the facilities or the knowledge to handle antique garments and probably shouldn't be trusted with your wedding gown.

Start with the obvious: Get out the yellow pages and call every dry cleaner in town. The longer they've been in business (look for one that's been around twenty years or more), the more likely they are to have seen some of the special garments you might have to be cleaned. Ask them how they dry clean. What are their methods? Do they do the work themselves or send it out? Do they do hand dry cleaning? Do they have a silk presser on staff? Do they pre-test buttons and sequins? Do they take fragile garments?

In some more populated areas there are "restoration laboratories." These are cleaners that specialize in handling old garments, particularly wedding dresses. If you can find one, this may be your best bet. Re-creation or theatrical groups might know where to go. Ask them. Ask bridal salons whom they recommend as well.

Storing and Preserving

Once the wedding is over and you've had your dress cleaned to be put away (which you should do *right away*, whether it appears stained or not), you need to think about how you'll store it to protect it for the future. Your beautiful garment's greatest enemies are dirt, light, contact with other garments, and moisture.

I've included some sources for special acid-free papers, storage boxes, and desiccating canisters (for controlling humidity) in the appendix. Prewashed muslin or all-cotton sheeting can be used to wrap your dress as well. When you're researching dry cleaners, ask how they box or hang wedding gowns and what kind of liners, garment bags, or boxes they use.

Your garment can be hung and covered, rather than boxed, although I would discourage this for dresses cut on the bias, heavy with beadwork, or made out of very sheer fabric. Never use plastic bags for storage! They trap humidity, attract dust, and can easily get small holes. Keep your dress in a dark, dry closet, where the temperature is relatively constant, and you or your descendants should happily be able to wear it again.

Flourishes

✣ As you research your dress, gather pictures of dresses you like and hang them up on a bulletin board, on the refrigerator, or with double-sided tape on a closet door. I have a space in my office where I put up postcards, calendars, reproductions of old marriage certificates—anything relating to Victorian weddings. It makes my office "Victorian," and I get into my "time machine" each time I look up!

✣ Find out what your mother's wedding was like, your grandmother's, or a favorite aunt's. Take notes—you may discover some ideas you'd like to repeat as a custom. On my parents' fortieth anniversary, I gathered information on their wedding from my aunt and wrote them a story recalling the day. Accompanying it were little tokens that related to the story. They've never forgotten it!

✣ As you do your research, if you find old family photographs that haven't been organized, offer to put them in an album and label them, then buy a pretty photo album and do it.

✣ Take the little things and turn them into events. There are opportunities all around you. Photograph your trips to the fabric store. Write in your journal about the woman who sold you those fabulous buttons. Live in the moment . . . the wedding will come soon enough!

✣ Get yourself a pretty fabric-colored blank book to keep your research notes in and a good pen. It will get you in an old-fashioned mood and will later become a permanent record of your wedding planning.

✣ Stop at an art supply store and pick up a sketch

book, pencils, and an art eraser. Even if you don't consider yourself an artist, try your hand at sketching your ideas. You might surprise yourself and discover a hobby shared by many Victorian women, including the queen herself!

✣ Start a scrapbook, keeping small swatches of the materials you've chosen and any stories behind them. Add your friends' fabrics when they marry or pieces of material from other important occasions.

✣ When you go to museums to do research, ask your mother, mother-in-law-to-be, sister, or fiancé to go along with you and make a day of it.

✣ Sew some Victorian-inspired pure cotton fabric bags and pouches with drawstrings to store bridal accessories in. You can add lace and trim for an extra romantic touch. Lined with acid-free tissue, these should provide an attractive way of taking care of your wedding things for years to come.

✣ When you make your garment, sew the lining separately with each piece so that later, alterations will be easier to make.

✣ Once you've stored your dress, either in a special container or in a bag, make a cotton cover to match your accessory bags. Now, wherever you store them, they'll look pretty *and* be protected.

✣ After the wedding, find out about joining a "living history" or re-creation group that includes your time frame or become a volunteer at a local house museum. This can be a rich source of interesting friends and acquaintances for you and your new husband.

CHAPTER FOUR

MEMBERS AND GUESTS

*I cannot help forming some opinion of a man's sense
and character from his dress.*

Lord Chesterfield

THE GROOM, BEST MAN, USHERS, AND FATHERS

Now that you've got a pretty clear idea of the period and style of your own gown, let's turn our attention to the groom and the other members of the wedding party, as well as the guests you've invited to celebrate with you.

Think about the weddings you've attended. How often did the men seem totally stiff or simply lost in the background? It's so easy to let this happen. Sure, a woman's wedding day is special, but there are lots of other people who have been a part of her life up until now. Yet the entire wedding industry is set up to cater to the bride and her every wish. A spoiled child's dream, but not a terribly attractive way to begin a life to be shared intimately with another!

The great celebrations in life, including the celebration of marriage, are joint ventures—a concert, if you will. The many instrumentalists and soloists assembled for the event can be guided by the bride to play a beautiful melody, where each participant's distinct "sound" is brought together in harmony. That's the ideal anyway, and I think it's a good one to aim for. So, please, don't forget the men!

A theme wedding, be it Victorian or otherwise, is so delightful because it provides lots of opportunities to include those you love and wish to say thank you to in a special way. Consulting your fiancé, his groomsmen, his father, and yours, explaining something about your Victorian wedding to them, and offering examples of how they might participate early on in the planning process is more than a courtesy. It's essential!

If the men in your life are interested in history or always wished they could be in the movies, you've already got it made. Tell them you'd like your wedding set in the era of the Civil War or the time of Wild Bill Hickok and Jesse James, of cowboys and Indians and *High Noon*, and see what reaction you get.

Promise your fiancé he can dress up as a southern gentleman like Rhett Butler, a Union Army officer, Bat Masterson, or a dapper Sherlock Holmes in opera attire. Connect the theme to something he's already interested in or can relate to.

My husband happens to be a Civil War buff and is a devoted fan of the old television and B-movie westerns. When we were planning our Victorian-inspired wedding, I reminded him we were talking about the same era and settings, and he agreed to wear tails. However, he asked if he could wear his dress cowboy boots and his antique "formal" Colt .45s. I sweetly smiled my most long-suffering smile and said yes. When our wedding day came, the pistols and boots were forgotten. Sometimes just being willing is enough . . . .

While you're doing research on your own dress, make sure to include the men in your life, especially the groom. Show him costume books with photos and illustrations. Find pictures of people from the time he would recognize or look at movies that depict the period, such as *Gone with the Wind, Glory, Life with Father, The Magnificent Ambersons,* and *Dances with Wolves,* or television shows, such as the miniseries "North and South" or PBS's "Sherlock Holmes" or "Upstairs, Downstairs." Point out what the men are wearing so he begins to notice details. Again, it's a matter of training the eye.

Don't push; suggest. Let your enthusiasm and delight be infectious. Listen and try to find solutions that everyone is comfortable with. If the men involved in your wedding are an adventurous bunch and like the idea of dressing up, get their ideas and try to work along with them.

In case they're really resistant to the idea of formal Victorian garb (which was even more formal than our twentieth-century formal wear), I've included some ways of approximating the more casual dress of the period (which can be somewhat less formal than a modern tux). I've given you guidelines as well for choosing modern formal wear that would be most compatible with the Victorian dresses you might have chosen for the ladies. Remember that time of day could influence your choice of casual over formal as well.

Luckily, men's clothing hasn't changed that much since the Victorian era in basic styling, especially when you look at formal wear. It's not that difficult to adapt slightly out-of-date clothing to the Victorian period. All it takes is a few added details and accessories.

I'll provide you with ideas for both formal and casual wear that will allow you to make your own from scratch or buy or rent the appropriate attire.

This antique wedding portrait illustrates the minimal change in men's fashions over the past 150 years. *Photo courtesy of the State Historical Society of Wisconsin.*

MEN'S CASUAL ATTIRE

If the men in your party really don't relish the idea of wearing a tux, a Victorian theme wedding is perfect—they don't have to! This fact alone may make them eager to accept wearing period costume if they're assured they need not dress up in the hated "monkey suit."

In the early Victorian period, men's dress was fairly formal all the time. Later, however, a looser, more informal suit called the sacque, or sack, suit became the fashion, and it didn't look unlike the modern three-piece suit. If you're interested in sewing one, there's a pattern available from the State Historical Society of Wisconsin's "Patterns of History" collection (see appendix) for a three-piece casual suit based on one from 1876. It could be made in wool, linen, or a linen-look fabric, depending on the season, and would be appropriate for the entire 1870s and close enough for the 1860s. There are even period notes along with the pattern to help the sewer adapt the pattern to an earlier or later period, and the pattern comes in multiple sizes. Another, later, version (1903) available from Past Patterns (#111) would be fairly authentic for the 1890s as well.

This would not have been what the average well-dressed man would have worn to his wedding; it was his everyday business attire. However, today, with the appropriate accessories, it can seem quite dressy, and if your own dress is less formal, a man's day suit might work very well. It could be coupled with the classic bowler hat of the period (also known as a derby), and the same suit could be used for groomsmen and fathers.

A dark suit of modern vintage that a man is already likely to have in his closet, coupled with a brocade vest, stand-up collar, broad or bow tie, and bowler would be a ready-made alternative. The vest and shirt can be purchased (see appendix) or sewn (Folkwear Patterns Victorian shirt #202 and vintage vests #222, which includes a tie). Hats, walking sticks, gloves, and spats can all be ordered by mail from sources listed in the appendix. The Folkwear shirt, by the way, could easily become your own favorite accessory after the wedding. When you see the pattern, you'll want one for yourself—and you might want to steal the vest, too (the pattern includes one tailored for a woman).

If you're going for a later period (1890s) casual look, the classic Gibson Girl dress or skirt and blouse I mentioned in chapter 3 could easily be coupled with the male sporting suit (#891M) and casual shirt (#891S) patterns from Old World Enterprises. You know this one . . . it looks just like what barbershop quartet members wear—striped jacket, light-colored pants, turned-down white-collared shirt, bow tie, and boater.

Again, think about the atmosphere you want to create and what would be enjoyable for those involved.

FORMAL MEN'S ATTIRE

Victorian formal wear for men was *very* formal. For most of the century it was strictly white tie and tails. This is *not* comfortable attire, and most men really don't like dressing up to that extent. It's also at the top of the price range to rent.

Although the frock coat was actually everyday attire for the business or professional man and would have been worn with a top hat, gloves, and a walking stick to the office, from our twentieth-century perspective it seems quite proper and dressy and has that old-fashioned look. For your modern-day Victorian wedding, this would look perfectly fine with just about any style of wedding dress from any decade of the period. It may not satisfy purists, but they would probably know what was absolutely authentic anyway and dress accordingly.

A simple solution for this outfit would be a black or charcoal gray frock coat (the closest rental item would be the morning coat) with fawn or gray trousers and a waist coat (with lapels) that matched the trousers or was in a third fabric (brocade, for instance). The trousers of the period were actually wide and baggy, without creases, and to our modern eye the groom and his men might look a lot like Charlie Chaplin. You probably will want to stick with modern trousers unless you want inadvertently to engender a few laughs (or want to explain the unusual tailoring in your program).

Look at the shirt styles for men in costume books or facsimile catalog illustrations. You can find rental items that are similar. If coupled with a broad tie or ascot, the groom will look the proper Victorian gentleman to the average eye. Of course, you can use the patterns I mentioned and make a shirt or buy one from one of the mail-order sources I've given you. The one from Amazon Drygoods comes with several styles of disposable, detachable collars and collar buttons.

Gloves would be best in gray or a pale fawn color to match the trousers, but make sure the groom knows he should not wear them during the ceremony. White gloves

were worn with a complete set of tails only. If worn to a dance, they would have been left on, but again, use them as an accessory only after the ceremony.

The walking stick was another important Victorian men's fashion accessory. I was corrected when I called it a cane, as this refers only to the type used by an incapacitated person. The proper "stick" should be of a dark wood and have an ornate brass, gold, or silver head—not a sporty one with a duck head or other animal. Some sticks even concealed knives or swords (probably not a requirement for your wedding)!

Spats can be added to modern men's shoes to make them look old-fashioned. These are available from mail-order sources and even turn up in vintage clothing stores on occasion.

If you really want to tackle sewing men's formal garb, I'm told it's not as difficult as it sounds. Here is a short list of patterns available, just to give you an idea of what's out there. Be advised, however, that those from Professional Patterns are exactly what they say—*professional* patterns. They have no instructions and are for the experienced, professional theatrical costumer:

- 1860s male evening suit (#861M) from Old World Enterprises
- 1890s male evening suit (#892M) from Old World Enterprises
- Gay nineties men's evening outfit (#VG9601) from Professional Patterns
- Late Victorian men's evening outfit (#LV603) from Professional Patterns
- Edwardian men's evening outfit (#E701) from Professional Patterns
- Mid-nineteenth-century dress shirt (#007) from Past Patterns
- Men's nineteenth-century drawers (#006) from Past Patterns
- Trousers 1851–76 (#710) from Past Patterns

A professional theatrical costume designer gave me some notes on sewing men's clothing from vintage patterns: seams for men's coats, for example, don't fall where twentieth-century clothing does—directly at the underarm and at the top of the shoulder. The patterns are correct for the period and are cut to authentic clothing of the time. For fabric, choose 100-percent wool or no more than 10-percent nylon or polyester mixed with wool—lightweight wool for summer, heavier weight for winter. Also know that sizes of patterns often *do not* correspond to department-store sizes. *Take your fiancé's measurements* and use the size that corresponds to these correct measurements!

If you don't mind making a fairly substantial investment, the groom can have an entire man's Victorian costume for about $500 from mail-order and local sources. This would include a frock coat, a vest, trousers, an authentic shirt with a set of ten detachable collars in different styles and collar buttons, period shoes, a top hat, gloves, and a walking stick. It would be costume quality and not entirely authentic, but would do the job. An investment of about the same amount or a little less might buy an outfit made by a competent seamstress complemented by store-bought accessories.

If you and your groom are interested in period recreation or dance, he could be completely outfitted for a Civil War reenactment, Victorian ball, mystery weekend (like those held at various period resorts nowadays), or Sherlock Holmes Society event, ready to pursue your hobby after the wedding. It could easily cost $100 or more to rent a tuxedo, hat, shoes, and other accessories that he would wear once and have to return, with nothing to show for it. What a nice wedding present for him, if this is something he'd enjoy!

Remember, too, if you're doing a lot of the wedding yourself or are having a small at-home wedding, or if friends are contributing their skills in other areas, you will be saving money and may want to put a little extra into the groom's attire that he will want to wear again. (He'll never be stumped for a Halloween costume, either.)

A word about renting clothing from theatrical costume rental places—these would be fine for guests who want to participate in the fun, but clothing from these places is generally a little too worn and not of good enough quality for the wedding party. It might be worth checking out what's available, but make sure to look all items over carefully and have them tried on beforehand to avoid any surprises.

There are companies that sell used tuxedos sometimes for less than you can rent new ones for. They're usually wholesale only, but I have a source in Nebraska that can put together tuxedos for your whole wedding party, and she has access to costume companies who make reproduction clothing as well. The company owners are Civil War reenactors, so they know all about the period you're trying to re-create. Just call or write Kari Geiger of The Millinery Shop (see appendix), give her the sizes of the men in your group and your budget, and she'll try to get you what you want.

Musicians, who are notoriously short of cash but who need to have at least one tux in their wardrobe, have their sources, too. They've been known to haunt used clothing shops and thrift shops for used tuxedos. You might also want to contact your local formal-wear rental stores and ask them what they do with used items when new styles come in. By combining, say, trousers from a used tux (and possibly a vest) with a frock coat you've bought or made (sometimes you can even find an old-fashioned tux with a frock-coat–style jacket or morning coat), a period shirt, and some accessories, you can put together an authentic look for the same price as, or less than, you might spend to rent a tux. And, again, the outfit is yours to keep.

If you're really on a tight budget, another solution is to have all the men, fathers included, simply wear a dark suit, adding a period-looking shirt, a vest, spats, a top hat or derby, and an ascot or bow tie. Even male servers at your reception can be put in period dress, and this is an easy way to do it. Just have them wear regular trousers, a button-down shirt with bow tie, a vest, and a skimmer or bowler, and maybe add garters at the arms.

Did you know that in some places you can even rent

vintage clothing for the entire wedding party? Nan Altman Guzzetta of Port Jefferson, New York, has a business that does just that—renting vintage clothing for events. You may find such an unusual supplier in your town. Just seek out your local vintage clothing maven and ask about this service.

MAID OF HONOR, BRIDESMAIDS, AND MOTHERS

In some weddings of the period, all the women in the wedding party wore a dress almost identical to the bride's. The object was to confuse evil spirits that might be lurking to spoil the bride's rosy future.

When trying to outfit the women in period garb, however, it might be far more interesting to consider having everyone dressed quite differently. This adds to the pageantry of the occasion and gives everyone more leeway to find a flattering color and style. For example, each female attendant could wear a different ball gown with distinct colors and accessories. Or each could wear a dress from a different decade.

If you prefer a more cohesive look, you might have the same pattern made up in different colors, trim, and accessories. You might want to work with each bridesmaid separately, finding the color, accessories, and style that suit her best, or if everyone agrees to one style you can then work with each attendant separately to individualize her ensemble.

Another suggestion is to use a variation of the same pattern as the bride's dress and simply change the fabric. This is what I did. I selected a pattern that was flattering to all four of us—myself, my matron of honor, and my two bridesmaids (which happened to be my grown daughters). Each picked her own fabric based on a series of samples I had selected. My matron of honor wanted a dress longer than my daughters', but shorter than mine, which was floor length. She chose her own jewelry, for an individual look, and my daughters wore matching antique cameos on black velvet ribbon and black stockings and shoes. This way we

This solemn wedding portrait shows the best man and maid or matron of honor in their wedding garb. *Photo courtesy of the State Historical Society of Wisconsin.*

were all basically consistent, but each of us was able to make some individual choices.

If you're having your own dress made by a seamstress, you may want to have all your attendants go to the same person (this goes for men's clothing, too, if you're planning on having it sewn). You should get a better overall price and consistency of workmanship.

You also might want to consider mail order for your attendants' dresses. Look into both nineteenth-century reproduction suppliers and conventional catalog companies with bridal catalogs. You might be able to find basic Victorian lines in a ready-made bridesmaid's dress and simply add details (lace, hat, gloves, etc.).

Amazon Drygoods has two dresses that might work well for the bridesmaids and your maid (matron) of honor, even the mothers if they're game. They're listed in the catalog as the "magnolia dress" and the "Georgia peach." These come in a variety of solid-color taffetas. They can be used plain with a hoop or with added lace, extra bows, or silk flowers to customize them—perfect for the Civil War period of the 1860s.

Also be aware that Jessica and Scot McClintock clothing (some of it quite suggestive of the Victorian era) is available in major department stores and that there are several McClintock warehouse outlets around the country. Items there are often at a 50-percent savings, but no alterations will be done. You can even find hoops there (because they also sell bridal fashions) at marked-down prices. Of course, not everything is available in every size.

Whatever you're doing for the groom, groomsmen, bridesmaids, and any other members of the wedding, remember to research your options early and allow plenty of time (double what you're told) for ordering by mail or having things made.

LITTLE PEOPLE

Children naturally love to dress up, and there are so many styles readily available in stores that are reminiscent of the

Know you what it is to be a child? It is to be something very different from the man of today. It is to have a spirit yet streaming from the waters of baptism; it is to believe in love, to believe in loveliness, to believe in belief; it is to be so little that the elves can reach to whisper in your ear; it is to turn pumpkins into coaches, and mice into horses, lowness into loftiness, and nothing into everything, for each child has its fairy godmother in its soul.

Francis Thompson

Children add special charm to a wedding; include them if you can. *Photo courtesy of Lambert Photographs, Columbus, Ohio.*

Victorian era. Kate Greenaway and similarly styled dresses and pinafores are easy to find in both pattern books and department stores. Boy's knicker suits can usually be located there, too.

The bridal sections of conventional pattern books have outfits for children coordinated with wedding dress styles. Accessories such as flower baskets and ring pillows are available locally or through mail-order catalogs. Whether they are participating in the wedding as a flower girl or ring bearer or just as honored guests, encourage children to be a part of your day.

refresher oil, is another idea. Consider fragrances such as old English rose, lavender, violet, lemon, or jasmine. These are available by mail order, in local gift shops, and in specialty stores.

Sachet was a perfumed powder used by Victorian women and men to scent clothes, linens, and note papers. Fabric bags of the powder tied with a ribbon became known as sachets. These are another gift you could make yourself, maybe even from the fabric used to make your wedding dress, trimmed with lace and ribbon. The ladies who made my wedding dress took leftover pieces of lace and fabric and made Victorian Christmas ornaments from them, which they later gave us for the holiday.

There was also something known as "sweetbags," which were muslin bags filled with coarse sachet used for fragrance and storage. These can be handmade or ordered from sources I've listed in the appendix. Another scented gift of the time is the pomander ball, which can be hung in a closet to freshen clothes. Instructions for these are easy to find in Christmas craft books.

Flower waters such as rosewater make another period gift. These were used for scented finger bowls, as a skin freshener, on a lace handkerchief, or in cooking.

Or give a traditional tussy-mussy—a little nosegay of dried flowers and herbs, with a center of roses. There was also a silver or silverplate posy holder of the same name (sometimes with different spelling), and exquisite reproductions have become available, as well as tussy-mussy lapel pins that can be worn with dried flowers or a few small buds.

Food gifts can work well for both male and female attendants. A company called Wines by Design, Inc. offers a selection of moderately priced wines, personalized with your own labels with your names ("Especially bottled for the wedding of . . ." is one way you might word it), a wedding picture, or a special message. Be advised, however, that the minimum order is one case (twelve bottles) of one type of wine with one label design (see appendix).

How about a basket of French wine, crackers, packaged meat, and cheese? After the wedding, the recipient can relax with a light repast and his or her particular sweetheart.

Or consider tea for one or two. In a basket or other suitable container place tea cups and saucers, a box of fine English tea, a package of crumpets, clotted cream or lemon curd, and the *Book of Afternoon Tea* (see appendix). Fill in with dried moss or tissue (which will also serve to prevent breakage) and weave a ribbon around it.

And what's more romantic than lace? A lace lingerie pillow can be purchased or made and commercial pattern companies have patterns for other period-look accessories. Many of these can also be purchased by mail, along with moire and lace keepsake boxes, picture frames, and hatboxes.

Jewelry is the traditional attendant gift, but why not make it appropriate to your theme? I've given you a list of sources in the appendix to choose from.

If some members of your wedding party are from far away, why not fill a basket, writing case, or lap desk with stationery, a letter opener, stamps, maybe a good pen, a Victorian rubber stamp, and a copy of *Gift of a Letter*?

You might want to pamper your maid of honor with a Victorian hatbox filled with rose perfume and bath products. These can be purchased fully assembled or made up yourself.

If someone is an avid reader, how about ordering some personalized bookplates? The appendix includes companies with period reproductions.

For the sewer or quilter, a pair of antique reproduction sewing scissors or a vintage-look sewing kit would be perfect.

Decorated baskets can be adapted to reflect the personal interest of each person in your wedding party and filled with the appropriate accessories. Sports, gardening, sewing, crafts, reading, hobbies, cooking—all can be adapted to a basket.

Think about the use of the basket afterward, too. Can it be used to hold magazines? As a wastebasket? On a desk to hold mail? As a sewing basket? In the kitchen? The Victorians used baskets to hold everything from keys to individual colored ribbons and laces, and they trimmed them with everything from fabric, dried or silk flowers, fringe, tassels, needlework, and beads to natural objects such as pine cones and moss.

Another gift can be the attendants' clothing itself. You can make part of their ensemble or have it made, or give them some of their accessories. A fan, a parasol, crocheted gloves, or a hat could become their attendant's gift.

Another idea is a Victorian reproduction frame to be filled later with your wedding picture in the appropriate size.

As with any gift, intentions are everything and possibilities are endless!

FLOURISHES

+ Have a movie party at your house where you invite your wedding party and view period movies to discuss what they might wear. Serve drinks and foods of the time (see chapter 6 for ideas).

+ If you've found a particular costume or photo book that has been especially helpful in your research, you might want to give a copy to each of your attendants, so you're all operating on the same wavelength.

More gift ideas for your "best people":

+ Frame a decorative hand-lettered quote from the period that reminds you of the person.

+ Pick a theme—such as bells or angels or birds—and give each attendant a different representation of it. One could be crystal, another porcelain, a third silver or gold plated—each should remind you of the recipient.

- If you have a married couple in the wedding—he's a groomsman, she's a bridesmaid—how about an outfitted picnic basket for two? You can order them ready-made (some with antique china and linens) or put one together yourself. My husband and I received one of these as a wedding gift and use it constantly.

- Give a book that expresses your sentiments. How about *A Token of Friendship* by Barbara Milo Ohrbach, "a collection of sentiments, thoughts, gift ideas, and recipes for special friends"? It features nineteenth-century botanical engravings, quotes, and instructions for making everything from ruby cordials to an herb-leaf bookmark.

- How about an antique-look frame with a picture from the past of you and your bridesmaid? The same idea could be used by the groom for his men. If you decide on this ahead of time, you can even arrange to get pictures before the wedding of you and your fiancé with these special people without their knowing what the pictures are for!

- Is your bridesmaid or maid of honor your sister? A very touching gift might be a copy of your grandmother's or mother's wedding portrait in an antique or reproduction frame. There's a company called Elbinger Laboratories in Michigan that will copy and restore old photographs—black and white, sepia, and oil coloring are available—and they promise the finest museum-quality "archival" reproductions. I've provided you with their address and phone number in the appendix.

- Another idea for the men—a smoking jacket (they don't have to smoke, that's just what it's called!). These are easy to make and are especially luxurious in a satin fabric or velvet with satin cuffs, collar, and pocket. Add a silk cord tasseled belt and they'll be right in nineteenth-century fashion.

✢ Gifts for the ring bearer and flower girl might be a period game, book, or toy—remember cat's cradle, jacks, and pickup sticks? This gives them something to do if they get bored during the reception. You can do this up in a basket, too, with a variety of small, portable games and toys and a few old-fashioned sweets to chew on.

Overleaf: Photo by Tom Eckerle.

PART III

CELEBRATION

*The time to be happy is
now,
The place to be happy is
here,
The way to be happy is to
make others so.*

ROBERT GREEN INGERSOLL

CHAPTER FIVE

A PLACE TO WED

Love all love of other sights controls,
And makes one little room an everywhere.

John Donne

The setting of your Victorian wedding is probably one of the single most important elements for transporting guests to a bygone era. Through the total experience—sight, smell, sound, and feel—of the place you choose, you can create exactly the atmosphere you want, bounded only by where you are located, your budget, and a few basic practical concerns.

In this chapter we'll consider location possibilities for both the ceremony and reception. We'll look at where Victorians would have wed, and then explore modern alternatives and how to locate resources near you. We'll cover the at-home wedding in depth, conventional locations and how they can be adapted, authentic locations, off-beat settings, and multiday and long-distance weddings. I'll give you lists of questions to ask to help you organize your information and make your final decision, and we'll discuss ways to deal with audio, video, and photographic equipment to minimize their negative impact on your romantic atmosphere. Finally, we'll look at various modes of transportation for the bridal party that can add a period flair.

Where would Victorians have wed?

For the most part, young nineteenth-century ladies would have been married at home—either in their family home or that of a close friend or relative. This was especially true in the early part of the century.

Later, beginning with the Civil War, church weddings were a growing trend, and marriage by clergy was the norm—so much so that by the 1870s, it was no longer considered proper by many "to have a marriage solemnized by a justice," whether in a church or at home. Then, according to the book *Civil War Etiquette*, "When the ceremony is completed, and the names of the bride and bridegroom are signed in the vestry, they first leave the church together, occupying by themselves the carriage that waits to convey them to the house of the bride's father and mother, or that of the guardian, or friend, by whom the bridal breakfast is provided."

We modern-day Victorians need not be restricted, however, by what was done before—it's that "best of all possible worlds" I mentioned earlier. We can use locations that are evocative of the era and yet have the freedom to be married wherever we choose, by whomever we wish.

Before you begin your search in earnest, I suggest you go back to the exercise we did together in chapter 1 in which you closed your eyes and imagined your ideal wedding. Maybe you've written your thoughts down already, but you've read and seen a lot of new things since then, so I think it's worth repeating.

Start with the blue sky (no limits but your imagination) and then come back down to earth. What kind of setting do you see in your mind's eye? Perhaps you'll want to describe the place you've imagined in detail into a tape recorder or in your journal. Or maybe you'd just like to make a spontaneous list and then pick out the three or four ideas that most appeal to you.

Next, ask your fiancé to perform the same exercise when he's by himself (so he's not influenced by wanting to please you or inhibited in any way), and then come together and compare notes.

You may come up with a childhood setting that has

a special magic. Or perhaps you recall some romantic place the two of you have shared that has a deep significance for you both. Or maybe your dream location is a complete fantasy—one you're not sure even exists or could possibly fit within your budget. No matter; this is just the first stage. Wishes are free and dreams are the beginning of great things.

Once you and your intended have shared your ideas, your next goal is to incorporate your fantasies. However far apart they may seem at the start, think about what compromises might be made to satisfy you both. Did both of you come up with the same place? Are there some similarities? For example, maybe you both picked an outdoor location, but not the same one.

Then look at logistics. How many people are you thinking of inviting? Are several guests coming from far away? Do you plan to invite people who need special access or facilities, such as the very old, very young children, or the disabled? (At our wedding, a close friend who attended was in a wheelchair at the time. We needed to choose a location on the first floor with a minimum of steps, and someone was assigned to help him to the restroom, which was in another building.)

Come up with a list of "musts" and then look at your own wish lists again. Which locations meet the necessary requirements (or can be altered to do so)? Your choice of location may also determine the time of day of your wedding or vice versa. It may put constraints on your guest list, too.

When we decided on the perfect place for our wedding, we were told it would accommodate only fifty people and the reception had to be over by 4:00. We decided to pare down our guest list to include only our closest friends and family and continue the celebration at home with an informal after-wedding party, where we were joined by still more guests. If you think creatively, there's always a solution!

Now that you've got things a little more narrowed down and both of you have had a chance to express your desires, you can start looking.

CHURCH WEDDINGS

If you've decided on a church wedding, it may be at the church you've attended since childhood or one you've grown into. However, if you're not affiliated with a particular church, you may be able to find a Victorian one or one that was built in the 1700s and was in use through the nineteenth century.

A picturesque church right on my own town's main street was built in the 1840s and is now used as a meeting house. It is surrounded on both sides and across the street by historic homes built in the eighteenth and nineteenth centuries. Newly restored, roomy, and simple, this white-steepled building is a real New England country church, and it would take very little to decorate it and make an impact.

A second, much larger stone church across the street is in the grand Gothic style and was also built in the 1800s. This one is Episcopal and has a much more opulent and somber feeling to it—beautiful, too, but in a totally different way. The point I'm making is, again, to think about what you want to create. Do you want a small chapel in the woods decorated with daisies or a great cathedral filled with white lilies and candles?

Look a little farther than your own backyard. Is there a historic district nearby? A large city? Within a relatively short distance from our home are several well-known period churches, including a spectacular Gothic built by Samuel Colt, the firearms manufacturer. Although built during the Victorian era, this church was used by some friends of ours for a medieval theme wedding and provided the perfect backdrop for their exquisite High Tudor garb.

Decorating the Church

You can bring your Victorian theme into the church by bringing in the appropriate flowers (which I'll discuss in detail in chapter 7) and adding a few simple touches. Fix big, soft lace-and-ribbon bows to the end of the pews—make sure you leave the streamers extra long. Or how about a

Architectural details, such as this delicate stained glass window, create unique opportunities for dramatic and romantic wedding pictures. *Photo courtesy of Lambert Photographs, Columbus, Ohio.*

flower-trimmed fan? (Crafts stores sell them with florist foam already attached.) In my local crafts store there are scads of books on Victorian wedding crafts using silk and dried flowers, ribbons, and lace. If you like, you can substitute fresh ones and achieve the same effects.

Another way to add drama and atmosphere to a church ceremony is with candles, especially if the church lighting can be made soft or it's an evening wedding. The church may have pew tapers (holders that attach to the pews for special occasions) you can use. Ask when you meet with the officiant.

You may also want to set up a unity candle arrangement. This is done by placing three candles in a line—the outer two are lit, the center one is not. The bride and groom each take a flame from one of the end candles and join to light the center one, a symbol of their hearts and minds coming together as one. This display is another opportunity to add floral and ribbon decorations. Perhaps you can rent or borrow ornate silver candlesticks if the church's are more modern or plain.

VICTORIAN-INSPIRED LOCATIONS

The perfect setting for your Victorian wedding might be an authentic one—a structure that was actually built sometime between 1837 and 1901. There are so many architectural styles to choose from—Gothic, Italianate, Queen Anne, or stick style. There are lots of books with pictures to guide you—some of my favorites are the *Painted Ladies* series of books by Michael Larsen and Elizabeth Pomada, and there are lots more available in bookstores or your local library.

You also might consider using a building from an earlier period that was in use through the nineteenth century as meeting place, eating establishment, or whatever. Or perhaps there's a modern building in your area that has been designed to imitate the Victorian style. This can do just as nicely, and you have the added advantage of modern facilities.

As you search the area, consider all of these options.

Using the following short list of some general categories to explore, you should come up with several good locations to choose from:

- ✤ Mansions and estates
- ✤ Museums, house museums
- ✤ Resorts
- ✤ Art galleries
- ✤ Vintage yacht or train
- ✤ Bed-and-breakfasts
- ✤ Historic hotels or inns
- ✤ Community centers or halls
- ✤ Restaurants (with banquet facilities)
- ✤ Parks
- ✤ Gardens
- ✤ Wildlife sanctuaries or nature centers
- ✤ Other outdoor locations:
  On a beach at sunrise
  On the shore of a lake
  In an orchard at apple blossom time

Use your imagination!

The Victorians loved nature and spending time outdoors. They spent their leisure time at the ocean or picnicking by lakes and streams. They even held picnics in cemeteries, considering this a way to visit their lost loved ones and enjoy the peaceful landscape surrounding them (today we'd probably be arrested!). Although weddings would not have been held in such places as these in times past, they are definitely evocative of the Victorian spirit. If you're considering an outdoor location for your Victorian wedding, do so with confidence. There a lots of ways to evoke the period with activities, dress, and food. However, there are some basic questions you need to ask before you select your outdoor location:

1. Is it accessible? Remember, everything will

have to be carried to the site. Also think about who will be attending your wedding and whether getting to the site will be a hardship.

2. Is it legal? Check with the proper authorities about any restrictions or permissions.

3. Is it beautiful? The site may be lovely in early spring or late fall before the crowds come and after the mosquitoes have been laid to rest, but what about your wedding day?

4. What if it rains? Can you put up a tent?

5. Will there be privacy? If your location is a public park or nature center, is there a way to keep curious onlookers from gawking or interrupting the ceremony? If not, you may want to consider reserving this site for the reception only.

6. What about sanitary facilities? Are they well kept and easy to get to, or will you need to provide portable facilities? Can you?

How to Find Your Ideal Location

Perhaps some of the following suggestions may seem a bit obvious to you, but in talking to brides who are planning their Victorian weddings, it often amazes me that they have overlooked some of the simplest and least expensive resources. Maybe it's that syndrome common to us all—we tend to be so familiar with what is around us every day, we don't really see it anymore.

The first place to start is with your local phone book. In the directory for my area, which includes several small towns and two medium-size cities, I found listings in the yellow pages for "Historical Places," "Museums," "Parks," "Art Galleries," "Arts Councils," "Banquet Rooms," "Boats—Rental and Charter," "Churches," "country clubs" (under "Clubs"), "Inns," "Hotels," "Information Bureaus," and "Nature Centers," just to name a few. In the white pages I looked under each town name and found more listings for historical societies and chambers of commerce.

Call your local chambers of commerce, information or tourist bureaus, historical societies, and museums and tell them what you're planning to do. They may either rent out locations for weddings or know of groups or organizations that do. "Let your fingers do the walking" first, just by making a few phone calls and asking the right questions.

When you're looking in the phone book under "Restaurants," try to recall if there are some you have visited that either *are* Victorian or *look* Victorian.

Consult with some of the people you're already considering for other aspects of your wedding—your caterer, bakery, photographer, or bridal salon. They've had lots of experience doing all kinds of weddings in all kinds of places and may have some ideas for you. If they're good business-people, helping you will only make it more likely that you'll use their services when the time comes.

Think of buildings in your area that were constructed during the Victorian period or before. There may be a community center, an old theater (honest, it's been done, and beautifully), a club (consider fraternal organizations such as the Elks or Masons, men's clubs—*former* men's clubs, it is hoped, professional organizations, and country clubs), or even a commercial or government building that can be used for your event (our local town hall contains a large ballroom with a complete caterer's kitchen and is rented out by the town).

Branch out and consider some state sources, too. Look in the state and municipal pages of your phone book. Call your state parks commission and see if you can get a listing of all of its properties. My stepson was married in the garden of a beautiful castlelike mansion on the Connecticut River. It was once a private residence, but now happens to be a state park. So don't just think "picnicking, camping, and hiking" when you think of state parks!

Don't overlook schools and universities, either. You

may be able to use a historic chapel for your ceremony or some other facility may be available. It never hurts to ask.

This is the time when a wedding consultant could be a real lifesaver. He or she should be very familiar with all the best locations near you, what facilities they have, and the costs involved. The time and effort a consultant can save you may be well worth the cost of a consultation.

Another professional that may be able to help is a special events planner. Some planners may not actually plan weddings, but specialize instead in planning benefits, fundraisers, or corporate events. They still would have a working knowledge of facilities in the area and may be willing to consult with you for a small fee.

If you'd rather track down your own information, don't forget your neighborhood gold mine—the library. Check the index for your local newspaper and browse through any regional magazines for your area. Talk to the reference librarian about your search as well. He or she may know of some guides, brochures, or reference books that will help you. By now, after all your costume research, you two should be old friends anyway!

One professional planning tool you should know about is the *Places* directory, subtitled "A Directory of Public Places for Private Events and Private Places for Public Functions." You might be able to find a copy in your local library or you can order one if you don't mind spending the money (I've included ordering information in the appendix). This directory covers New York; Boston; Philadelphia; Washington, D.C.; Atlanta; Dallas and Houston; Chicago; Los Angeles; and San Francisco and their outlying areas, although its listings are most complete for New York. *Places* lists information about a wide variety of settings, including ballrooms, boats, clubs, galleries, gardens and terraces, museums, restaurants for private functions, townhouses, and mansions.

I thought the best way I could show you how to research the options in your area would be to do a similar search in mine and tell you how I did it, so here goes:

Because I'm a regular reader of *Victoria, Victorian*

Homes, and *Nineteenth Century* magazines, I went through back issues and wrote down any house museums, gardens, or inns mentioned that were in my area. I then called to find out whether they allowed weddings and what their facilities were like.

Next, I called the Association of Bridal Consultants and discovered a bridal consultant who specialized in Victorian weddings located in my state.

I talked to several photographers and caterers, told them I was planning a Victorian event, and asked if they had any experience doing weddings or events set in that period or knew anyone who had. My interviews yielded several more locations that needed to be checked out.

Next I went to the business office of my local phone company (you can do this at the library, too) and looked through phone books for several of the larger communities surrounding mine under the same headings I'd used earlier to scan my local directory.

Here's just a small sampling of what I found:

- ✢ A former country club (circa 1920s) overlooking Long Island Sound has a 300-person-capacity ballroom, overnight accommodations for 14, and full in-house food service.

- ✢ A community center less than a half hour away was built in 1896 and can seat 150 people. It has a kitchen and most utensils, a center hall that could be used for dancing, and a wraparound porch ideal for cocktails.

- ✢ A rose-colored Victorian cottage and carriage barn would be ideal for a medium-size wedding.

- ✢ A historic Victorian home is currently owned by a justice of the peace, who performs the ceremony and even coordinates the reception, with fifteen rooms and beautiful grounds with a gazebo and pool.

- ✢ The oldest state house in America, located just one hour from my home, is now rented for

weddings and special events; it has a fabulous staircase especially suited for dramatic entrances and tossing wedding bouquets. Although built in the colonial period, it would easily lend itself to a spectacular Victorian wedding.

❖ A company that rents vintage yachts for private parties has some that were built in the twenties that would lend themselves nicely to late Victorian garb; they are truly luxurious. The sea provides a completely different atmosphere, too, reminding us of exotic places with its very own rhythm and sense of time.

❖ A complete re-created Victorian village has buildings that have been moved from towns all over Connecticut and Massachusetts, including a carriage house, a schoolhouse, a general store, and an adorable Victorian-era chapel. There's even a horse and carriage with costumed driver for rent to carry the wedding party from the chapel to the "Red House," or reception hall, which includes an inviting parlor, old-fashioned bar, dressing room, and large dining area. I was so intrigued by what I heard I just had to go and visit. Now I want to do my wedding all over again!

These are just a few of the locations I found within an hour to an hour-and-a-half drive from my home. If you do your homework, your search should yield similar rewards.

As you begin to call and visit locations in your area, you'll want to collect some essential information to help you decide whether a place is truly the one for you. Here's a list of questions you might want to ask (you can probably think of more):

1. What are the available dates?

2. Are there any restrictions? This is often true

of old mansions and public parks or buildings.

3. Can it accommodate the number of guests you're planning?

4. Is there a place for musicians and other entertainment? For audio/video equipment? For dancing?

5. Can you decorate with flowers or other materials?

6. What do they provide? Seating? Catering? Alcohol? A place to dress if the ceremony is to be held there as well as the reception? Rooms for overnight guests or accommodations nearby? Table linens or decorations of their own (and, if so, what do they look like)? How many staff and service personnel are included in the price? Would they be willing to wear some period accessories or dress in costume? If catering is provided, can they meet your requirements for a Victorian-inspired menu or are you restricted to a limited choice of modern fare?

7. What is the rental fee, and do they require a security deposit?

8. If you need to bring in your own catering service, what kind of kitchen facilities do they have—full or warming only?

9. How many hours is the rental period?

10. Is there adequate parking?

11. Do they have air-conditioning? The only real glitch in our own wedding was the fact that the inn where it was held in early September had turned off the air-conditioning for the season. As luck would have it, temperatures were well into the eighties and we all sweltered. It was so warm in the dining

room, the wedding cake began to melt! So make sure the facility not only has adequate cooling (or heating, if your wedding is to be a winter one), but that it will be operable on the date of your wedding.

12. Does the facility require extra insurance? Some historic locations will ask you to pay an insurance fee to cover any damage that might occur.

13. Are china, glassware, flatware, and serving pieces available if you're bringing in your own caterer, or must you rent these yourself? What style are they? If they're very modern or unattractive, you may want to rent your own anyway.

14. Are there any other weddings or parties going on at the site at the same time? If so, how intrusive will they be? (You might want to stop in and see for yourself during a multiple wedding booking.)

15. Is your date guaranteed? Yes, it *has* happened—a wedding has been bumped to make room for a larger party. Make sure of the policy and get it in writing.

16. What, exactly, does the price include? Are there any overtime charges?

17. If the facility provides the food or has its own caterer, can you sample the food?

18. How long before the wedding can you have access to the facility for setup and decoration? Is there any place for storage?

19. Who cleans up?

Decorating the Hall

Once you think you've found your place to wed, you can begin to explore ways to make it more inviting and more reminiscent of the period.

If your ceremony and/or reception is being held indoors, perhaps you can bring objects from home to give the hall a greater feeling of intimacy and sense of family. One special-events planner I know did a wedding in a stately Victorian mansion on the West Coast. Although sumptuous and beautiful, palatial homes like this can have a coldness about them, especially because they aren't lived in and are devoid of the former inhabitants' human touches.

As guests entered the foyer for the ceremony, a fire was lit (it was a chilly San Francisco morning) and the mantle and occasional tables were filled with family pictures going back several generations, carefully placed in reproduction frames and arranged on crisp linens and crocheted doilies. Guests delighted in telling stories after finding themselves, their parents, or their grandparents in the photos. This is certainly an icebreaker, and what a great way to personalize a somewhat impersonal place!

The addition of greenery can bring a lot of warmth to a large, open space as well. The Victorians were great indoor gardeners, and many vintage homes had glass solariums or conservatories. You can buy (and then bring home) or rent some potted plants—palm, Norfolk pine, and ficus are good varieties. Or how about some small, balled shrubs and trees placed in containers, to be planted later in the bride and groom's own yard? There is actually an old wedding tradition whereby the bridal couple is gifted with two cedar trees that are then planted side by side in their yard. As the trees grow together, the custom goes, so does their love.

Mantels, shelves, window sills, and lighting fixtures all provide opportunities for decoration, and of course, the seasons suggest materials—evergreens and mistletoe in winter; spring daffodils and daisies; summer greenery, fruits, vegetables, and flowers; autumn's colorful gourds and squashes and burnished leaves.

The hall may come with its own artwork hanging on the walls, but perhaps you could replace it for the day with some from home you especially like or some you have borrowed. Did you know that framed prints can be taken on loan from many libraries? Find out if yours has this service and what artists of the period might be included in the collection. Look for works by the Pre-Raphaelites or the Impressionists. If you aren't allowed to remove existing art, you may be able to place yours strategically around using existing furniture or easel stands. Don't forget to make a list of what you've brought, however, and assign someone to see that all of it finds its way back home.

Flowers, of course, will likely provide a major part of your decorations. Make sure that your florist knows that arrangements need to be in proportion to the size of the rooms and its furnishings. If you're using a period mansion, home, or any facility where the activity will take place in several rooms, you may want to have flower arrangements placed throughout. I'll discuss floral decoration at length in chapter 7.

Lighting is not only functional, it's a decoration—both the fixtures themselves and the kind of light they produce. Carefully check out the lighting of the facility you've chosen. Try to view it at the time of day when you'll be holding your wedding. What kind of atmosphere does it create? Is it what you had in mind? Dim lighting, partial lighting, candles, and colored lighting can all be used to soften the mood. You'll need to know ahead of time, though, what you can and can't do. It may be as simple as unscrewing a few bulbs or replacing them with lower-wattage ones, but you'll need to get permission.

On the other hand, if you want a bright, festive atmosphere, you may have to add lighting or up the wattage to create the effect you want. Make sure the fixtures can accommodate higher-wattage bulbs.

The furnishings and their placement are another consideration. Is there something unsightly or that takes up too much room? Find out if it can be stored or moved to a different area. Can you add furnishings of your own or some you have rented?

We all know that scents can be very evocative. They fix events in our minds and trigger our memories. Can you use flowers, potpourri, incense, or scented candles to complement your theme?

Your color scheme (the one you've chosen for your

wedding attire) will be an essential element to add continuity and an overall atmosphere to the hall—it's what will hold everything together. Look at all the ways you can bring it out—in linens, accessories, flowers, favors, decorations, and furnishings.

If your wedding is in a public park or garden, Nature will do most of the decorating for you. Some simple satin bows on the trees where the ceremony will take place or some handmade satin banners or windsocks in the bridal colors to ripple in the breeze make some colorful additions. Whatever you decide to use, make sure it's portable!

THE AT-HOME WEDDING

After searching far afield (or you may know it in your heart right from the outset), you may ultimately find that the best location for your Victorian wedding is "home, sweet home."

The advantages of the home wedding are many. The atmosphere is intimate and friendly. You are surrounded by all the familiar things you cherish. Marrying at home is a way of emphasizing the joining of families and pasts, and reflects pride in the family and heritage.

Home weddings are less fatiguing. The hassles of dealing with so many service people are pretty much eliminated. People can dress more casually. You can still encourage them to wear vintage-style clothing and accessories, but more informal styles would be in order.

An at-home wedding can be planned according to *your* schedule—there's no waiting in line for the availability of a particular location. You're completely free to arrange things the way you want, when you want. Rearrange furniture, redecorate the rooms—as long as it's your house or your parents don't mind.

A home wedding generally costs less, so the money saved can be put into the honeymoon, a new home, some extra-special wedding food and drink, or period clothing.

It's easy to add other period activities as part of a home wedding. Turn the reception into a Victorian lawn

On sweetly solemn thought
Comes to me o'er and o'er;
I am nearer home today
Than I have ever been
before.

Phoebe Cary

party—everyone dresses in summer whites and gathers after the ceremony to play croquet and shuttlecock. Set up an area for period amusements and games. You might even assemble some common parlor entertainments such as reading tea leaves and telling fortunes (there are simple books to guide you), consulting the Ouija board, conjuring (magic tricks), playing tiddledywinks, gathering around the spinet to sing, or looking at slides through a "magic lantern." I've given you some sources for these in the appendix.

Children are a lot easier to handle at a home wedding. They can occupy themselves with toys and games (remember the toys and puzzles basket we suggested in chapter 4?) and even bed down for a nap if they get sleepy. There's a convenient place to warm a bottle or change a diaper, too.

If this kind of wedding suits you best, here's a list of things to consider as you make your plans:

1. Can the home accommodate the number of guests you want to have?

2. Are the restrooms adequate, or will you need portable facilities?

3. Is there enough parking? If not, can you work out a car or van pool arrangement, where someone is assigned to chauffeur guests back and forth from a central parking lot?

4. What service personnel will you need?

5. What equipment will you need to rent? Tables? China? A tent? Outdoor lighting?

6. Is your electricity adequate for outdoor lighting and band equipment?

7. In case of bad weather, what alternative plans can you have? Although you've rented a tent, it could turn cold and nasty, even in the summer (evenings in July in Connecticut can dip down to 55 degrees). Should you rent propane heaters, just in case? On the other hand, if your home isn't air-conditioned,

how will you handle sweltering heat? (Air conditioners can be rented, too.) Have dry hay handy to spread on a rain-soaked lawn the morning after a thunder shower, if this is where the ceremony is to be held.

Decorating for the Home Wedding

Decorating your home for a wedding means observing the familiar and looking at it in a new way. How can you transform the familiar stage where life's little daily dramas unfold and make it special?

The Victorians took their usual household furnishings and adorned them with symbols of the interdependence of the natural world and theirs. They used flowers and greenery to bring the outdoors in. The diary of one girl describes the wedding of another:

The rooms were decorated with ferns and flowers; a large palm at the end of hall and high vases of roses at front entrance. At top of stairs in the turn stood a large palm. The front drawing room mantel had banks of daisies and ferns—the fireplace filled with ferns. . . . The sitting room with palms against the long mirror, mahogany table against it with large glass punch bowl and glasses—high bouquets on mantel. The music room and back of it, bouquets of roses. The dining room, above the sideboard . . . with candles burning in front and vases of pink clover blossoms. From the dome over the table, festoons of pink clover blossoms.

Think about the various distinct and separate parts to a wedding. First, the guests arrive; then they gather for the ceremony. Next, the wedding party enters and the ceremony begins. Following the ceremony are congratulations

Flowers and other decorations can transform a home into the perfect setting for your wedding celebration. *Photo by Tom Eckerle.*

and best wishes, and the transition into the reception, which includes food and beverages and possibly entertainment and activities. It all ends with joyful good-byes, as the bride and groom set off for their honeymoon.

In your decorating and planning, you will want to help create the transition from each part of the wedding to the next. For example, you can create a signal that the ceremony is about to begin by having the bridal party enter from another room or down a staircase. To help form an aisle, you can use seating or have stands with ribbons or rope swags tied across and decorate them with flowers and ribbon streamers.

You may want to separate the ceremony from the reception by holding them in different rooms. The ceremony, for instance, can be held in the living room and refreshments can be served on a porch, in a sunroom, or out in the yard. Or perhaps a partition can be constructed or a screen or latticework used to form a barrier.

Include a place for guests to store coats and handbags and for dressing and last-minute primping. Have it organized and well supplied, and don't forget the decorations!

Some of the same ideas I listed for public places can be easily adapted to the home wedding. In addition to borrowed artwork, inexpensive reproduction posters would work well, especially those from museum stores.

Again, house plants and other greenery can be used to complete the decor, and consider other natural decorations such as fruits and vegetables, pinecones, or rocks.

Reevaluate the lighting in your home for the time of day and the mood you want to create. Do you need to add to or take away from existing lighting? Can you use tiny white Christmas lights or paper lantern lights to good advantage? Of course, period lighting for much of the Victorian era would have been gas, oil, kerosene, or candlelight. Can some of these be used safely? If yours is an evening wedding, you can really splurge on candlelight. Consider luminarias (made by cutting a design in a paper lunch bag, filling it with sand, and setting a votive candle in it) to light the outside walk or patio. If you cut out a design appropriate to the theme and use a delicately colored bag and trim with ribbon, they'll look lovely. You can add to the impact of candlelight indoors by positioning candles in front of mirrors and setting any other reflective objects nearby.

Consider the current placement of furniture. How can it be rearranged or removed to create a better use of the space available? If the existing furniture is modern, can you borrow some wicker or wrought iron to suggest a different time? How about covering some furniture with fabric or attaching bows, greenery, or flowers? There are even some easy-to-sew covers specifically designed to transform folding chairs into romantic seating. Sewn out of a floral chintz and tied with big, floppy bows, these would work wonders and can be used again and again. (You'll probably have to keep track of who borrowed them last, though!)

The Victorians loved to collect things and displayed them prominently in their homes. Do you have a collection of antique fans, pretty shells, lacy old-fashioned valentines, or vintage toys you could set out? Or perhaps you can create a vignette, or little scene, using some everyday articles from the period. I have arranged one of these on a table in my bedroom consisting of a glass box, some dried flowers caught in lace, a pair of crocheted gloves, and a period hat. Look at magazines such as *Victoria, Victorian Homes, Victorian Sampler,* and *Victorian Accents* for lots more ideas. It is even better if you can put something together from members of the family and close friends for your special day. Maybe you have an old-fashioned dollhouse that could be decorated for your wedding and set up on a table.

Take a look at Allison Leopold's book *Cherished Objects: Living with and Collecting Victoriana.* In it she shows how to use pictures and collectibles to create the Victorian ideal of a domestic Eden. Many of these could be adapted for your wedding decor. By adding some subtle touches— such as linens and doilies on the mantle, cabinet shelves, and tables—your collections or the same objects you've always displayed can take on a vintage look. Even if your home is modern, you can use fabric, needlework, and artifacts to "set it back" a hundred years or more.

In this smaller, more intimate setting, scents are especially effective. The natural smells of food cooking or warming, a crackling fire, or garden flowers in bloom are the best of all. Just be conscious of this part of the environment and look for ways to enhance it. Perhaps you'd like to augment certain odors with scented candles, incense, or simmering potpourri.

There are some props such as arches, gazebos, tent-like arches, trellises, and netting you may want as part of your decorating scheme. These can usually be rented from party rental companies or maybe even theatrical supply companies. Check your local phone directory. You can even rent dance-board sections to create a dance floor if there isn't room for dancing elsewhere.

A plain veranda or porch can be "Victorianized" with hanging plants, flowers, and portable lattice work.

One modern Victorian wedding reception I know of was held in a garden using white wrought-iron furniture for casual seating. A dance floor was created on the patio using trellises woven with artificial ivy and flowers to surround it and suggest a gazebo. A lighted fountain was rented for the evening to add sparkle and charm.

Think about the season. There's a difference between early spring, midsummer, and early fall. The flowers are different, the yard is different, and the weather is different. Decorate accordingly. Create a "midsummer night's dream" inside a screened porch or tent with tiny votive candles and fairy lights in the trees and fill the table with the abundance of flowers, fruits, and vegetables that are summer. Decorate the house for a Victorian Christmas for your winter wedding, with spiced cider simmering on the stove and a fire glowing in the living room.

Again, an overall color scheme can do a lot to tie everything together. Look for all the opportunities around the house to bring it out—furnishings, flowers, favors, decorations, china, and linens.

SPECIAL CONSIDERATIONS

The Multiday and Long-Distance Wedding

In times past, wedding celebrations were multiday affairs, sometimes lasting weeks. The reason then was that people had to travel long distances and it seemed incumbent on the host to make their journey worthwhile. Attenders indulged in food and drink, and the festivities were designed to give an atmosphere of plenty, promising financial success and fertility for the bride and groom.

Sometimes the wedding moved. An infare, or reception, at the groom's home was usually held on the second day. One source, *To Love & to Cherish* by Linda Otto Lipsett, describes a Texas wedding that involved the entire wedding party traveling on horseback to the groom's home:

There were three fiddlers in the party, one having been hired to play for the dance. He became tired around twelve o'clock and quit the job and went to *bed, but another took his place and they danced on until break of day, with plenty of coffee and cake to keep them going, the coffee being made in a sizable wash pot and kept hot over the coals in the fireplace.*

The multiday wedding is coming back because, again, families are spread out and sometimes must travel a long distance for just one day. These celebrations are usually scheduled over a long weekend, with prewedding festivities on Friday and Saturday and the wedding on Sunday. Or if the bride and groom are not leaving immediately for their honeymoon, the wedding can be held on Saturday, with a relaxing postwedding get-together on Sunday.

Some bicoastal couples have been known to plan two small weddings, one on each coast. One I remember from some years ago took place in a prominent New York hotel. The couple then flew to Los Angeles for an informal outdoor reception near the groom's hometown and departed for their Hawaiian honeymoon the following day.

Multiday or multiple weddings take very careful planning or else things can get awfully confusing. If everyone else is doing the traveling, the hosts need to consider meals for their guests and social events to keep them busy. Perhaps an aunt or good friend could host one of these events. An informal Friday-night supper (even a pot luck, if there's a substantial contingent living in the wedding locale) is one idea. If the wedding is in the afternoon or evening, a wedding-morning breakfast or brunch would be another.

The day after the wedding could include a picnic or lawn and croquet party, a see-the-Victorian-sights party, a bon-voyage bash for the honeymooners, or a tea where the wedding gifts could be displayed in true Victorian tradition. Some fresh dishes could be added to leftovers, to minimize waste and maximize economy. Continental breakfasts, brunches, and teas are simple and can be planned from store-bought foods but take care of breakfasts and lunches quite nicely. There are plenty of menu suggestions you can pull ideas from in the next chapter.

If you're planning a wedding long distance, make sure you have one person, and only one person, acting as your representative. Make sure you communicate with that person regularly and that he or she understands and is excited about the theme and has a sincere desire to follow your wishes. Your representative should get everything in writing, just as you would if you were there or if that person were planning his or her own wedding.

You will probably want to be at the wedding location at least a week in advance to handle any last-minute glitches. And make sure your guests know where to reach you at all times.

Transportation

Because the automobile was barely a Victorian invention, authentic transportation is not your red convertible.

Some period modes of travel would have been horseback, horse and carriage, horse-drawn sleigh, bicycle (a later Victorian invention), train, boat (remember the Mississippi riverboats of Mark Twain's Hannibal, Missouri?), and your God-given conveyance—your own two feet! Oftentimes the ceremony was held in the neighborhood church down the street, so everyone walked or rode to the reception with the bride and groom leading the way.

I went back to my local telephone directory to see what I could find for transportation in my area. Under a listing for "Hay Rides" the ad said that horse-drawn sleigh rides could be arranged as well, at your location or theirs. I next called a series of shops listed under "Riding Apparel & Equipment" and "Saddlery and Harness" and learned about several stables that rented out complete rigs with driver just for weddings.

Another option you might consider, if you and your groom are good riders and you've had some practice riding sidesaddle, is leaving the church on horseback. If you're in a rural area, this would be practical, memorable, and perfectly authentic!

If the reception is nearby, you might want to consider a bicycle or even one built for two (rental places sometimes have them available). Just be sure your dress is secured out of the way of the pedals and chain.

If an automobile is the only way to get where you have to go, then a vintage automobile might be a good choice. Although an anachronism, there's something wonderful about an old Rolls or Bentley. Limousine services often have one or more of these cars to rent, and there are sometimes even services that specialize in vintage auto rentals.

Favors

Favors are part of your decorating scheme but also give your guests something to take home with them. If they're given some thought they can emphasize your theme long after the wedding is over.

I've compiled a list of suggestions for you, many of which you can make yourself or cost very little to buy.

- A packet of seeds for a spring wedding
- A Victorian-style votive holder and candle
- Seashells wrapped in netting or in a small box or basket
- A paper fan
- Jordan almonds wrapped in net or lace
- Instead of almonds, some old-time penny candy, rock candy, saltwater taffy, or licorice
- Other creative ways of wrapping candy—miniature parasols, Victorian reproduction paper boxes, or a small beribboned basket
- Long-stemmed chocolate roses
- Marzipan—a favorite at Christmas
- Net or lace bags of potpourri
- Tiny picture frames with a picture of the two of you (maybe your engagement picture), or send a wallet-size of your wedding photo to go in the frame

- Bud vases with a single bloom
- Sachets
- A monogrammed box with a piece of wedding cake or groom's cake, tied with a ribbon
- Seasonal gifts: an Easter egg or Christmas ornament, for example, or if your dresses are handmade, Christmas decorations could be made from leftover fabric and trim
- Wedding programs
- A single bloom (rose or carnation, fresh or silk) fashioned into a lapel pin for the gents and a hairpin for the ladies
- Small potted plants from living centerpieces used to decorate tables

You'll probably think of lots of other ideas, but these are a few to get you started. Keep your eyes open for more in crafts books and magazines.

Handling Audio and Video Equipment

There's nothing worse than dressing authentically, finding a historical location, decorating according to the period, and then having musicians or video technicians completely spoil the look and mood of your event. Sometimes there's really no way around it, but let's at least discuss some of the ways to minimize the negative impact these people can have.

We'll talk a lot more about period music in chapter 8, but while we're on the subject of the hall, I thought I should at least mention it. The more authentic the music, meaning music that uses acoustic instruments with no amplification, the less of a problem it will be to "hide" unsightly audio equipment. If, however, you must have amplification, one of the best ways to hide unsightly speakers and microphones is with greenery. Palms and ferns are bushy, yet offer no impediment to sound. A sheer fabric screen might be constructed and decorated as another solution.

Consider having your musicians dress in period costume, too. Using the ideas I gave you for Victorian accessorizing, they should be able to achieve a compatible look.

The same can be done with your video technician, if you're having one. The best way to avoid the intrusion of modern-day technology is, of course, to eliminate it altogether, but I, for one, get great pleasure from watching our wedding video. Let the person who will run the camera know that you want him or her to be as invisible as possible. Using various camera techniques, he or she can zoom in on the action without standing right in the middle of everything.

Photography

During the first thirty years of photography, few wedding portraits were taken, or at least few have survived. Those that do survive were often taken a year or more later and focus largely on the bride alone. Actual bridal portraits show up more frequently after 1870 and increasingly resemble those of the twentieth century. In her book *Wedding*, Barbara Norfleet surveys wedding photography from 1850 to 1976. In this fascinating study, she describes the practice of wedding photography in the Victorian era this way: "Wealthy couples began to hire photographers to make portraits of the bride and groom together, often set in the home, where the couple is surrounded by the props of Victorian stability and opulence."

Again, a photographer at your Victorian wedding can abruptly remind everyone that this is the 1990s, not the 1890s. Period dress would help, but so would a period-looking camera. Large- and medium-format cameras somehow look more old-fashioned than the standard 35 millimeter. Ask your photographer about using a box enclosure and a wooden tripod to disguise the chrome and plastic of the modern camera. One photographer I interviewed specializes in vintage-look wedding photography. She uses such an enclosure for formal portraits and uses infrared indoors to avoid the intrusion of flash. The results are grainy and ethereal, and she makes sepia-toned prints, which she then hand colors.

The personality of the photographer has a lot to do with how much he or she stands out. You want someone who knows how to blend into the background, that you barely distinguish from the guests.

I was an attendant at one wedding where the photographer was a complete clod. He was disheveled, loud, and boorish, cracking stupid jokes and forcing divorced parents together into photos that looked like prison portraits. You couldn't help but notice him—he was the only one who looked completely out of place!

With your wedding and reception sites chosen and secured, your decorations planned, transportation arranged for and technical help provided, you can now turn your attention to the remaining ingredients for your celebration: food, flowers, and entertainment.

Flourishes

- Check with your local lumber or home decorating store for mirror squares—the kind used to create mirrored walls. These used individually as a candle base multiply the light and add to the magic. You can glue lace or trim around the edge to make them even more romantic.
- Have someone collect all the candle stubs from your ceremony and reception and put them aside. Melt them down later and pour into a candle mold, creating one large candle you can decorate with pressed flowers and burn at your first anniversary.
- Make your picture gallery a collection of photos of both of you growing up—from baby pictures to your yearbook photo and beyond. Include other memorabilia from childhood, such as trophies, report cards, locks of hair, or an old doll or teddy bear—whatever you and your parents may have collected.

+ Ask a friend to save the ribbons from the church or at-home ceremony. Use them later in sewing and crafts projects around your home.

+ Paint an old-fashioned boardwalk photo prop—the kind with a scene and holes large enough for someone to fit his or her face through—and position it in the backyard. Then take pictures with an instant camera and display them for everyone to see.

+ If there's a pool or pond on the property, set floating candles on it. Children's water safety rings can be used to encompass plastic containers filled with flowers and then set to float on the water.

+ Here are some alternatives to throwing rice (which is deadly to birds): Pass out bubble liquid and wands and blow bubbles or substitute birdseed, grass seed, or puffed rice (rice in this form does no harm).

+ Attach a special note or clever rhyme written in calligraphy to each favor with a ribbon. You can include your names and the date of your wedding as well.

+ Place a fresh flower bouquet in the women's powder room for an extra-special touch.

+ Another theme for a photo display could be a collection of wedding pictures. Ask each couple invited to bring their wedding portrait for prominent display.

+ Have your photographer take old-time photo portraits of everyone who comes in Victorian clothing. Put these in your album and make a copy for a gift to the subjects.

CHAPTER SIX

ROMANTIC REPASTS

It's food too fine for angels; yet come, take
And eat thy fill! . . .

Edward Taylor

You've chosen the most fabulous bridal gown, outfitted your groom and your bridal party, and found the perfect location for your Victorian wedding. But what food are you going to serve at the reception? Somehow the usual selections—prime rib or chicken cordon blue—just don't seem to fit the bill. But how can you make your reception meal Victorian? What would a nineteenth-century meal have consisted of and how would it have been prepared? What would the table look like? And would a Victorian wedding celebration have included an open bar?

Just how much influence you will have on the food selection and presentation will depend somewhat on the location you've chosen. You will probably find yourself in one of three situations: Your location has its own caterer or food service, you will be bringing in your own caterer, or you'll be doing it yourself.

Regardless of which of these three options you've chosen, you can bring in your theme. Of course, if you're doing it yourself (with lots of competent help, I hope), you'll have the most control over what is served and how. If your reception site has its own caterer or in-house food service, you may be more limited in your choice of menu (but not necessarily). And finally, if you're bringing in your own caterer, you'll need to know how to find one that will create a menu with nineteenth-century flavor.

In planning your menu, from hors d'oeuvres to the wedding cake, you can combine modern convenience with the Victorian love of fine dining. *Photo by Tom Eckerle.*

But before we talk about handling these three different situations, we need to know what kind of food we're talking about and what special arrangements a Victorian-style reception might require. In this chapter, we'll take a brief historic look at Victorian food and dining. I've presented menus for four different types of receptions with some sources for recipes and some presentation ideas. I've done the same for four different pre-wedding celebrations I've talked about in previous chapters: the engagement party, a work party for addressing and stuffing invitations, a bridesmaid's tea, and a costume and history research party. These events you would most likely be doing yourself or with a friend or relative. However, if you're planning a large engagement party (or someone is planning it for you), you might be enlisting the services of a caterer.

I've also provided suggested menus for several post-wedding celebrations, including a honeymoon breakfast. There are menu ideas for a lawn party, hot-dish supper, and open house, should there be out-of-town guests you or your family will be visiting with after the wedding.

As much as possible, I've tried to present actual vintage menus taken from cookbooks, magazines, or written records of the day; I explain unfamiliar terms and suggest substitutions where a particular dish either would not generally be to modern tastes or includes ingredients that might be difficult to obtain. In some cases I've put together my own menu using recipes from Victorian cookbooks. I've provided plenty of useful sources for all, so you should have little difficulty locating recipes for yourself or your caterer.

Next there's a section on finding and working with a caterer, along with a list of essential questions to ask before you decide which caterer to hire.

We'll take a detailed look at the wedding cake—how it would have been presented in Victorian times and some modern-day alternatives. I've even given you the names of some wedding cake artists who specialize in creating Victorian confections in the appendix.

As with any part of your Victorian wedding, you can incorporate as few or as many as you want of the ideas presented here. Any of the suggested menus could be interchanged, rearranged, condensed, expanded, or combined. They're just a place for you to start, whether you're doing the meal yourself or working with a caterer.

DINING IN VICTORIAN AMERICA

The history of food preparation and dining customs is just as fascinating as that of costume. In this modern day of fast foods, fad foods, and nouvelle cuisine, I find it especially comforting to go back to the old recipes handed down from my mother's and grandmother's kitchens. Although I was given an up-to-date version of the *Boston Cooking School Cookbook* as a new bride, I still prefer my Grandmother Kase's 1939 edition, which is decidedly more fun to read and contains many recipes that originated in the Victorian era, missing from its modern counterpart.

As you begin to put together your menu, keep in mind that there were distinctly different foods favored by various ethnic groups, regions, and classes, in England as well as in the United States. American taste differed from English, and high society in this country actually preferred to imitate French cuisine rather than that of the mother country. A good book to give you an understanding of American Victorian dining (and a source for many of the recipes you'll need to complete some of the menus suggested here) is Susan Williams's *Savory Suppers and Fashionable Feasts*. Not just a cookbook, this volume describes nineteenth-century table manners, dining rooms and their furnishings, and food fashions of the times and gives menus and recipes for just about every common and uncommon occasion.

Victorian America saw the founding of the Boston Cooking School in 1879, made famous by Fanny Farmer. It was the age of the great hotels, and best-selling cookbooks were written by Alexander Filippini (longtime chef for the House of Delmonico), Oscar of the Waldorf, and Hugo Ziemann, steward of the White House.

If the truth must be known, all affectations and pretense aside, the dinner, the world over, is the symbol of a people's civilization. A coarse and meanly cooked and raggedly served dinner expresses the thought and perhaps the spiritual perception of a nation or family. A well-cooked and a prettily-served dinner will indicate the refinement and taste of a nation or family.

Robert Laird Collier

Isabella Mayson Beeton's *Book of Household Management* was the domestic bible on both sides of the Atlantic. It was written in four years while the young Mrs. Beeton translated novels; wrote articles on fashion, cooking, and, domestic life for her husband's *Englishwoman's Domestic Magazine*; ran a household; conducted an active social life; traveled extensively; and gave birth to two sons, one of whom died three months after his birth—all this before she was twenty-five!

Beeton's book first appeared in its entirety in 1861, and the title itself reveals something about middle-class Victorian lifestyles. Although during the Gilded Age dinners might include as many as twenty-seven courses, along with appropriate wines, servants were plentiful and cheap, and the mistress of the house was more often a "manager" than the actual cook. She might make a special dish on occasion, but the daily cooking was handled by the help. Mrs. Beeton's chapters titled "Domestic Servants" and "The Housekeeper" advise the home manager how to handle these employees. "As with the commander of an army, or the leader of any enterprise, so is it with the mistress of a house," she declares!

By the 1870s, a large number of women were completely devoted to homemaking and child rearing and were not making a direct contribution to the household income. The mark of a successful middle-class man was to be able to support his family in leisure. Coupled with the fact that families were shrinking in size, women had more time and money to invest in activities such as formal balls and suppers and ladies' luncheons. Increased mobility and more disposable income meant more travel and, therefore, the influence of regional and foreign cuisines.

Don't suppose, however, that all women ran their houses like Mrs. Beeton suggests or met the ideals of *Godey's Lady's Book, Peterson's Magazine,* or the etiquette books of the day. As we discovered about courtship and marriage customs, diaries, letters, journals, and other written documents and artifacts show that some followed the dictates of these "authorities," but many didn't. If you read nineteenth-century writers such as Mark Twain, Henry James, or William Dean Howells, the meals described are not unlike what we enjoy today. Actual records of family life indicate that people were more concerned about budget and nutrition than some overstuffed published menus would indicate. Just use them as guidelines and pare them down to suit the occasion and the guest list.

If you think the size of the menus seems a bit daunting, consider the implements you might be required to recognize and use properly at a formal meal—many of them so specialized, we scarcely know the use for them anymore!

There are, however, some period touches you might like to include for your event. The use of the finger bowl, usually before the fruit and dessert course, was a must for delicate ladies and gentlemen. And the folded napkin was truly an art. Another practice I like is that Victorians never put manufactured food products in their original bottles or cans directly on the table—they either went into a clever concealing container or were emptied into a bowl or pitcher.

The appearance of food-processing companies (the Heinz company was founded in 1869) meant new ingredients were available and gave the middle class access to delicacies previously out of reach financially—things such as oysters, crab, and lobster. Better transportation in the 1870s meant availability of unusual fruits (bananas and oranges) and spread the influence of French food (fondues, ices, lettuce salads, bonbons, sweet oils, tomatoes, and fricassees). By the turn of the century, American cuisine included German, Chinese, Turkish, Jewish, Italian, Russian, and Scottish cooking.

As with all the other aspects of your Victorian wedding, planning and preparing food for your special occasions can be a way of putting you in touch with your own heritage. What did your mother cook? Your grandmother? Are there recipes handed down within your own family you might use?

My ancestors emigrated from Germany, England, and Switzerland. The inn where my husband and I were married specializes in Swiss/German-style food. I included a beef dish, a fish dish, and a fowl dish, much as the Victorians would have. The only obvious omission was game, because it wasn't offered. However, the wedding was small and the establishment quite flexible—if I'd wanted to pay extra, I probably could have arranged for it.

Game was plentiful and varied in Victorian America. A single day's menu from the Astor House in New York City (circa 1863) gives all these choices, in addition to nearly thirty other selections of beef, fowl, fish, and organ meats: broiled plover, roasted quail, teal duck, mallard duck, broiled woodcock, larded partridges with game sauce, roast grouse, and saddle of venison with current jelly. The menu also includes green turtle soup, the lack of which on the modern menu is a testament to our spoiled environment. Sweetbreads and tongue were also common fare, but our modern taste and concerns about light eating make them all but extinct for most.

A List of Some Edible Flowers

Apple blossoms
Carnations
Chrysanthemums
Clover
Cornflowers, or bachelor's
   buttons
Cowslips, or primroses
Daisies
Dandelions
Daylilies
Elderflowers
Hawthorne
Hollyhocks
Honeysuckle
Hyacinths

Jasmine
Lilacs
Marigolds
Nasturtiums
Orange blossoms
Pansies
Peonies
Pinks
Roses
Snapdragons
Sunflowers
Tulips
Violets
Wisteria

The Victorians had available the freshest ingredients, including fresh flowers and herbs, which they used generously in their cooking. This is an unexpected delight and easy to incorporate even into modern dishes, but a word of caution: If you want to try recipes using fresh flowers, be sure they are *completely* pesticide free. I've given you some mail-order sources in the appendix for fresh flowers and herbs for cooking, but, of course, growing your own is the best. Just make sure whatever you use in cooking hasn't been sprayed or systemically fed with any chemical pesticide.

WINES AND LIQUORS

Claret, the Victorian favorite, can no longer be purchased under that name, because it's too vague and misleading to be legally viable. According to Mrs. Beeton,

> All those wines called in England clarets are the produce of the country round Bordeaux, or the Bordelais; but it is remarkable that there is no pure wine in France known by the name of claret, which is a corruption of clairet, a term that is applied there to any red or rose-coloured wine. . . . The clarets brought to the English market are frequently prepared for it by the wine-growers by mixing together several Bordeaux wines, or by adding to them a portion of some other wines; but in France the pure wines are carefully preserved distinct. The genuine wines of Bordeaux are of great variety, that part being one of the most distinguished in France; and the principal vineyards are those of Medoc, Palus, Graves, and Blanche, the product of each having characters considerately different.

Choose a light, dry red wine and you'll have an approximation of a claret. They are especially good served with lamb, beef, game, and cheese. My wine merchant recommended those from the merlot grape, such as a Saint Emilion or Pomerol. If you have a knowledgeable wine merchant, ask what he or she would suggest. Try a few different types and see what suits your taste.

White wines popular during the period were Madeiras (the driest kind served with soups, the sweeter as an aperitif) and sauternes (drier types with white meats and seafood, sweeter ones as a dessert wine).

There was always dry sherry, served as an aperitif or with canapés. After dinner usually meant bringing out the port (served by itself or with apples, walnuts, and Stilton or blue cheese) or brandy.

Champagne meant romance and gaiety, and the Victorians drank it often. When Dominique Pérignon created it he is said to have exclaimed, "I am drinking the stars!" Not only for toasting, champagne was also used to make champagne cup and in cooking. Other drinks included kirsch, gin, spiced apple wine, hot buttered rum, and mulled cider.

Cocktails made a solid appearance in Victorian America as well, although some critics abhorred them. Some period drinks mentioned by Charles Dickens in 1842, which he encountered in the bar during his stay in a Boston hotel, include the "Gin-sling, Cocktail, Stingaree, Mint Julep, Sherry-Cobbler and the Timber Doodle." The daiquiri was introduced at the close of the Victorian era by some American engineers working in the Daiquiri iron mines of Cuba. They invented the cool lime and rum drink around 1900 as a refresher for the end of a hot day's work. At around the same time, another American, also in Cuba, invented the rum and Coca-Cola.

These are just a few historical culinary tidbits to get you thinking. You can get as authentic as you like—it will only add to the fun.

✣　✣　✣

Four Victorian Wedding Receptions

The Wedding Breakfast

WEDDING BREAKFAST MENU

Oyster Soup, served in a tureen

Roast or Boiled Fowl or Game

Venison

Country Ham

Roast Lamb

Pressed Beef

Game Pies

Lobster Salad

Chicken Salad

Fried Oysters

Salmon, Broiled, with Lobster Sauce

Pâtés

Aspics

Cheeses, decorated with herbs

Deviled Eggs

Tarts, dinner and sweet

Water Ices

Cakes

Cookies

Bonbons

Coffee, Tea, Cocoa

Most Victorian wedding receptions were known as wedding breakfasts, but they hardly looked like a breakfast at all. They were usually held closer to lunch time and could be very sumptuous meals. The wedding breakfast could be served either buffet-style from a sideboard, where guests seated themselves, or as a regular sit-down meal. The same menu could easily be for a wedding supper, also a common practice. You can decorate the table lavishly with mosses, flowers, and ferns and have lots of tall potted plants in the room, including the essential parlor palm. Victorians used food as decoration too, making towers of fruit and putting cakes and confections on tiered servers with flowers and greens.

Your wedding breakfast can be adapted to include mostly hot dishes or cold ones or a mixture of both. The menu on page 133 is similar to one in Mrs. Beeton's book.

You might adapt this to the season and to an outdoor or an indoor setting. Many of the meats could easily be served cold for an outdoor summer reception. Most of the recipes are in *Mrs. Beeton's Victorian Cookbook*, a modern reprint of the original *Book of Household Management*, but you can probably find modern versions in any general cookbook. Pressed beef is a cold, pickled beef. Dinner tarts usually contained meats and vegetables; sweet tarts could be cream filled with fruit on top or filled with fruit only.

The Formal Dinner Party

Dinner parties were the most important of social occasions. Dress was extremely formal, and short-sleeved gowns with low-cut necklines were in order, as they also were at balls. Etiquette books admonish guests to be sure they have clean hands and nails; a proper conversation never included religion, politics, controversial topics, or anything vulgar. Men escorted ladies to the table in careful pairings usually assigned by the hostess.

Guests at a formal dinner party could have as many as twenty-four pieces of silverware to contend with and seven or eight glasses. Each person would have his or her own individual salt, and introduction of a personal finger bowl would signal the end of the meal—sometimes with a slice of lemon in it or with rosewater and usually made of glass with a doily under it used to wipe the fingers after dipping.

Coffee might be served immediately or offered a half-hour later in the drawing room, possibly with brandy. In the early part of the Victorian age, men usually separated from women and went to a special smoking room or stayed in the dining room to partake of cigars and brandy, while the women retired to the drawing room.

1895 DINNER PARTY

Raw Oysters, on ice and lemon

Mulligatawny Soup

Roast Turkey
Oyster Sauce
Turnips
Boiled Ham
Cranberry Sauce
Potatoes
Pickled Peaches
Chicken Salad

Ice Cream
Cake
Fruit

Coffee

This menu is from a fall dinner party held in 1895. It is simple compared to some described by Isabella Beeton. All of the recipes are recognizable, I think, except the mulligatawny soup (also spelled in some cookbooks mullagatawny). This was made by boiling chicken (or sometimes rabbit) to make a stock, adding the meat after it's been browned, and then adding curry powder, other seasonings, and rice. A modern version in *The Joy of Cooking* includes vegetables, diced apples, and cream. It's a simple, economical, hearty soup that would be easy to make for a large crowd.

A Victorian Ball

The ball "season," both in England and America, was in winter. A ball was usually held in the wee hours, requiring some to take a nap between supper and the event. This would make a lovely evening wedding reception, especially if you can provide period music and dance instruction or demonstrations and if your location is a vintage home or other building with a large, opulent room for dancing. In chapter 8 I've given you the names of some organizations that will actually provide demonstrations and instruction for period dance. With this reception, the emphasis is less on food and more on costumes and music. A large ornate punch bowl or two would provide the centerpiece of the meal surrounded with lighter foods. At right is a period menu from *Mrs. Beeton's* for a ball supper for sixty people.

The menu for a ball should provide lighter fare and plenty of beverages for dancers. *Photo by Tom Eckerle.*

WINTER BALL

Boar's Head, garnished with apple jelly
Mayonnaise of Fowl

Small ham, garnished
Iced Savoy Cake
Epergne with Fruit
Two Boiled Fowls, with Bechamel sauce
Tongue, ornamented
Trifle, ornamented
Raised Chicken Pie
Tipsy Cake
Roast Pheasant
Galantine of Veal
Lobster Salad
Fruited Jelly
Biscuits
Prawns

Custards, in glasses
Small Pastry
Raspberry Cream
Meringues
Vanilla Cream
Charlotte Russe
Swiss Cream
Blancmange

Claret Punch
Champagne Punch
Lemonade
Coffee, Tea, Cocoa

Chances are you'll want to skip the boar's head!

Savoy cake is similar to pound cake and may be iced for special occasions. There is a recipe for this in the original *Mrs. Beeton's*, but not in the recent version (although there is one for Savoy biscuits). A good pound cake recipe would probably produce adequate results. An epergne is a type of serving dish.

Tongue is usually not appreciated by many people, so you'll probably want to eliminate it, but the roast pheasant would add some real glamour to your buffet.

Trifles are rich and spectacular-looking layered desserts, and tipsy cake is a molded sponge cake soaked with sweet wine or sherry and brandy and filled with custard and blanched almonds. The recipes for both are in the new *Mrs. Beeton's*.

Charlotte Russe is a dessert composed of gelatin, whipped cream, and lady fingers, originally named in honor of Princess Charlotte of France. Recipes for this abound, as do variations on blancmange (a cold molded dessert, which literally means "white food" and is usually served with jam, jelly, light cream, boiled custard, or fresh or stewed fruit) and creams (sometimes strictly a molded dessert similar to a Bavarian, sometimes including wine-soaked cake as a base).

Recipes for both claret and champagne punches or "cups" are in the new *Mrs. Beeton's* and almost any other good reference-type cookbook that includes beverages.

A *Fête Champêtre*

A French term originating in the eighteenth century, *fête champêtre* means "outdoor festival." In actual practice during the Victorian age, a fête was an elaborate dinner party, where the participants sought to impose civilization on nature with elegant linens, china, and silver brought into the woods. (Actually, it's not unlike bringing a recreational vehicle completely outfitted with all the modern conveniences into the woods to "camp out.") A reception following this theme could include activities such as archery, wading, nature collecting, games, and fortune telling (how about a scavenger hunt?).

A *fête champêtre* would be perfect if the location you've chosen is in a park or nature center. Although this could be a fairly elaborate affair, the mood is casual and relaxing and especially nice if there are going to be a lot of children present. You could hang colorful lanterns and banners from trees and bring along rugs, as the Victorians did, to lay on the ground to sit.

FÊTE CHAMPÊTRE

Cold Cucumber Soup

Quiches
Fish and Meat Pies
Fried Chicken
Sliced Country Ham
Cold Meat Loaves
Tossed Salad, made with flowers
Potato Salad
Coleslaw
Baked Beans
Pickles
Relishes
Mustard Butter
Horseradish Mayonnaise
Pickled Beets and Eggs

Fresh Fruit
Pound Cake

Lemonade
Rhubarb Cooler
Iced Tea
Frappés

Wines: Port, Brandy, Apolinaris Water
Claret and Champagne Punches
Soda Water

Musicians in the party could bring along their instruments and guests could be encouraged to sing along. Bring in plenty of baskets to carry away dirty dishes—rental dishes are usually heavier and less breakable. Just make sure whatever you bring in with you goes out the same way!

Just for chuckles and to show you how elaborate a Victorian picnic could really be, here's Mrs. Beeton's list of items not to forget:

A stick of horseradish, a bottle of mint sauce well corked, a bottle of salad dressing, a bottle of vinegar, made mustard, pepper, salt, good oil, and sugar. If it can be managed, take a little ice. It is scarcely necessary to say that plates, tumblers, wine glasses, knives, forks, and spoons, must not be forgotten, as also teacups and saucers, 3 or 4 teapots, some lump sugar, and milk, if this last-named article cannot be obtained in the neighborhood. Take 3 corkscrews.

She also recommends taking a half-pound of tea, three dozen quart bottles of ale, ginger beer, soda water, lemonade, sherry, claret, champagne "à discrétion," and brandy. Sadly, her direction "Water can usually be obtained so it is useless to take it" is no longer true.

Frappés are creamy drinks, usually with fruit and sometimes with liqueur added. You might try one with oranges or orange juice concentrate and orange liqueur. Mustard butter and horseradish mayonnaise are easy to make and just add a little zip to the usual spreads: add two tablespoons of mustard, one teaspoon lemon juice, and a dash of cayenne pepper to one-quarter pound of softened butter for the first; one tablespoon horseradish to one cup mayonnaise for the second.

Cold cucumber soup recipes can be found in many cookbooks, including *The Joy of Cooking*.

PRE-WEDDING CELEBRATIONS

A Valentine Engagement Party

As I suggested in chapter 1, you could announce your engagement at a Valentine's Day party, because the Victorians made so much out of these and it would give you a superb opportunity to introduce your theme. Decorate with hearts, cupids, bows and arrows, horseshoes, and love knots—all sentimental Victorian symbols of love. Paper lace doilies, lots of red fabric, ribbons, lace accessories, and flowers should complete the picture. This could easily be done as a buffet or a sit-down dinner, complete with congratulatory toast.

VALENTINE'S DAY DINNER

Scalloped Oysters
Pastry Puffs, filled with Lobster Salad

Cream of Love Apple Soup

Salmon, in caper sauce
Lemon Chicken

Lemon Curd and Strawberry Cream Tarts
Coeur à la Crème
Small Almond Puddings

Coffee, Tea, Cocoa
Champagne

The scalloped oysters recipe in *Mrs. Beeton's* is authentic and doesn't take long to make. (I made it one morning for a Sunday brunch using canned oysters and it took only 45 minutes.) Other good cookbooks have recipes as well.

Coeur à la crème can be a molded heart-shaped spread made with cream and cottage cheeses, sour cream, garlic, and herbs (see *Victoria* magazine's February 1990 issue) or can be made as a dessert, as I've used it here (see *The Joy of Cooking*).

"Love apples" are actually tomatoes, so all we're talking about is a simple cream of tomato soup, which could be served in a white tureen to make it a little more special.

Lemon curd was used at tea time, but also as a filling. It can be bought in a jar or you can easily make it yourself: Just beat three eggs lightly and add the grated rind and juice of two large lemons, one stick of softened butter, and one-half cup of sugar. Heat in the top of a double boiler until the sugar dissolves and curd thickens, stirring constantly. Pour into jars and cover immediately. Simple cream tart recipes may be found in any reference-type cookbook.

The small almond puddings are molded—both puddings and molded foods were very common, often made in fancifully shaped tin-lined copper molds. You'll find the recipe in the new *Mrs. Beeton's* along with those for salmon in caper sauce and lemon chicken.

Invitation Work Breakfast

The idea for this event is to make addressing and stuffing envelopes a special and shared occasion. It may be something you put together just for your female friends (although some of the men I know do gorgeous calligraphy and have the best handwriting!), or you could start out that way and the gentlemen could join you for breakfast later.

This 1876 menu is taken from Mary F. Henderson's *Practical Cooking and Dinner Giving*, where she virtually introduced the idea of the breakfast party. It was probably more closely akin to what we call brunch today, because it was prescribed for 10:00 A.M. to noon, although she felt an even earlier hour was better. You can decorate with fruit and flowers and be sure to use some lovely linens.

1876 BREAKFAST PARTY

A Havana Orange for each person, dressed on a fork

Larded Sweetbreads, garnished with French pease
Cold French Rolls or Petits Pains
Sauterne

Small Fillets or the Tender Cuts from Porterhouse Steaks, served
on little square slices of toast with mushrooms

Fried Oysters
Breakfast Puffs

Fillets of Grouse (each fillet cut in two), served on little thin
slices of fried mush, garnished with potatoes à la Parisienne

Sliced Oranges, with sugar

Waffles, with maple syrup

This is a huge meal for even a large work party. If you eliminate the sweetbreads, which might not be to the taste of many, and the grouse course, you would have the beef on toast and the waffles, plus fruit and rolls.

You can make the meal more like our modern steak and eggs if you substitute an omelet for the waffles. Add some homemade or extra-special store-bought jams, jellies, preserves, or conserves, and your party's complete.

If you're wondering what "pease" means, it's simply the plural of pea (now you know what "pease porridge" is in the nursery rhyme). Fried mush is cornmeal cereal that has been chilled, cut into slices, and fried.

Broil or grill the fillets of beef and make a light gravy with the mushrooms. The recipe for fried oysters can be found in a variety of cookbooks.

Almost any good homemade rolls right out of the oven will do just fine, even better than bakery rolls, but if you have a good bakery, you can get them fresh that morning. The breakfast puffs Mrs. Henderson mentions were probably potato puffs made from mashed potatoes. You'll find the recipe in *Savory Suppers and Fashionable Feasts*.

Pink Bridesmaid's Tea

Victorian teas took many forms: drawing room, nursery, farmhouse, after sport, garden, and others. The one I've described here is a traditional ladies' tea (which I've set up as a light meal of tea sandwiches and baked goods). If you'd like to find out more about the proper tea, there are lots of fascinating books on the subject, including Marika Hanbury Tenison's *Book of Afternoon Tea* (I've listed others in the appendix).

Delicate china and gleaming silver make even the simplest tea an event. *Photo by Tom Eckerle.*

LADIES' TEA

Cucumber Sandwiches
Egg and Watercress Sandwiches
Rose Petal Sandwiches
Salmon Mousse

Crumpets
Scones
Muffins
Tea Cakes
Victoria Sandwich

Clotted Cream
Jellies and Jams
Honey Butter
Lemon Curd

Stewed Apples
Frosted Peaches
Fresh Fruit

Coffee, Tea, Cocoa
Pink Lemonade

Recipes for everything here can be found in almost any good, complete cookbook. For this tea, use color to pull everything together. Decorate in pink and white (I've even given you plenty of "pink" in the food selections). Use pink flowers, pink ribbons, a pink tablecloth with a white lace overlay, pink napkins, and pink candles. You can even wear pink and white, if you like! (Why not get carried away?) You can mix other colors, of course, like red or peach or mauve, but pink should definitely predominate. Use lots of leafy greens and dusty green and gray mosses to fill in, and don't forget to combine herbs along with your flowers for decorations on the table and on the food itself.

Rose petal sandwiches are simple—just make sure the blooms are chemical free. Before using, remove the bitter white heel from the bottom and carefully wash and dry it. Look for the most aromatic blossoms, since this will mean a rosier flavor. You can just spread cream cheese on brown bread and arrange the petals on the cream cheese or use white bread with just a little unsalted butter.

Nasturtiums are great to eat too and are very colorful and showy. They just shout summer! You can also use flower waters in cooking—rosewater can be gotten from health food or specialty food shops or you can make your own. The Victorians used rose hips for jellies and in cakes and sauces—they're higher in vitamin C than tomatoes, oranges, or lemons.

Honey butter is really easy to make, too: Just take one-half pound of softened sweet butter, add one-half cup of honey and a little cream, and beat with a mixer. Serve at room temperature.

Also known as Devonshire cream, clotted cream takes a day to make and requires fresh, unprocessed milk. To approximate it you can substitute a spread made of three ounces of cream cheese with one-half cup of heavy cream beaten in until smooth. You can also use one-half cup ricotta cheese instead of the cream cheese and use one-half cup of yogurt to replace the heavy cream. It's not quite the same, but an approximation. If you want to try the real thing, some of the tea books I've included in the appendix tell you how.

A Victoria sandwich is actually a sponge cake made in two layers with jam or butter-cream icing in between and confectioner's sugar sifted on top. Frosted peaches (recipe in *Savory Suppers and Fashionable Feasts*) are fresh peaches dipped in egg whites, then twice in powdered sugar (drying in between). They are arranged in a glass dish on the table and garnished with green leaves.

Costume and History Breakfast or Tea

The purpose of this event is to get your wedding party (and possibly, parents) together to familiarize them with your theme and work on clothing for each of them. Have plenty of books with photos and illustrations for them to look at, and you might even consider showing videos of some of the movies or television shows I listed for you in chapter 4. This menu lets you do most of the work ahead, leaving you plenty of time to prepare materials for your guests.

BREAKFAST BUFFET

Vegetable Quiche
Seafood Crêpes

Lettuce Salad
Sliced Tomatoes

Rosewater Sugar Cookies
Lavender Meringues

Iced Lemon Mint Tea
Iced Orange Cinnamon Tea
Sauterne
Cordials
Brut Champagne

Quiches and crêpes would not exactly be typical for tea, but they were made by the Victorians (who loved every-

be able to approximate a Victorian menu by pulling several together.

When choosing your own caterer, make sure you get references and recommendations. It's not out of line to ask whether you can sample some of a potential caterer's cooking, either. A caterer can show you an album of beautifully appointed tables with elaborately presented dishes, but the proof of the pudding is in the eating.

Meet with several potential choices, take notes, and be prepared with information on the number of guests you're anticipating, a firm budget, and the reception site. To communicate what you're trying to do, show them this book and the menus I've provided here. If you already have your own menu in mind, share it with them and get their reaction. How flexible are they? Caterers have definite styles of their own, and you're trying to match the caterer with the theme, style, and location of your Victorian wedding, so don't be afraid to keep looking for the right match.

Some other questions you'll need answers to are

+ Is there a minimum or maximum number of people the caterer is willing or equipped to handle?

+ How many servers will he or she provide and what is the ratio of servers to guests? Will the cost per person be less for a buffet-style event?

+ What appointments does the caterer provide? Linens? Serving dishes? Candlesticks?

+ What about beverages? Does the caterer really understand wines and liquors? What about nonalcoholic beverages? You'll need to make a decision as to whether you want to have a modern open bar or want to offer spirits in the Victorian manner—at the table or in a punch or cup. This could actually save you the expense of a bartender and also puts the consumption of alcohol back where it belongs—as a complement to the meal, not an end in itself.

+ In order to complete your menu, does the caterer need any special equipment not included in the cost of the site?

+ Is your deposit returnable if the contract is canceled within a reasonable amount of time? After what date will you be penalized? How much is your deposit and when is your final payment due? Are tips included in the price? How much are they and for whom?

+ Can you have *recent* references? If not, *don't* use that caterer! Ask whether you can visit a reception or at least observe the preparation stage.

+ Does the caterer have liability insurance?

+ Are the servers and other food-service personnel willing to wear period costumes or accessories (as we discussed in chapter 5) or possibly follow some clothing guidelines?

+ If you are planning a buffet for a large number of people, does the caterer offer ideas for traffic flow and table arrangement at the site? Make sure there are enough tables for food and enough duplicate dishes to serve the crowd quickly.

THE WEDDING CAKE

Queen Victoria's wedding cake can only be imagined. It reportedly weighed 300 pounds, measured three yards across and fourteen inches high, and was decorated with roses and topped with an ice sculpture of Britannia surrounded by cupids.

By the Civil War, the white wedding cake had emerged as the popular favorite, although earlier it was just as likely to be a dark fruit cake, and in some regions a rich pound cake was traditional. Often two kinds of cake were served—the fruit cake, offered as a separate groom's cake

Whether plain and simple or highly elaborate, the wedding cake is the centerpiece of your romantic repast. *Cake by Jan Kish of La Petite Fleur. Photo courtesy of Lambert Photographs, Columbus, Ohio.*

and topped in white (sometimes used as the top layer of the bride's cake) and the bride's cake. This second cake would often be sliced and sent home with guests.

A traditional pioneer wedding cake was called "stack cake." Each wedding guest brought a layer of cake, which when spread with applesauce was laid on top of the layer before it. The more beloved the bride, the more stacks and the more layers!

Superstitions about wedding cake are plentiful. One says it's bad luck for the bride to bake her own wedding cake, and she's never to steal a crumb before it's cut. Another dictates if she saves a small piece, she'll ensure fidelity. But one custom is constant even today: The bride is to cut the first piece (in the Victorian era it was believed if she didn't, she'd be childless).

The cake might be iced with a butter cream or egg-white frosting and possibly filled. It could be several tiers or only one layer and might be topped with real, silk, or sugar flowers or an elaborate sugar "sculpture."

One modern Victorian bride used a white porcelain tree of life as a cake topper (a motif you often see in period quilts), because it was a symbol that reached its greatest popularity in the Victorian era and best expressed this couple's sentiments about their marriage.

The Victorian era was the height of confectionery art, and there are still bakers capable of building similar creations today. I've given you a list of some in the appendix. If these are nowhere near you, use the same methods I suggested for finding a caterer and uncover the hidden talents that may be residing in your area.

FLOURISHES

- ✧ Have menus printed up for each table (or photocopied), using a fancy border from one of Dover's Victorian border books and calligraphy. Mount them on cardboard and display on a small easel. If you are having a buffet or smaller event, use one at each end of the table.

- ✧ After the meal, serve fresh fruit along with knives to pare and a confectioner's sugar shaker (there are beautiful glass ones that are antiques, but a modern hobnail pattern would be a good substitute).

- ✧ On a picnic, cover anything that's modern and would jar the mind back into the twentieth century with fabric. Cover coolers and boxes. Use as many period containers as possible, especially baskets, that can be decorated with flowers and ribbons.

- ✧ Make your own picnic hamper by lining a sturdy picnic basket with quilted fabric (or pad it with batting and sew it strategically together with some durable fabric), using a glue gun to hold it in place.

  Then put together plates, linens, utensils, and beverage glasses for two. I prefer using heavier china and glassware and some mismatched stainless or silver to plastic (perhaps you have some odd pieces, or check your local thrift stores and flea markets). Small quilted bags can be sewn to protect them, tied with ribbons.

Make sure to include a cutting board and a sharp knife with protective sheath (some Chinese cooking knives have these), a can opener, and a corkscrew. And take everything you brought into the woods back with you (unless, of course, you were thoughtful enough to bring along some special food for the wildlife).

✧ Freeze flowers and fresh herbs in ice for decoration—again, make sure they are pesticide free.

✧ Start your own collection of Victorian recipes. As you try different dishes, copy the ones you like in a small book or on recipe cards. Be sure to include any interesting history and the source of your recipe.

✧ Ask members of your family to pool their favorite recipes for a family cookbook. Type the recipes into a computer or hand write them neatly (giving the name of their contributor and any family lore surrounding them) and have them duplicated. Make a nice cover for each and give them as gifts for Christmas. You may want to make a similar collection of your wedding-day recipes and give them out to your guests!

Chapter Seven

Flowers That Speak of Love

O the pretty brave things, thro' the coldest days
Imprisoned in walls of brown,
They never lost heart tho' the blast shrieked loud,
And the sleet and the hail came down;
But patiently each wrought her wonderful dress,
Or fashioned her beautiful crown,
And now they are coming to lighten the world
Still shadowed by winter's frown.
And well may they cheerily laugh "Ha! ha!"
In laughter sweet and low,
The millions of flowers under the ground,
Yes, millions beginning to grow.

Ralph Waldo Emerson

The wedding is probably the celebration we most associate with flowers, because they provide us with an ancient symbol of marriage as a living, growing relationship, needing careful tending and nourishment to flourish. Perhaps at no other time were flowers more a part of the rituals of love, courtship, and marriage than during the Victorian era. As you plan your wedding flowers, you may want to incorporate at least some of the sentiment and symbolism that the Victorians attached to flowers.

In addition to giving you background about nineteenth-century attitudes toward flowers and some common practices, this chapter will help you choose your wedding flowers—for decoration, carrying, and wearing. I'll assist you in finding a florist and give you ideas for inexpensive and simple ways to do your own wedding flowers. And when the wedding is over, I'll tell you how you can preserve your flowers as a keepsake, using both Victorian and twentieth-century technology. But first, let's take a brief look at how the nineteenth-century mind viewed the fruits of the gardener's toil.

The Victorians believed that flowers should be "loved." If treasured and held in high esteem, they thought, plants would last longer and bloom more abundantly. Not much different, it seems to me, from those today who advocate talking to plants and go so far as to play soothing music to help them grow! (It works, by the way.)

Nature held a special place in the Victorian universe. Flowers were a reminder of "what Eden was." Children were told that each flower had a fairy, and a whole world of mysterious "little people" frolicked in the garden unseen. Nineteenth-century Americans loved natural settings, and yet at the same time sought to cultivate nature and bring it under their control. They brought plants and flowers indoors and trained vines, shrubs, and herbs into topiary forms. They built conservatories of glass to house them, and some wealthy homeowners had elaborate greenhouses built, complete with carefully landscaped walkways and fountains.

Flowers, herbs, and greenery were cut, dried, and pressed and used in household and personal-care preparations and in cooking. And they were mirrored in nearly every nineteenth-century art form and artifact—poetry, painting, sculpture, fabric, china, silver, jewelry, needlework, and even music.

The Victorians collected and documented the natural world around them. They went on walks and picked wildflowers and grasses, capturing them in portable flower presses before they had time to wilt. Some kept their finds in pressed-flower diaries or herbariums, along with their names and information about where they'd been found. Others made flower booklets—somewhat smaller volumes

Nature was revered by the Victorians, and they sought ways to bring flowers, herbs, and greenery into every aspect of their lives. *Photo by Tom Eckerle.*

FLOWERS THAT SPEAK
OF LOVE

159

containing poems, quotes, or sayings along with pressed flowers to match the verse. These flower volumes were often intensely personal. They might describe one's own yard, a favorite walking place, or a country hike with a friend, and they aptly illustrate the intimate dialogue with nature treasured by so many Victorians.

Girls (including the future queen of the empire) learned to do watercolor sketches of flowers, both wild and cultivated, and had detailed copybooks to help them. They soon learned to grow a garden, and every well-bred Victorian lady knew how to arrange flowers. Trips to local florists or "swaps" with neighbors expanded the colors and varieties available, and children were often asked to gather wildflowers to add to the selection.

Indeed, in her *Book of Household Management*, Isabella Beeton told her readers, "We can imagine no household duty more attractive to the ladies of the house than that of making their tables beautiful with the exquisite floral produce of the different seasons, exercising their taste in devising new ways of employing the materials at their command. Young people should have their taste for arranging flowers encouraged, and be allowed to assist in decorating the table." But, she warned, "Care should be taken not to overload the table with flowers."

Early Victorian flower arrangements seemed to go by the rule "the more the merrier" and invited the greatest variety of colors, textures, and types of flowers, with little thought given to their complementarity or symmetry. They could include fresh, dried, or artificial materials—even odds and ends such as feathers, leather, seeds, beaded things, and seashells. The more unusual and cluttered, the better, and the vases used were large and ornate.

Mid-Victorian arrangers took a more organized approach, making recommendations for color coordinating flowers and filling in with green foliage. The highly ornamented container, however, was still prized.

By the 1880s, with the emergence of the new aesthetic associated with the Arts and Crafts movement, simplicity became the watchword of floral arranging. The arranger was to take cues from the order and form of nature itself and consider the flower in its natural state. Only one or two varieties were to share the same vase, which should be simple and, preferably, clear glass. Mrs. Beeton agrees, saying, "It is well to avoid many colours in one decoration, for, even if well grouped, they are seldom as effective as one or two mixed with white and green. . . . It is the fashion to have a single colour for a dinner-table decoration, this being often chosen of the same tint as the hostess's dress or the hangings of the room." And arrangements should *never* obstruct the all-important social conversation at teas, balls, or dinner parties.

THE LANGUAGE OF FLOWERS

Throughout history, flowers have had religious, mythological, and symbolic meanings, as well as culinary and medicinal uses, but in the Victorian era these evolved into an elaborate "language" for communicating love and friendship, a delicate rebuff, or disdain and rejection.

The appearance of floriography, or assigning meanings to flowers, gave women of the Victorian age a way to express their feelings within the bounds of a strict etiquette. The first flower dictionary, *Le Langage des Fleurs* by Mme. Charlotte de la Tour (Louise Cortambert), made its debut in Paris in 1818 and was an overnight sensation, appearing in eighteen editions and gaining popularity in Spain, England, and America.

Other guides appeared throughout the century, often contradicting one another, which made it essential that the communicants were using the same volume. In addition to meanings assigned to individual flowers, a bloom's presentation had something to say as well. If a flower was offered upright, it meant good news; down-turned signaled the opposite. Thorns left on a rose inverted its meaning. And the rose—the rose was in a class by itself; each color had a different meaning and various combinations changed the significance of the single rose. A fully opened rose, for example, placed over two buds stood for secrecy, while a white and a red rose together signified unity.

I've provided you with a brief list of some popular

Love's language may be talked with these;
To work out choicest sentences
No blossoms can be meeter;
And, such being used in Eastern bowers,
Young maids may wonder if the flowers
Or meanings be the sweeter.

Elizabeth Barrett Browning

Victorian herbs and flowers and their meanings. Your own wedding flowers can draw from it as much or as little as you like. If you would like to learn more, I've listed some sources in the appendix. This is simply by way of background and not meant to confuse or overwhelm you. Just play the "flower game" for fun and add yet another dimension to your Victorian wedding.

The Meaning of Some Flowers and Herbs

Azalea. Temperance.

Bay leaf. "I change but in death."

Bittersweet. Truth.

Chrysanthemum. Red ones declare love; yellow stands for love refused; white stands for truth.

Daffodil. Regard and chivalry.

Daisy. Innocence; associated with children and with fortune-telling ("He loves me, he loves me not . . .").

Dogwood. Durability.

Fennel. Worthy of all praise; strength.

Flowering almond. Hope; an especially appropriate wedding gift, I think, to be planted in the couple's yard.

Forget-me-not. True love; remembrance.

Holly. Foresight.

Hyacinth. Sorrow; in some floral dictionaries the hyacinth stands for sport or play, and a white hyacinth stands for unobtrusive loveliness.

Ivy. Fidelity, because it clings, and once it has taken hold it can never be separated. Also stands for marriage, making it especially appropriate to be included in the bridal bouquet.

Lavender. Distrust; in some dictionaries, luck.

Lilac. First love; it is said that if one lilac is cut down in the garden, the others refuse to bloom.

Lily. Purity; one of the oldest flowers in the world.

Lily-of-the-valley. Return of happiness; the symbol of May Day.

Linden tree. Conjugal love.

Marigold. Grief.

Marjoram. Blushes.

Mint. Virtue.

Mistletoe. "I surmount difficulties."

Moss. Maternal love.

Mustard seed. Indifference.

Myrtle. Love and marriage.

Orange blossoms. "Your purity equals your loveliness."

Orchid. A belle; although this might seem like an exotic flower, wild orchids grow in English fields and hedgerows.

Peony. Shame and bashfulness.

Peppermint. Warmth of feeling.

Phlox. Agreement; unanimity.

Rose. The queen of flowers; in general, the rose symbolizes love, but different types and colors stand for the many aspects of love. White is for pure and spiritual love; yellow, for infidelity or diminishing love. The cabbage rose is the ambassador of love, while the musk rose emphasizes capricious beauty and the Damask rose means brilliant complexion. Only the bud, if it is white, signifies a heart ignorant of love, or girlhood. A red bud means "pure and lovely."

Rosemary. Remembrance, friendship, and fidelity; wedding guests were presented with gilded sprigs of rosemary tied with colored ribbons.

Sage. Esteem or domestic virtue.

Sweet basil. Good wishes.

Thyme. Activity.

Tulip. Declaration of love, says the red tulip; hopeless love, says the yellow.

Violet. Modesty.

Zinnia. Thoughts of absent friends.

YOUR WEDDING FLOWERS

I might as well tell you—I'll take fresh flowers over artificial ones any day, no matter how well executed they may be. Even though I admittedly have some silk flower arrangements in my home here and there, I still prefer to buy fresh

Loveliest of lovely things are they,

On earth, that soonest pass away.

The rose that lives its little hour

Is prized beyond the sculpted flower.

William Cullen Bryant

ones (a part of my weekly budget is devoted just to flowers) or bring them in from my garden. Fresh flowers are luxurious. Their colors, textures, and aromas can't be duplicated. Through them we connect with nature on a daily basis, reminding us of the continuity of grace, beauty, and life itself.

Putting my obvious prejudice aside, however, there are distinct advantages in using silk flowers for weddings. They don't fade or break. They can be made far ahead of time, they don't require refrigeration or especially careful handling, and they can be kept forever without any additional cost to preserve them. However, silk flowers are usually more expensive than fresh, unless, of course, the fresh flowers you're using are exotic or out of season.

You don't necessarily have to have all silk or all fresh either. You could, for example, have the bouquets and boutonnieres done in silk and the flower arrangements in fresh-cut flowers.

Think about the effect you want to achieve as well as what will please you the most. For me, an abundance of fresh flowers at my wedding was essential. They were on the veranda where the ceremony took place and in profusion in the dining room for the reception. The women in the wedding party carried them and wore them in their hair, and the men's boutonnieres were fresh rosebuds. There was even a cascade of fresh flowers decorating the wedding cake.

Whatever you decide, determine your budget and then work within it. Do some of the work yourself, if you need to stretch your wedding dollars.

DECORATING THE CHURCH AND THE HALL

In chapter 5, I discussed many of the ways you can enhance the locations of both your ceremony and your reception, including the use of flowers. I talked about creating an atmosphere or mood, and how to make impersonal spaces more inviting. What kind of effect or feeling are you trying to achieve, and what does the location itself suggest? If your ceremony is in a church, is it a formal cathedral or a country meetinghouse? Is it dark and somber or bright and sunlit?

flowers with long stems for you that morning, which can then be tied together with a ribbon and carried as an arm bouquet. Or how about some fresh-picked wildflowers? Be careful, though—take only those that grow plentifully, such as Queen Anne's lace, buttercups, or the various kinds of daisies. Many wildflowers are now on the endangered species list. Fortunately, though, more and more wildflower seeds are being sown and many people have burgeoning wildflower gardens of their own. Depending on how far in advance you are planning your wedding, maybe you can sow a meadow with wildflowers yourself, to be used in your bridal bouquet and ever after.

Tussy-mussies are easy to make and very Victorian. They had their own vase- or horn-shaped holders, which could be held in the hand, clipped to one's clothing, or set on a table. Reproductions of these are available, and should you choose to have your bridesmaids carry tussy-mussies, the holders make lovely gifts and were often given in the same way by Victorian brides. There are even buttonhole tussy-mussies that the male attendants can wear, which hold a single bloom with a little greenery quite nicely.

To make a tussy-mussy, take one important flower—a rose, for example—and place it in the center. Encircle it with rings of smaller flowers, herbs, and a final circle of leaves on the outside. Wire the stems together gently and push the bunch through the center of a paper lace doily or surround with a ruffled circlet of lace or dried Queen Anne's lace. Wrap the stems with wet paper towels, foil, and then green florist's tape, working from the top down. Add a pretty ribbon and you're ready to go.

Variations on the tussy-mussy make a lovely bouquet for the bride and/or her attendants. *Photo by Tom Eckerle.*

One way to make flowers go further in a bouquet is to couple them with other materials. Use lace in your bouquets, woven through, rolled up as rosebuds or in streamers. The same can be done with ribbon. Decorate a fan or a parasol with flowers, lace, and ribbon or use small decorated baskets.

You will probably want a separate bouquet for tossing, preferring to preserve the one used during the ceremony as a keepsake. In nineteenth-century America, the bride often threw several bouquets, one to each bridesmaid. In one was hidden a ring, and the woman who caught it was the next to wed. A small tussy-mussy (or several small bouquets, if you'd like to follow the Victorian tradition) would do nicely and could be made out of fresh, dried, or silk flowers. A small herbal bouquet would work well for this, too, but make sure to include some rosemary (remembrance), parsley (festivity), and sweet basil (good wishes).

OTHER FLORAL PIECES

A single bloom, coupled with an herb sprig or some baby's breath, makes a fine boutonniere. Mothers' corsages can be made up as wristlets, and again, you might want to include some fragrant herbs. When planning for flowers that will be close to the face, be conscious of those who have severe allergies. At my own wedding, we had a special silk flower corsage made for my mother, who has a serious asthmatic condition coupled with allergies. She has been known to end up in the hospital after being in close contact with someone wearing perfume!

Hair clips, headpieces, and circlets are some other beautiful ways to use flowers for your wedding. When shopping for your headpiece, make sure your hair is arranged the way it will be on your wedding day so it will fit properly, and let your florist *and* your hairdresser know what you're planning.

Flowers can be used as favors, as well. A single bloom can be laid across a plate or tucked in a napkin. Or each guest can be given a boutonniere.

Baskets for various purposes—holding wedding programs, favors, or flower petals or birdseed for throwing—can be decorated by gluing moss and dried flowers around the edge or on the outside. Streamers of ribbon or ruffles of lace will add to the romantic look. There are plenty of crafts books to show you how to make lovely decorated baskets, and you might even want to use tiny ones filled with Jordan almonds or some other treat for your favors.

If you're going to use fresh flowers for hairpieces,

for favors, or as a decoration for your wedding cake, make sure you plan for them in your floral order. The little extras can add up, so try to determine *all* the flowers you'll need ahead of time to avoid any surprises.

For those of you who are doing your own flowers, you'll probably want to buy wholesale, if at all possible. Plan out your flowers, making a list with quantities. Include fillers and greenery. You'll need a fairly large quantity for a wholesaler to be willing to do business with you, and in some areas wholesalers may not be willing to sell to you at all if you don't have a tax number.

Many wholesale florists deal in dried and silk flowers, as well as accessories and floral supplies. Look in your yellow pages under "Florists—Wholesale" and "Florists' Supplies" and make some phone calls. If wholesalers aren't willing to deal with you on a wholesale basis, ask if they sell retail. The retail section of a wholesale floral supply house can be less costly than a florist who does retail only. Get prices and compare.

There are some definite advantages to using a professional florist. It's one less thing you have to think about the week of the wedding, and a professional will have access to all the right sources for the wedding arrangements and bouquets you want. Arranging flowers is an art, and some of us (I include myself in this!) are not all that artistic or experienced with arranging flowers. A florist will also know which flowers are in season at the time of your wedding and, therefore, the least expensive. They will know which flowers are especially perishable and which will hold up best.

If you decide to use a professional florist or silk flower arranger and it's within your budget, try to find someone who knows something about Victorian-era flowers and their meanings and the use of herbs. This may sound harder than it really is. People who love flowers are often interested in their history and the customs surrounding them, and many have an avid interest in herbs.

If you can't find someone with an interest in Victoriana or floriography, simply finding an open-minded and creative florist might be enough. Together, with your own background and some of the sources I've provided for you, you should be able to come up with an acceptable plan.

Here are some more tips for finding and working with a good florist:

- ✣ Go window shopping and look at their displays.

- ✣ Get recommendations, especially from friends interested in Victoriana or from locations with a Victorian slant.

- ✣ Ask to see pictures of the work they've done for weddings.

- ✣ Get estimates from several florists, not just one.

- ✣ Show your floral arranger what the dresses in your wedding will look like and bring color swatches. Bring pictures, too, of bouquets you like from magazines and books.

- ✣ Ask your florist to make suggestions, using flowers that will be in season at the time of your wedding if you're on a tight budget.

- ✣ Come with a list of flowers you like, either for their meaning, their significance to you, or their overall appearance, and let your florist know at the outset if you're going to be using herbs.

- ✣ Be flexible. I had my heart set on gardenias, one of my favorite flowers, for my bouquet, but after considering the expense and the fact that they can turn brown when handled, I changed my mind.

Don't be afraid to work with a home-based floral business, if the owner has a good reputation and has been in business for a while. I found one for my own wedding who had a special affinity for flowers from the Victorian era. Her business thrives on word of mouth and, because she has very low overhead, her prices were quite reasonable. We worked out a flower scheme using swatches of material and looking through flower books over coffee at her dining-room table. She had a fan made from my dress fabric and lace to hold my bouquet and fabricated a lovely gift basket for my matron of honor. Her service was friendly and personal—in fact, we've been friends ever since!

PRESERVING YOUR WEDDING FLOWERS

Rather than having only pictures to remember your flowers, there are many ways to keep them "alive" long after your big day is a fond, mist-filled memory. Victorian flower crafts are thriving and would be a wonderful way to turn your Victorian poseys into a keepsake. You can try them yourself, or there are plenty of flower craftspeople ready to do them for you. Don't be surprised, however, if the colors of your flowers change through the various preservation processes—they can either lose color or deepen, depending on the flower or the technique that's used, but these new hues have a beauty all their own.

Preserve your bouquet, as in this glass dome, and it will surely become a treasured decoration for your home, filled with meaning and sentiment. *Photo by Tom Eckerle.*

Pressed Flowers

Your bouquet can be disassembled and pressed, then reassembled into a picture or several small ones, made into a tray or arranged under glass on a tabletop. You can use your pressed wedding flowers to frame your invitation or a wedding photo (use a black-and-white or sepia-toned print for an antique look). Most flowers press well, except those that are especially succulent, such as bearded iris and gardenias.

I've listed some books for you in the appendix that give clear, step-by-step instructions for pressing flowers, as well as ways of using them in completed projects. Just be aware that the actual pressing should be done when they're as fresh as possible, so if you're not inclined to do it right away, you'd be better off letting someone else do it for you. I've given you sources that provide special insulated containers for overnight shipment of your flowers. All you need to do is make arrangements in advance and they'll take care of everything.

Potpourri

Another Victorian custom for preserving wedding flowers is to make potpourri. Combining the dried petals and blossoms with herbs and spices, and using fragrant oils to refresh them (I've given you sources for these, too), is a delightful way to bring your wedding-day memories into your home. There are many beautiful containers for potpourri, or you can probably find interesting containers right in your own cupboards. Your bridal potpourri mixture can also be sewn into a pillow or sachets.

Drying your flowers whole is another way to preserve them as a keepsake, and there are several methods to choose from, each with its own advantages and disadvantages. As Dody Lyness, editor of "Potpourri Partyline," a newsletter for floral professionals, puts it, there are three basic choices: "You can freeze 'em, bury 'em, or hang 'em by their heels."

The three methods she refers to are freeze-drying (a relatively new technology), using a desiccant (such as silica gel, alum, borax, or hot sand), or air drying.

Freeze-Drying

Freeze-drying requires costly equipment and must be done by a professional. I've given you the name of an organization that will supply you with a professional in your area, if this is the route you'd like to take. It's the one I chose and I was very happy with the results.

The professional who dried my wedding bouquet says she can successfully dry nearly every flower or fern, with only a few exceptions. Certain varieties of daisies and mums don't preserve well; nor do some tulips, but not all varieties of these flowers are a problem. The best thing to do is call in advance as you're planning your bouquet and to ask how well the flowers you're thinking of using will keep. You'll also want to know if you can expect a lot of fading, since certain varieties do fade more than others.

The advantages of freeze-drying are that colors are

sies at the breakfast table. These small, inexpensive floral touches add color and beauty to each day and remind you not to hurry.

✧ Use seasonal flowers as the Victorians did. The flowers that are in bloom locally should be fresher, less expensive, and more authentic for your Victorian wedding and any other time.

✧ After the wedding, continue to use herbs in your arrangements. Learn about their household and medicinal uses (I've given you some sources in the appendix to find out more).

✧ To perk up dried or artificial flowers that have been stored, either before or after the wedding, put your tea kettle on the stove and gently let the steam blanket the flowers. Fluff them up with your fingers between brief trips through the steam.

✧ If your bouquet includes some greenery that can be rooted, such as ivy, don't forget to start some new plants for your home.

✧ If you're not going away on your honeymoon immediately or you're driving to a nearby location, take as many of your wedding flowers as you have room for. Use them to add extra romance to your bridal suite, at home or away.

✧ A wonderful gift would be a basket of seeds or small plants to start a "bridal garden." Your bridal garden basket could follow a theme, concentrating on herbs, cutting flowers, wildflowers, or a culinary garden. If someone asks what you'd like for a wedding present, say you'd like a garden!

CHAPTER EIGHT

MUSIC AND ENTERTAINMENT

Love, sweet love is the poet's theme,
Love, sweet love is the poet's dream;
What is the love of which they sing?
Only a phantom, unreal thing!
'Tis but the dalliance, the dalliance of youth and maid,
'Tis but the passion, the passion of vows that fade;
'Tis not the Heav'n, the Heav'n implanted glow,
That true hearts call love,
Ah, no! ah, no!

Popular Victorian song

The music of Victorian America was one of rich variety, heavily influenced by Europe and the various ethnic groups flooding the shores of the young nation and heading westward toward "the promised land of opportunity." Yet the music of the period had its own impetus and direction, developing into a sound that was uniquely American.

So, what music did American Victorians hear? If you were to attend a ball, a political rally, or a country fair, what melodies might have orchestrated the event? And what songs were played on the parlor spinet or hummed on the street?

At a ball during a typical social "season" you might hear a grand waltz by Strauss, as lavishly dressed ladies and properly attired gentlemen floated around the dance floor.

On September 11, 1850, you might have paid several hundred dollars just to listen to three vocal numbers by the plain and diminutive "Swedish Nightingale," Jenny Lind, singing angelically to a packed house at New York's Castle Garden concert hall in her American debut.

Throughout the 1850s in theaters and halls both in the North and the South, you could be entertained by the Christy Minstrels—black-faced white men playing the five-string banjo and singing songs like "Dixie" and "Old Dan Tucker," imitating the accent and mannerisms of the plantation slaves, not knowing this form of entertainment would later develop into ragtime, jazz, and vaudeville.

If you lived in rural America, you might be very likely to travel to hear an itinerant preacher leading a camp meeting, often lasting several days. In the words of one observer, there would be "groaning, weeping, shouting, praying, singing. Some are converted, and make the woods ring with joyful shouts of 'Glory,' and these exhort others to come and get religion." The gospel songs and popular hymns characteristic of these revivalist services were rousing enough to move men's souls to repent and avow themselves to heaven.

You could have sung the new patriotic hymn, first introduced in 1831 by a group of schoolchildren, titled "America." This familiar tune from the mother country, known in England as "God Save the King," was given new lyrics by a young music student (who later became a minister) named Samuel Francis Smith.

If you were part of high society in "little old New York," you might very well have attended the opening concert in 1842 of the first permanent orchestra, the Philharmonic Society of New York, which was later to grow into today's world-renowned New York Philharmonic.

In cities and towns, in concert halls and barns, you could have been entertained by the Hutchinson or the Baker family, some of the many folk-singing troupes that yodeled

Period music can help create a feeling of nineteenth-century gentility at your ceremony and reception. *Photo by Tom Eckerle.*

and fiddled their way across America in the 1840s, 1850s, and 1860s. Awakening people to the pleasures of choral music, their songs helped to further social causes such as abolitionism, temperance, and religious revivalism.

The Victorians loved classical music, but what they heard was dominated largely by European composers and musicians. They listened to Mendelssohn, Brahms, Bach, Beethoven, Handel, and Haydn. German and Italian opera had made its way to America (the New York Metropolitan Opera House opened in 1883 with a performance of Gounod's *Faust*), and chamber music concerts were also quite popular. The first foundation to encourage the arts was established by George Peabody in Baltimore in 1857.

A phenomenon of the Victorian age was that of traveling virtuosos—pianists, violinists, vocalists, entertainers, and sometimes literary figures who were adored and even worshiped, not unlike rock musicians of today. These musical and literary celebrities would go to all the major American cities, and their arrival was touted in newspapers as a major social event. When Charles Dickens came to America in the 1840s, for example, he was only twenty-nine and was adored as if he were royalty. And it was no accident that Jenny Lind's promoter was the notorious P.T. Barnum.

Although most of the classical music Victorian Americans heard had taken root on foreign soil, some was notably home grown. Probably the most important American composer at the turn of the century was Edward MacDowell. He wrote lovely piano tone poems, the most well-known being the *Woodland Sketches*, which includes "To a Wild Rose" and "To a Water Lily." He also wrote some major works for symphony orchestra, and if you're thinking of using authentic Victorian American music for your wedding ceremony, you might want to familiarize yourself with his work.

A more "experimental" American classical composer of the day was Charles Ives, although his work was virtually unrecognized until the 1930s and 1940s.

Popular music of the days before and after the Civil War included sentimental ballads and nonsense songs, many

The dance was a way for men and women to become acquainted under the watchful eye of Victorian society. *Art courtesy of the Flying Cloud Academy of Vintage Dance.*

of which have simply not held up to the test of time. Some you might be familiar with, though—because they were redone in more recent years—are "Listen to the Mocking Bird" (1855) and "Where, O Where Has My Little Dog Gone" (1864).

Perhaps the single composer most associated with the Victorian era and popular music is Stephen Foster. His songs have become a lasting part of our American music heritage, especially those of his golden years from 1850 to 1860. Songs like "Oh! Susanna," "Old Black Joe," "Old Folks at Home," "Camptown Races," "My Old Kentucky Home," "Jeannie with the Light Brown Hair," "Beautiful Dreamer," and "Come Where My Love Lies Dreaming" were the superhits of the mid-nineteenth century.

The Civil War brought its own music, most notably Julia Ward Howe's "The Battle Hymn of the Republic," George Frederick Root's "Battle Cry of Freedom" and "Tramp, Tramp, Tramp the Boys Are Marching," and Patrick S. Gilmore's "When Johnny Comes Marching Home."

The music of the Reconstruction included the songs

of the trainman and the cowboy. Construction of the first transcontinental railroad began in 1863, and by 1890 there were more than 125,000 miles of railroad in operation. Songs like "She'll Be Coming 'Round the Mountain," "Nine Hundred Miles," "The Midnight Special," and "I've Been Working on the Railroad" became a part of our musical heritage, many of their melodies taken from African-American spirituals.

Cowboy songs like "Streets of Laredo," "Old Chisholm Trail," "Poor Lonesome Cowboy," "I Ride an Old Paint," and "Home on the Range" were all written and sung widely during the Victorian era, along with folk songs like "Tom Dooley" and the ballad "Jesse James."

After the Civil War, minstrel shows remained popular, but black groups emerged, writing and performing their own music. Most notable was James Bland, the first major black popular song composer, who wrote such American classics as "Carry Me Back to Old Virginny" and "Oh! Dem Golden Slippers." Meeting with raves in Europe, Bland gave command performances for Queen Victoria and the Prince of Wales.

The years following the Civil War saw the growth of vaudeville and the music halls and the popularity of singing stars such as Lillian Russell. The public fondness for circuses made "The Man on the Flying Trapeze" a hit in 1868, and songs about the new popular sports and games such as croquet, baseball, and poker soon followed.

Sentimental songs like "I'll Take You Home Again, Kathleen," "Silver Threads among the Gold," "When You Were Sweet Sixteen," and "Sweet Adeline" could be heard everywhere. Some, such as "Rock-a-bye Baby" (written by fifteen-year-old Effie Crockett in 1887 when she was babysitting for a restless child) are still familiar to all of us, whereas others with titles like "Why Did They Dig Ma's Grave So Deep?," "Cradle's Empty, Baby's Gone," "The Picture That's Turned Toward the Wall," "If the Waters Could Speak as They Flow," and "Say Au Revoir but Not Goodbye" we've probably never heard and might best be forgotten.

LOVE, LET US WANDER.

WALTZ.

(SONG AD LIB.)

Words by ARTHUR J. LAMB.

Music by GEO. SCHLEIFFARTH.

Come,........ let us wan-der, my love, thro' pur - ple bow-ers go

stray - ing; Come,........... let us wan der, my love,

Two lit - tle hearts both a- may - ing; We........... will a

As the nineteenth century came to a close, America's music had become big business. Every parlor had a piano, and sheet music sold by the million copies. Here's a quick list of some popular songs and events to give you a feeling for the authentic music of the day and perhaps some ideas for your own Victorian wedding.

1887. "Oh Promise Me," now a wedding standard, was written.

1891. "A Bicycle Built for Two" was penned by Englishman Harry Dacre during a visit to America, its success bolstered by the new fad for bicycle riding, one of the earliest sports embraced by women.

1883. John Philip Sousa played at the World Exposition; his two greatest marches, "El Capitan" and "The Stars and Stripes Forever," were written in 1896.

1892. "After the Ball," written by Charles K. Harris, became the first popular song to sell several million copies of sheet music.

1894. "The Sidewalks of New York" was written and performed, adopted as the anthem of the largest city in the world.

1895. John E. Palmer composed "The Band Played On," after hearing a German street band in New York City.

1898. "Gold Will Buy Most Anything but a True Girl's Heart" was a best-seller, extolling the virtues of a young lady who knows the value of true love over money.

This is just a smattering of what Victorians heard in concert halls, neighborhood churches, barns, and music halls and sang in drinking establishments and their own parlors. If you'd like to learn more, I've given you some resources in the appendix. "But how," you may be wondering, "can I adapt this music to the various parts of my Victorian wedding?"

Choosing Your Wedding Music

As with each of the other elements of your wedding we've considered so far—location, decorations, flowers, clothing, and food—music makes a very important contribution to the tone of the day (formal or informal, intimate or grand) and can emphasize your Victorian theme. But how can you use music of the Victorian period in your ceremony and reception?

Before you actually get down to making selections and adapting them to your plan, first find out what music means the most to you and your future husband, without considering what point in time the pieces are associated with. Just be as comprehensive in your music soul searching as you can. Are there particular melodies or lyrics that mean something special? Is there a particular hymn you've always liked singing in church? Is there a folk song you sang as a child that still makes you smile when you think of it? Are there any classical melodies you find particularly romantic or emotionally moving?

If your musical taste tends toward the contemporary, try listening to some classical music, traditional folk music, or lighter opera together. Many libraries have records and tapes (some have a sizable collection of CDs, too) to lend. Using some of the background I gave you on Victorian music, listen and get a feeling for what the Victorians treasured. Listen to as many different kinds of music as you can before you make your final choices.

You might start with some of the romantic or impressionist composers: Rachmaninoff, Tchaikovsky, Ravel, Debussy, and Saint-Saëns. Try Chopin, Lizst, Schumann, Shubert, and Beethoven. Two Victorian favorites were Mendelssohn and Brahms—these composers are extremely accessible, even to the listener who is not that familiar with classical music.

Some of my personal favorites are Respighi's "The Pines of Rome"; almost all of Debussy, Ravel, Rachmaninoff, and Chopin; and Saint-Saën's *Carnival of the Animals*.

Another composer who held a special excitement for

the Victorians was Bach. Although he died in 1750, several previously unheard pieces were discovered during the nineteenth century. One, the "Passion According to St. Matthew," was uncovered by Mendelssohn and performed for the first time since Bach's death in 1829. Some of Bach's compositions would work very well for the ceremony.

To locate recordings of works by these composers, just check the audio card catalog in your library or ask your librarian for help. If you want to purchase current recordings in a record store, ask the sales clerk if you can see a copy of Schwann's (their publications are *Opus* for classical recordings and *Spectrum* for popular). These are sort of the music world's version of publishing's *Books in Print* and will list the title, artist, and record company, along with a number for ordering purposes.

Add some elegance to your next candlelight dinner and have Mozart playing softly on the stereo. When you're in your car, tune in the classical station once in a while. Take note of the composers and the names of pieces you like. I've given you some suggestions for each part of the ceremony and the reception, but they are *only* suggestions. Your own personal choices will always be the most meaningful.

If you're looking for more ideas, discuss possibilities with musicians who have done weddings before or the music director of your church or synagogue.

Look for pieces that have a marchlike quality to them or a definite rhythm you can walk to evenly. You'll need a fairly slow one for the processional and a slightly quicker one for the recessional. Then look for soft, dreamy music or light, jaunty music (depending on the feeling you want) for the prelude (arrival). If you hear piano, guitar, or vocal solos you really like, they can be used during the ceremony (although you may want to keep them short), or I've suggested some selections from popular Victorian music that would do nicely. The most important goals in choosing your selections are that the music evokes the mood you want, each selection is a good indicator of the various parts of the ceremony, *and* you and your fiancé really like it.

After you've written down several choices for each part of the ceremony and, perhaps, some ideas you may have for the reception, start narrowing them down to a program. Then see if the music fits the activity it goes with. Try actually walking to the processional and recessional. Do they keep a comfortable pace? Where among the words spoken in the ceremony will the solos go, and are they compatible? How about length? Are they pieces that can easily be duplicated by a solo musician you can hire, or do you need a sound system to play them? Do you want all live music, all prerecorded music, or a combination of both?

Of course, you may decide to use more contemporary music for your wedding, and we'll discuss some possibilities later on in this chapter that might blend very nicely with your Victorian theme. Or you may want to use some earlier music (which, by the way, could also be called "authentic," because everything that went before, theoretically, could have been heard by the Victorians, right?). But if you've decided to "go all the way" and carry your theme throughout, the following suggestions should help you move ahead.

The Ceremony

For the ceremony, you will be making your selections from classical, sacred, popular, or folk music. If you're being married in a church or synagogue, you first need to be sure about what rules there are governing music, if any. If a park, a mansion, a garden, or your own home is the site you've chosen for your ceremony, you might want to key your music to the general feeling evoked by the specific location.

If your church has a choir, you can talk to the music director about having it sing at your wedding. Expect to pay the director and the accompanist, however, and ask at the outset what's required. You also may want to hire the church organist, and, again, find out the fee. You'll need to know, too, about the sound system in your church or

Not a Sparrow Falleth,
But its God doth know,
Just as when His mandate
lays a monarch low:
Not a leaflet waveth, but
its God doth see;
Think not, then, O
trembler,
God forgeteth thee!

W.S. Passmore, from the song "Not a Sparrow Falleth," music by Franz Abt synagogue, the rules for using the equipment, and what personnel must be present to run it (and how much you'll need to pay them).

Then you need to break down the various parts of the ceremony and select music for each.

Prelude Music

You'll need some music to accompany the arrival of the guests before the ceremony, whether it's being held at a house of worship or another location. This could be a small string or wind ensemble, a classical guitarist, organ music, or any other light, welcoming music and can be live or prerecorded.

At the time of my own wedding, I was studying the folk harp. My instructor also happened to have a lovely voice, and she and her flutist husband played medieval and Renaissance music for our wedding ceremony. The sound of the harp and flute together drifted delicately through the air while people were greeted and gathered on the veranda for the ceremony. With her long, blond hair, beautiful hand-carved troubadour harp and soft, flowing peasant dress and his lilting tones, they added a romantic appearance as well as delightful accompaniment.

Suggestions:

> **Bach.** "Suite No. 3 for Orchestra"
> **Debussy.** "Prelude" to *Afternoon of a Faun* (1892)
> **Handel** "Air in F"
> Piano pieces by Chopin, Debussy, or MacDowell

Processional

Your selection for the processional needs to have a definite rhythm, suitable for a slow walk. This part of the ceremony is often broken down into two parts, with one piece of music for the entrance of the wedding party and something different (usually Wagner's "Bridal Chorus" or Mendelssohn's "Wedding March," although both are often used as a recessional) that announces the bride. However, if you're doing the processional the way many Victorians did, the same piece can be used for the entrance of the entire wedding party, since the bride and groom enter first.

Suggestions:

> **Bach** "Andante" from *Brandenberg Concerto No. 2*
>
> **Wagner.** "Bridal Chorus" from *Lohengrin*
>
> **Mendelssohn.** "Wedding March" from *Midsummer Night's Dream*
>
> **Handel.** Largo or Allegro Maestoso from the *Water Music Suites*
>
> **Purcell.** "Trumpet Tune and Air"
>
> **Clarke.** "Trumpet Voluntary" (also known as "Prince of Denmark's March"); often used as processional or recessional in British royal weddings
>
> **Guilmant.** "Wedding March"

Hymns

If you're having a religious ceremony and you intend to include hymns, why not look through the hymnal and find some that were written by Victorian Americans? Here are some composers and titles you might find:

> **Mason.** "Nearer My God to Thee," "My Faith looks up to Thee," and "From Greenland's icy mountains"
>
> **Hastings and Toplady.** "Rock of Ages"
>
> **Webb.** "Stand up, stand up for Jesus"
>
> **Bradbury.** "He leadeth me" (Aughton), "Just as

I am, without one peal" (Woodworth), "Savior, like a shepherd lead me" (Bradbury), and "Sweet hour of prayer" (Consolation, Walford, Sweet Hour)

Lowry. "Shall We Gather at the River?"; a companion to this well-known gospel song is "Shall We Know Each Other There?"

Solos

VOCAL

Here's where you can bring in a definite Victorian touch, especially through lyrics, to reinforce your theme in music. Of course, you can use classical solos, which would likely have been used at an actual Victorian wedding. Or you might want to include some popular sentimental Victorian songs that expressed nineteenth-century ideals of love and marriage.

Suggestions:

Classical
Schumann. "Thou Art Like a Flower"
Schubert. "Ave Maria"
Popular
Dana. "Flee As a Bird" (c. 1842), an absolutely precious soprano solo based on the 11th Psalm

White. "Trusting" (c. 1873), a somewhat operatic but touching solo or duet for soprano and tenor with a religious theme

Teschmacher and d'Hardelot. "Because" (1902)

Bond. "I Love You Truly"

Bingham and Molloy. "Love's Old Sweet Song" (Actually, this selection and "Because" were a tad after the Victorian era, but typical and familiar enough to be worth including.)

de Koven and Scott. "Oh, Promise Me" (1889), the old stand-by

Rice, Brown, and Daniels. "You Tell Me Your Dream, I'll Tell You Mine"

Foster. "Beautiful Dreamer"

Herbert. "I'm Falling In Love with Someone," "Thine Alone," and "Sweethearts"

Romberg. "When I Grow Too Old to Dream" or selections from *The Student Prince*. Although post-Victorian, Romberg and Frimi (*The Firefly, Rose-Marie,* and *The Vagabond King*), like Herbert before them, were the giants of the operetta and their music captured much of the essence of Victorian romantic sentiment.

Whoever you select to perform these solos will have to do them completely straight, with no "camp" or melodrama, although some vocalists might be tempted. It might be nice to feature an arrangement done in harmony by a small group of singers or as a duet—even better if you can arrange for the singers to perform in period dress!

INSTRUMENTAL

Some of the words of popular Victorian songs might seem a little too "schmaltzy" for the ceremony, but the melodies by themselves would make lovely instrumental solo material. Consider Herbert (composer of such operettas as *Naughty Marietta, Babes in Toyland,* and *Sweethearts,* many of them immortalized on film by Nelson Eddy and Jeannette MacDonald) or Romberg. Selections from these would also be quite suitable for dance music at the reception, especially the waltzes.

Perhaps a short piano piece appeals to you—maybe one by MacDowell, or how about "Clair de Lune" by Debussy? Be creative and try not to be too bound by convention—just pick a favorite piece of music that says either "joy" or "happiness" to you both.

Recessional

The recessional is usually more upbeat and has a slightly quicker tempo than the processional, befitting the celebration of your new status as husband and wife, and anticipating the festivities about to be held in your honor.

Suggestions:

> **Beethoven.** "Joyful, Joyful, We Adore Thee"
> **Mendelssohn.** "Wedding March" from *Midsummer Night's Dream*
> **Wagner.** "Bridal Chorus" from *Lohengrin*
> **Widor.** "Toccata" from the *Fifth Organ Symphony*, used as a recessional for the wedding of Princess Anne
> **Handel** "Air" from the *Water Music Suites*
> **Purcell.** "Trumpet Tune and Air"
> **Beethoven.** "Ode to Joy" from the *Ninth Symphony*

The suggestions and ideas I've provided for you here are tailored to your Victorian theme, but there are many styles of music that would be quite compatible with a romantic Victorian theme wedding. There are marvelous vocal solos from twentieth-century American musicals ("This Is My Beloved" from *Kismet* left many an eye damp when it was performed at one wedding I attended) and great romantic ballads from American composers such as George Gershwin, Cole Porter, Harold Arlen, and Hoagy Carmichael.

You can certainly use recent selections if you like, but I offer a word of caution here. Because these more contemporary songs have modern associations, they almost pull us away from the more nostalgic atmosphere we're trying to create and transport us rather abruptly into the "here and now." If a particular song has deep sentimental meaning for you and your fiancé, then, by all means, include it. Just take into consideration how it might affect the overall atmosphere you're striving for.

THE RECEPTION

The music you choose for the reception will largely depend on whether or not you intend to have dancing and how thoroughly you'd like to remain true to (or at least compatible with) your Victorian theme.

Music for Arriving and Dining

Although our own wedding had lots of Victorian touches, we didn't try to achieve a completely authentic re-creation, and the inn where we were married did not have a dance floor. Both my husband and I have a special fondness for the music of the big-band era and agreed that light jazz renditions of our favorites would be sophisticated without being pretentious and would be appreciated by our guests, most of whom were in the thirty-and-over category. We hired a jazz quartet, consisting of electric keyboard, saxophone, electric bass, and drums (the keyboard player had been a member of a band I sang with at one time and I knew him to be extremely talented and professional). Armed with a long list of our favorite songs to choose from and instructions to keep the volume low, we couldn't have been happier with the results. We were even able to sneak in a few dances in a vacant corner of the dining room.

Another musical style that might work well for your reception, especially if dancing isn't planned and the attire you've chosen is late Victorian, is ragtime. A child of the Gay Nineties, ragtime was American to the core. Along with the greatest composer of ragtime, Scott Joplin, there were other important figures such as Tom Turpin, James Sylvester Scott, Louis Chauvin, and eventually, Jelly Roll Morton and Fats Waller. Ragtime is happy, sometimes poignant and exciting music and would make a decidedly upbeat backdrop for your Victorian wedding.

Dance Music

If you were attending a ball in the nineteenth century, you could expect to find anything from a lone pianist hired for the evening to play music for dancing, to a small band consisting of piano, violin, and flageolet (less noisy than a horn), to a full string orchestra.

Vintage dance societies are often available for demonstration and instruction at wedding receptions. *Art courtesy of the Flying Cloud Academy of Vintage Dance.*

Should you have your heart set on a Victorian ball reception, complete with period dance instruction (sources for this in the appendix), you'll need to provide appropriate music.

One solution is prerecorded music, but if you'd rather have the added excitement only a live performance can offer, hiring just a pianist is a good alternative and much less expensive than a full band.

You might want to contact a local country dance group or vintage dance society and ask whether they know of any musicians for your event. They might also be able to help you prepare a list of prerecorded music if you want to go that route.

Typical dances of the Victorian period were the waltz and the polka, and others had exotic-sounding names like the mazurka, the schottische, the redowa, the quadrille, and the German. Many a ball ended with the Sir Roger de Coverly, which was simply a Virginia Reel with a different name. Many of these dances are not that difficult to learn, and if you've ever square danced, you'll have a "leg up" on everyone!

If you hire a small string ensemble for the ceremony, the same musicians might be able to play dance music for you, in addition to providing light classical selections during dinner.

In between dance sessions, you might consider having some singers performing Victorian parlor songs, a ragtime piano player, or a barbershop quartet as musical entertainment.

Compatible Contemporary Music

If a top-forties wedding band is really what you want, then have it. I do think, however, that contemporary rock-and-roll music would go a long way toward spoiling the mood you've worked so hard to create. Careful selection of the music to be played—choosing the "light" romantic ballads and dance tunes that so many radio stations play nowadays—would be a workable solution.

The standard ballads and dance music of the thirties and forties are both sophisticated and fun to dance to, and there seem to be more bands or small groups around that specialize in this type of music. Another bonus is that many people know the basic ballroom steps and wouldn't require instruction, the way they probably would for vintage dance.

A band that plays ragtime and Dixieland would be another alternative, as would a country-and-western band (fiddle, mandolin, and banjo are definitely period!).

Another solution, of course, is to use a disc jockey who will work with the music you choose. If he or she has a creative style, together you can design a program that emphasizes your Victorian theme, or at least says "romantic."

Live music adds excitement to any event, but it's more expensive and confines you to the style and repertoire of the musicians you hire. Prerecorded music is less expensive and gives you the widest selection of artists, instruments, and styles, and you can be sure of the quality ahead of time.

Hiring Musicians and DJs

Once you've decided what music you want and whether you want it to be live, prerecorded, or a mixture of both, how do you find the right musicians or DJ and what do you need to know to make the relationship a smooth one?

To locate solo musicians or a particular type of band, try the Musicians' Union Local in your town. Also contact area music groups such as community bands, choirs, or Sweet Adelines and barbershop quartets. Although some of those who participate in these groups may be amateurs, many are accomplished singers and musicians.

If you have a music school or a college or university with a music department in your community, tap resources there. Let the head of the department know what you are doing and that you are interested in working with someone to help plan a program using nineteenth-century music. College music students are also music history students and may be able to help you with suggestions.

Check the yellow pages under "Musicians" and don't overlook booking agencies. A booking agent can help you find exactly what you're looking for, whether it's a folk harpist, a ragtime band, or a classical ensemble. A group or soloist that's registered with a booking agent has the added advantage of being "tried and true." You'll also save time with an agent.

Colleges can be a good source for DJs, if they have a college radio station. Also try your local radio stations and the yellow pages.

For the reception, if you're considering more contemporary music, say 1930s and 1940s or jazz, try piano bars or nightclubs nearby. Watch the newspapers or call ahead to find out what bands or artists are playing when and what style of music they play. Go to hear them yourselves and then find out what agent you can book them with or how to get in touch with them directly.

When you've located a likely prospect, here are some tips to help you make your final decision and make your working relationship smooth.

❖ Be sure you hear a musician or musicians as they will appear for you before you hire them, no matter how highly recommended they come.

❖ Check references.

❖ Make sure you have a letter of agreement or contract. If a musician doesn't have one of his or her own, make one up yourself confirming date, arrival time, playing time, location, program agreed on, breaks, fee, and whether or not the musician is to be included at the meal. Outline the payment schedule (balance plus amount to be paid after the wedding). Make two copies, both signed by both of you, one for your files, one for the musician's.

❖ Check out the sound systems at both the ceremony and the reception location and make sure they are compatible with the needs of the musicians you're hiring. Make sure the electrical requirements of the location are adequate— both with regard to voltage and number of outlets.

❖ Hear a DJ, too, before you hire him or her. DJs have their own style and it may not be to your liking. For most weddings, that style and ability to act as master of ceremonies is desirable. For your theme wedding, you may want a less dominant leader or someone who is in the background altogether. Also, DJs often have their own records and equipment. How willing are they to work with your own program and recordings?

❖ When hiring a dance band, ask about their experience—how long have they been together, and specifically, which musicians will be present at your wedding reception? Make sure you name them in your contract.

- Does the band come equipped with "break tapes" (prerecorded selections to be played while they're taking their breaks)?

- If you hear a DJ you like at another wedding or party, be sure to ask for that person by name when you book your wedding; you may end up with a substitution otherwise.

- Do everything in writing, including the list of musical selections you'd like for the band or DJ.

- If you're using vintage instruments, there's little need to worry about being too loud or whether there are enough electrical outlets! Loud electrified music would, in my opinion, truly work against your theme. Go instead with electric instruments that sound acoustic or acoustic instruments that can be made to carry further through the use of microphones.

- Make sure you let the band or DJ you've hired know you do not want them loud. Tell them what you are doing and the mood you're trying to create.

Rigging Up Your Own Sound System

If you're on a very tight budget, you could enlist a couple of knowledgeable volunteers to handle prerecorded music for you, borrowing records from friends and family and taking them out of the library. You'd need to make a set of master tapes and use a cassette system. Make sure you get more than one person to volunteer, so they can share the time working the sound system and enjoy some of the celebration. Even if you've employed a nonelectrified group of musicians, you may still need a small sound system and microphone to make announcements.

If you're recording your own music, be sure to use only high-quality tapes and use sixty-minute tapes (thirty minutes on each side), because they're stronger and more reliable than longer-playing ones. Carefully label and write out your program.

You can rent a sound system or put together several systems in the family to get the coverage you need. This is done by chaining amplifiers together, using several sets of speakers, and adding a mixer. Leave this, however, to someone who is experienced and knowledgeable.

Then, set up the whole system for a trial run in a garage (or the actual hall if possible) and make sure it can do the job. If you're being married at home, a fairly small system will be all you'll need, but you will still need the mixer for smooth transitions and fadeouts.

OTHER ENTERTAINMENT

If you're looking for some different entertainment between band sessions or just want to provide a special treat for your guests, consider some other entertainment besides music. The Victorians loved country fairs and circuses, complete with side shows featuring magic acts, mentalists, escape artists, acrobats, and feats of strength. Particularly if you're having an outdoor wedding and if children are invited, you might want to include some of these at the reception.

Fortune-telling was a popular parlor game, whether the "reader" looked at your palm, read your cards, or divined the future from your tea leaves. There are people you can hire to do this, or perhaps a friend would like to oblige for fun—there are books that tell the fundamentals of palmistry, tarot card reading, and reading tea leaves, and it's a great way to break the ice at a party.

If you're having vintage dance music for your reception, part of your entertainment might be demonstrations of period dance for your guests. I contacted some of the vintage dance societies in our New England area, and all of them offered workshops, demonstrations, and dance instruction. Their members also dressed in vintage costume and would, by the way, be another good resource for help with Victorian wedding garb.

And if you really want to do something spectacular, you can always have a small fireworks display (done only by professionals, of course)—perhaps just as the bride and groom are ready to leave for their honeymoon.

FLOURISHES

- ✢ Ask your parents what kind of music they had in their wedding ceremony and use some of the same selections in yours.

- ✢ If you and your fiancé are experienced singers, consider singing to one another as part of the ceremony. Only do this, however, if you're sure you can pull it off. I sang for several years in a band and had a fair amount of experience singing in front of large groups of people, but my emotional state during our ceremony would have made it impossible for me to sing—I was trembling too much!

- ✢ Involve musical family members and friends in the ceremony and the reception. Find out what your talent pool is and include them as soloists during the ceremony or to fill in during band breaks.

- ✢ Have a song composed just for the two of you. If either of you is musical (if you both are, how about a collaboration?), you can write your own, or perhaps a songwriting friend would like to present it to you as a wedding gift.

- ✢ Don't forget the music for your honeymoon! Have a small cassette player and some carefully chosen tapes to take with you: How about some old Frank Sinatra, Duke Ellington, Harry Connick, Jr., Ella Fitzgerald, or Billie Holiday? Or make your own tapes of your all-time favorite songs. If you've prerecorded music for the wedding, why not take it along to enjoy your day for days to come?

✣ Rent a player piano complete with Victorian-era music rolls and use it for background music during the wedding meal or as a filler for band breaks.

✣ If you're inviting a number of children to your wedding reception, you might want to provide some special entertainment just for them. How about a folksinger, juggler, clown, or magician, or simply someone to read aloud, tell stories, and play games?

Overleaf: Photo by Tom Eckerle.

PART IV

KEEPING THE ROMANCE

The golden hours on angel wings
Flew o'er me and my dearie . . .
ROBERT BURNS

CHAPTER NINE

A MONTH

OF

SWEETNESS

With thee conversing I forget all time,
All seasons, and their change; all please alike.
Sweet is the breath of morn, her rising sweet,
With charm of earliest birds.

John Milton

The word *honeymoon* means, literally, "a moon of honey" and comes from the days of marriage by capture. For one month after the groom had captured his bride, the couple "hid" from her parents, drinking honeyed wine. I prefer to think of it as a "month of sweetness," and even if you're not able to get away for a month (who is?), the period leading up to your one-month anniversary is indeed a sweet time.

Your honeymoon is a time free of everyday demands when you can totally devote yourselves to one another and enjoy this new phase in the love relationship. It's a time to regroup after the hectic prewedding period. It's a time to rediscover each other, travel, relax, and have fun.

For the Victorian American bridal pair, the honeymoon was called the Bridal Tour and, for the wealthy, could mean as much as six months on an ocean liner or traveling through Europe or America. For middle-class couples it might have meant a trip to New York City, Cincinnati, Chicago, San Francisco, or the ever-popular Niagara Falls.

It's different today in our more mobile and sexually liberal society. The idea of the honeymoon as an adjustment period where couples discovered each other sexually just isn't necessary for most newlyweds. Many have experienced premarital sex, if not an extended period of intimacy, and some have been cohabiting for a year or more. How you spend your honeymoon depends on a whole different set of variables.

Before you settle on your honeymoon location there are some questions you might want to ask yourself and each other:

+ What's your honeymoon fantasy? If you had unlimited time and money, what would it look like? Spend some time on this exercise. Tuck as many of the details of this fantasy away as you can (maybe even write them down). Yes, you'll need to come back to reality, but there may be ways of fulfilling more aspects of your fantasy than you might think.

+ Is there someplace you've never been and always wanted to go for as long as you can remember? Perhaps you and your fiancé could fulfill a fantasy together.

+ Now, back down to earth. . . . Include money for transportation both to and from your destination, and figure in expenses while you are there, such as for food, accommodations, sightseeing, and souvenirs.

+ How long can you legitimately ask off from work? If it's not possible to take a week or more right now, plan even a short getaway—

you'll need it! Then you can take a more extensive trip later on when time permits.

✝ What type of climate does each of you like? Do you like tropical weather or cool mountain air?

✝ What time of year is your honeymoon? If you're having a winter wedding in the Northeast and you want a seashore vacation, your choice of location will be different than if you are marrying in July or August.

✝ Do you want to travel abroad or stay closer to home?

✝ How do you want to travel? By train, boat, car, or plane? Would you like part of your honeymoon to be by bicycle (cycling through Vermont in the fall, for example) or horseback (one of my husband's honeymoon suggestions was a cattle drive. . . . I said, "Some other time, dear.")?

✝ What kind of accommodations do you prefer? A luxury hotel? A cozy bed and breakfast or historic inn? A cabin? A private condo or villa? A tent?

✝ What kind of atmosphere are you looking for on your honeymoon? Do you want the excitement of a big city with lots to do or a slow, languid lifestyle where there's nothing to do but sleep, lie in the sun, and sip mint juleps? Are you looking for adventure? Do you want to be pampered? Do you want to meet new people or be alone? Do you want lots of activity or want to be lazy? Do you want to be in the city or the country? Are you interested in lots of nightlife?

✝ Take an honest look at your schedules for the months leading up to your wedding day. What other things besides the wedding are happening? During the months before our big day, my fiancé and I were fixing up and selling both our houses, moving, traveling a lot on business, and seeing relatives. Our idea of the perfect honeymoon was to take the phone off the hook for a week, sleep late, and enjoy our new home! We took our romantic honeymoon trip on our first anniversary.

✢ When you and your fiancé do things together on weekends, what kinds of things do you do? Do you spend most of your time engaged in sports activities? Shopping? Going to museums, shows, and films? Quietly puttering around the house and reading? What you enjoy doing on your time off is a good indicator of what you would find enjoyable on your honeymoon.

✢ How good a traveler are you? Be honest. Does moving from place to place, packing, and unpacking make you irritable? Do changes in eating and sleeping patterns upset your system? If you want to see several different spots together, but you know what lots of change does to you, maybe a more stationary vacation would be better. You want this trip to be smooth and enjoyable for both of you. I've been on the road with my husband traveling for business where we've been in as many as seven cities from coast to coast in less than three weeks, and I know I can handle a lot of change fairly well. However, because we've done that kind of travel so much, when we really want to relax and concentrate on each other, we take a cruise or go camping. We have to pack and unpack only once, the food is fairly consistent, and we can sightsee or socialize as much or as little as we want to.

✤ How much or little are you and your partner interested in Victorian history, architecture, art, etc.? If it's something you both have a passion for, then by all means, include some Victoriana in your honeymoon plans.

If you've answered these questions and have decided on a popular honeymoon spot such as Hawaii or the Caribbean, then a good travel agent should be able to steer you in the right direction and make all the arrangements for you. There's no cost to use a travel agent, and if you don't have your own, ask a friend or family member to recommend one. If you haven't decided where you're going yet, a trip to the library travel section should help you find some interesting locations. As you find locations that look promising, contact your travel agent and get up-to-date details.

This chapter is designed to help you carry your interest in Victoriana into your plans for a honeymoon. Rather than simply feature individual locations (although I will give you suggestions and examples), I thought it would be more helpful to organize them into theme ideas based on kinds of places to visit (the shore, the mountains, a country inn, a

Mountain resorts such as the sprawling Mohonk Mountain House offer fresh air, lots of outdoor fun, *and* Victorian architecture. *Photo courtesy of Mohonk Mountain House, New Paltz, New York.*

grand hotel), and then you can choose the location that's right for you and obtain the information you'll need (I've tried to help you with some sources in the appendix).

Once you decide where you're going, be sure to make your reservations well in advance, because, as with everything else, popular places are sometimes hard to book without sufficient lead time. Allowing yourself six months is not unreasonable. Making arrangements far ahead can also mean substantial discounts on accommodations and transportation.

Seven Victorian Honeymoons
The Bridal Tour

The Grand Tour was part of a complete nineteenth-century education and sometimes was a trip designed for the bridal pair. It might involve a transoceanic trip to Europe and then six months touring the Continent or more extensive travels into foreign lands. It was to be leisurely and culturally rich, exploring the intellectual and philosophical as well as seeing the sights.

Few of us today can even consider such an excursion, restricted by either time or finances, probably both. I did read recently, though, about a couple who fulfilled this dream later in life, taking their children with them—something they had prepared for over a sixteen-year period. The family embarked on a year's journey around the world, visiting twenty-two countries, and designed it to reflect the Victorian educational ideal of the Grand Tour.

Maybe you don't have the resources or the time for such an extravaganza, but if you're really eager to see a lot of different sights and have a couple of weeks to spend, you might want to plan a regional tour of a particular area, moving around to several locations during the course of your trip.

My husband and I have been working toward a cross-country tour since we first met. He has always wanted to visit historical locations significant to the Civil War and the old American West. I have a passion for Victorian house

museums and anything concerning nineteenth-century life-styles. I found two tour guides, one for the old West and one for the Civil War (see appendix), and have started a journal of places I'd like to visit that I've learned about from books, magazine articles, and word of mouth.

We're planning to take our trip a year and a half from now, combining our interests. We've already arranged for someone to live in our house for six months while we're gone and plan on leasing or buying a small van-camper. We've often commented on what a great honeymoon this would have been, had we been able to swing it at the time.

This kind of trip requires long-term planning and a lot of time flexibility, but a smaller "tour" could be done in a couple of weeks. You could choose one area particularly rich in your field of interest. South Carolina, for instance, is one state full of places significant to the Victorian era in general and the Civil War in particular. There's plenty there to keep the two of us happily busy for weeks on end.

One couple I know spent their honeymoon bicycle riding from country inn to country inn in Vermont. Another did a similar tour of the Pennsylvania Dutch country. My cousin and his wife are avid hikers and planned an extensive trip hiking sections of the Appalachian Trail. Other ideas include touring California wine country (there's a lovely Victorian inn in the Napa Valley) or following the Oregon Trail westward.

If this kind of traveling vacation appeals to you, make sure you're fairly rested *before* you leave, as it can be quite physically demanding, especially if you're not used to a lot of walking or other physical activity. If you're driving, you'll need to see to it that your car is in good working order. Plan short hops, allowing time to really see the places you want. Once you've decided on the places you want to visit, if you're a member of the Automobile Association of America (AAA), they will map out a customized route just for you with approved accommodations (hotels, motels, RV parks, and campgrounds).

Make sure you have a definite itinerary with confirmed reservations at each stop, though. There's nothing like a No Vacancy sign when you arrive tired and hungry in a strange town.

The Seaside Resort

There were once many large seaside resorts throughout the country, and a sun-filled seashore vacation was a Victorian favorite. Some of these old beauties have been torn down to make room for modern hotels; others have been lost to fire and other natural disasters. But there are still some magnificent nineteenth-century seaside resorts in operation, and if you ask your travel agent, you should be able to get a list of suggestions and some brochures.

A few areas I would recommend you look at are Newport, Rhode Island (which is absolute heaven for the lover of Victorian architecture); Cape May, New Jersey (ditto); and Coronado, California.

The Hotel del Coronado, which opened in 1888, is located near San Diego. It was designed by the famed architects James and Merritt Reid (who also designed the Fairmont Hotel in San Francisco), and the installation of the hotel's original lighting system was overseen by none other than Thomas Edison himself; it was the largest single installation of incandescent lamps in the United States at that time. Although there have been modern additions made to the original hotel, it retains much of its original character, and the surrounding city of Coronado seems almost enchanted. L. Frank Baum must have thought so—he wrote *The Wizard of Oz* there!

Victorian Costume Holiday

Increasingly, there are Victorian-era resorts and inns, historical houses and museums, and other places that organize Victorian-style weekends. Some involve solving mysteries; others are centered around vintage dance or Victorian lawn games such as croquet. Victorian garb is encouraged and there's usually some dance or game instruction available for the uninitiated. This might be just the thing to extend your Victorian wedding into your honeymoon and allow you to wear your carefully assembled wedding garb once again.

These weekends might take a little effort to uncover, but some of the Victorian lifestyles magazines often run features on these special events. Some larger inns and bed-and-breakfasts run Victorian festivals and weekends as well. Read the next section to find out how to get information on these.

Mohonk Mountain House (circa 1868), on Lake Mohonk in upstate New York, hosts a Victorian Holiday each fall. This year's three-day weekend event included lectures and workshops by experts in the fields of Victorian collectibles and ephemera, vintage dance, and crafts. You can make a tussy-mussy, learn to play croquet, and attend a Victorian dinner dance. My husband and I brought costumes for the croquet tournament and the dance. Because the house has one of the largest collections of Victoriana in use, you can surround yourself with the furnishings and objects of the period and actually use them, not just look at them in a museum. The grounds are rustic and vast, with hiking trails, horseback riding, and many more outdoor activities.

You might want to plan such a weekend as the beginning or the end of your honeymoon trip, perhaps as an adjunct to a city stay. Remember, too, that you'll have to transport your costumes without crushing them (packing a period ballgown, complete with hoop, is definitely a challenge) or have them pressed when you get there. This is probably easiest if you're traveling by car and have more room to hang or lay out your garments.

A Cozy Bed-and-Breakfast or Country Inn

If you've never stayed in a bed-and-breakfast (B&B), you're in for a treat! And if your idea of the perfect honeymoon is all the comforts of home away from home, then a country inn is for you. You can find one that is casual or elegant, quiet or bustling, depending on your fancy.

The advantage of this type of accommodation is the

personal service, uniqueness, warmth, and charm you just can't find in a big commercial hotel. Some B&Bs and inns have special honeymoon rooms. One I know of in Julian, California, has a separate fairy-tale cottage just for honeymooners.

A place I've read about and am dying to visit that seems the perfect place to spend a quiet, slow-paced, contemplative honeymoon is the Chautauqua Institution in western New York State. Most cars never find their way past the town gates. Visitors can take classes on embroidery or politics, sail, attend an opera, or just doze on a cottage porch.

Founded in 1874 as a place for sunday-school teachers to meet in the summer, the Chautauqua Institution has developed into a center for education, art, religion, and recreation. For anyone interested in Victorian architecture, there's plenty to see in this national historic district. During the two-month-long summer season there are concerts, lectures, operas, and plays. The center is a place where artists, writers, and ordinary citizens come to get in touch with themselves and replenish. Cottages are available by the week or for the season and there are several beautiful inns, hotels, and B&Bs. An accommodations guide and additional information are available for the asking (see appendix). In addition to Lake Chautauqua itself with its fishing, boating, and swimming, nearby attractions include Allegheny State Park and the Seneca Indian Reservation.

Inns and B&Bs don't have to be just "cozy"—you can get as fancy as you like. The Chateau Tivoli in San Francisco, for example, is as opulent as many grand hotels, and Norumbega, a B&B in Maine, is actually a small "castle."

To find a country inn or B&B, look in the library or bookstores for one of the hundreds of guides published on the subject. *Recommended Country Inns,* for example, from the Globe Pequot Press (also the contact for the American Bed & Breakfast Association, founded in 1981), has editions for New England, the Mid-Atlantic and Chesapeake region, the South, the Midwest, the West Coast, the Rocky Mountain region, and the Southwest. All have been personally visited and evaluated and are also indexed by type, including "inns for romantic getaways," "inns serving afternoon tea," "inns for the sports minded," "inns with separate cottages," and "inns that serve gourmet meals."

A separate set of guides for B&Bs is also available from Globe Pequot, and there are many, many others for you to choose from published by others. These guides sometimes list B&B reservation agencies for various areas, and they can help you make reservations for many B&Bs, guest houses, and inns throughout the central United States and Canada.

Grand Hotel

You may be planning a non-Victorian honeymoon otherwise, but would just like to stay surrounded in nineteenth-century opulence and luxury. To find one of these elegant Victorian "ladies," ask your travel agent. He or she might have to do a little digging, but ask to have a list of possibilities in the area you've chosen. If you're not satisfied with the choices, check your local library travel section and periodical literature. Then write away for brochures.

Victorian seaside hotels such as the Hotel del Coronado have always been popular honeymoon spots. *Photo courtesy of Hotel del Coronado, Coronado, California.*

One such famous hotel, used as the location for the movie *Somewhere in Time*, is the Grand Hotel (built in 1887) on Mackinac Island. The island sits at the juncture of Lake Huron and Lake Michigan and was renowned for its therapeutic environment. There are no cars allowed and visitors walk or ride bicycles to see the sights. Guests at the hotel are transported from a ferry by horse and carriage driven by Victorian-garbed hotel staff. Known for its period cottages in a variety of architectural styles, the island has many other attractions, including a fort, a nature center, and spectacular views. There are special events and festivals throughout the spring and summer, including an annual lilac festival and classical music festival.

Or perhaps you'd like to visit a spa, complete with private mineral bath and massage. Consider historic Saratoga Springs in New York State. A favorite with millionaire-industrialists, old New York families, and flamboyant celebrities such as Diamond Jim Brady, Saratoga boasted some of the finest hotels in nineteenth-century America and some of the best gambling casinos. Still others came to "the Springs" to partake of its therapeutic waters in hopes of a cure for some real or imagined illness.

Many of Saratoga's luxurious hotels and spas were torn down or otherwise lost, but the area has experienced a revival in the last twenty years. The Adelphi Hotel has been restored to its original Italianate grandeur and an elegant new spa has been built. Area attractions include the Saratoga Performing Arts Center (which houses the National Museum of Dance), the Yaddo artists' community, Skidmore College, the National Museum of Racing, and lots of places to visit for the Victorian architecture enthusiast.

Mississipi Riverboat Holiday

How would you like to take a slow-moving steamboat along Mark Twain's beloved Mississippi River? You can. And you'll see America in a unique way that's a special part of our Victorian past. Two such boats are the Delta Queen and the Mississippi Queen.

Mississippi riverboats such as the *Creole Queen* are available for honeymoon cruises, as well as wedding receptions and day trips. *Photo courtesy of Mariano Pepper & Company.*

You can book a trip from two nights to twelve, and you can choose from a wide variety of relaxing vacations. You can see the old South as you cruise from New Orleans to Memphis, plan a special fall foliage trip, or take in the Kentucky Derby. If you like to dance, you can sign up for the Big Band Vacation and travel with some of the great bands of the thirties and forties. Or celebrate the holidays aboard ship—from Thanksgiving to New Year's—and recapture the charm of old-fashioned holiday traditions.

Accommodations on both boats reflect the period, and some cabins have stained-glass windows and brass beds. You can sample the best of Southern cooking, listen to Dixieland and ragtime, play bingo or backgammon, or take calliope lessons. On the Mississippi Queen, there's even a fitness room, sauna, pool, gift shop, movie theater, and beauty salon.

If the majestic St. Lawrence River seems more to your liking, cruise the Thousand Islands or follow the whales to the Saquenay Fjord in Canada on the Canadian Empress or the Victorian Empress, both replicas of historic steamships. If you'd like to stay over in Montreal, Quebec City, Kingston, Toronto, or Ottawa, St. Lawrence Cruise Lines will take care of all the arrangements.

Romantic Stay-at-Home Honeymoon

If funds don't permit an extensive vacation, you'd like to save up for some future date, or you'd just rather relax in familiar surroundings, why not honeymoon at home?

Just because you're staying home doesn't mean your honeymoon can't be just as romantic as if you had gone to a luxury hotel in an exotic location. Did you know you can rent a portable hot tub? Why not have a caterer prepare your meals for a few days, use prepared foods from the market, or go out to local restaurants for dinner?

Decorate the house for romance. Order flowers, stock up on candles and champagne, shut off the telephone, and tell your families you're putting up the Do Not Disturb sign. Make sure you have plenty of bubble bath and other stuff for pampering each other: special snacks (my favorite is smoked salmon, my husband's is caviar), good music, a hammock, and some light reading.

Because everyone else is probably working, maybe you have friends or relatives with a pool you can use during the day while they're away. Just make sure you leave things the way you found them.

A honeymoon at home can be just as romantic as a honeymoon trip—and far less hectic. *Photo by Tom Eckerle.*

Get brochures and contact your local chamber of commerce and State Parks Department. Plan some day trips to the local attractions you somehow never seem to get around to seeing. With the money you'll save on travel you can go out on the town as often as you like and not feel guilty, and because you're not dragging luggage across airports or trying to find your way around in a strange place, you'll be rested and full of energy and might be up for some strenuous exercise (of course, you may have other plans . . .). You can even plan a bike trip or a hike if you live in the country or a walking tour if you live in the city.

Sometimes there really is no place like home. For us this was the perfect solution after a very hectic year before our wedding. Our new home happens to include a swimming pool, so we felt like we were at our own private resort. There was no pressure to be anywhere, no need to make travel connections, no luggage to carry, nothing to pack, no schedule to keep, no reservations to make. It was heaven!

Honeymoon Tips

+ You may want to book a hotel nearby for your wedding night or stay at home until it's time for your trip. Keep your location quiet unless you don't mind uninvited guests.

+ Leave plenty of time to get to the airport, train station, dock, or whatever.

+ Give yourself scheduling options. If you've chosen a location where there's a lot to do, you may be tempted to try to do too much. Decide ahead of time that you're not going to push and that what's important is spending quality time together.

+ Call your parents and anyone else who might be concerned (I needed to call my children!) when you reach your destination and let them know you've arrived safely. Don't forget to say thanks.

- Take traveler's checks and credit cards, rather than lots of cash.

- Keep a list of both credit card numbers and traveler's checks in a separate place.

- Label your luggage inside and out. That way if the tag is ripped off, you can still prove it's your luggage. You might want to come up with some identifying mark or sticker to help you separate your luggage from the rest, because lots of suitcases look alike.

- Make a list of what you're taking in case you need to make a claim later on.

- Leave a copy of your itinerary with your families in case of an emergency.

- Check to see if your homeowner's or renter's insurance covers losses of property like video and still cameras, jewelry, etc. while traveling. What do you need to cover them—register ID numbers, model numbers, or proofs of purchase? Does your policy cover any gifts you might have gotten as wedding presents and might be taking with you? Increase your coverage if it doesn't.

- Bring the documents you'll need with you. They might be your driver's license, marriage certificate, passport, and/or visa. Keep them all in a folder or pouch and in a safe place.

- Pack in advance to avoid rushing at the last minute. Don't overpack, but do consider changes in weather conditions.

- If you're leaving right away, arrange for someone to take care of your wedding gifts, particularly depositing the checks and cash.

- Have someone check on your house or apartment while you're away. Arrange to stop the paper and the mail delivery.

Flourishes

✛ While you're on your honeymoon, dress romantically. Wear a graceful cotton floral jumper over a white T-shirt rather than shorts. Wear a full-brimmed straw hat (decorate it yourself with silk flowers and ribbon) instead of a cap. How about a white lace petticoat peeking out?

✛ Concentrate on the other person. Take care of each other. Leave time for a back rub, for taking a shower together, for watching the sun go down.

✛ Cut large red hearts out of contact paper and stick them on each piece of your luggage. You'll pick them out every time!

✛ You don't have to go out to eat every meal during your honeymoon. Stay in the room for a few meals. You don't necessarily have to order from room service, either. We often go to an epicure shop or large grocery store after we arrive and get settled in our room. We'll put together a sumptuous meal of precooked shrimp, pâté, caviar, salmon, fruit, and cheese (if you forget to pack it, you may want to pick up a small knife), so we can eat whenever we feel like it. Add a bottle of wine or champagne (don't forget the corkscrew), some ice (we fill the sink with water and ice to chill the champagne quickly), and voilà!

✛ Don't just visit the typical sites that most out-of-towners do. Go to the local library, the town hall, or a small neighborhood market. Once, when visiting a tropical island, I spent an hour observing a session of traffic court. It gave me more insight into the workings of the government, the nature of the people, and the differences in culture than any tourist attraction ever could have. On another trip, we attended the local Grange's annual chicken supper. We made lots of new friends and even swapped recipes!

✣ While you're on your honeymoon, make a habit of taking afternoon tea. Many hotels, inns, and B&Bs are serving tea these days. It's relaxing, terribly civilized, and may be a custom you'll enjoy keeping when you return.

✣ If you're staying in one place for a while, order some fresh, fragrant flowers for the room.

✣ Don't forget to bring candles and candleholders, some bubble bath, and maybe some massage oil. Pamper yourself and each other.

✣ Bring a special blank volume just for recording your thoughts and feelings. You may want to include in its pages small tokens from your travels—a cocktail napkin, a flower pressed between its pages, or a brochure from someplace you truly enjoyed together. Get as sentimental as you like—this honeymoon journal will become more precious with each anniversary.

✣ If you have room in your suitcase, bring a small cassette player and some romantic music. You may want to follow the suggestion I made in chapter 8, if your wedding music was prerecorded. Bring along a copy of the tapes and relive your wedding once more.

✣ Unplug the television and vow that during your honeymoon you won't look at it once (or buy the newspaper, either)!

✣ Bring some travel sachets to scent your luggage and your room. You can buy or make the kind that hang on the doorknob. Just don't forget to take them with you when you leave.

✣ Bring a book of your favorite poems and read them to each other. Repeat your vows—this time privately, to one another alone.

CHAPTER TEN

A HOME FOR THE TWO OF YOU

When we come home, we lay aside our mask and drop our tools, and are no longer lawyers, sailors, soldiers, statesmen, clergymen, but only men. We fall again into our most human relations. . . . We cease the struggle in the race of the world, and give our hearts leave and leisure to love.

James Froude

The Victorian home was the center of a woman's universe and a man's refuge from the world. In his book *The Light of the Home: An Intimate View of the Lives of Women in Victorian America*, Harvey Green describes the Victorian home as

The opposite of the man's world; rather than an environment that bespoke commerce and trade, it was a miniature universe of culture and education for family and visitors. Here the arts and sciences of the museum, concert hall, and schoolroom were translated into the shells and other curios adorning the parlor, the prints and paintings on the walls, the piano and organ in the parlor, and the books in the library. Women were the organizing force and marshals of this domain.

Times have changed and the home is now a shared enterprise. Usually, a woman is no longer financially dependent on her husband, unless by choice, and men generally take more interest in home design, decoration, and maintenance. Many women have demanding careers and some have even switched traditional roles with men, supporting their families while their husbands or others care for their children.

When we look closely at the treatment of women in the nineteenth century, few of us would wish to return to that unenlightened time. However, there was a respect for the home and its activities, an emotional investment in family life, and a belief in the moral influence of an orderly and aesthetically beautiful retreat from the world of "commerce and trade" that I believe we are returning to.

In this chapter, we'll take a brief tour of the typical Victorian home of the latter nineteenth century, examine some ways to bring Victoriana into the modern environment, and provide sources for household furnishings with a Victorian flair. We'll see how Victorians might have dedicated the bridal home and how that custom might be adapted for the modern bride.

Some of you may actually live in a vintage home and be restoring it. Others may be apartment dwellers. Still others might live in raised ranches, capes, contemporaries, or colonials. But obviously you have an interest in Victoriana and might be wondering how you can bring your wedding theme into your home. We'll explore ways of bringing Victorian touches to every room in the house, regardless of its architectural style.

If you're thinking of buying a vintage home or would just like to help save a Victorian landmark in your community, two sources should help you get started. First, write to the National Trust for Historic Preservation (NTHP). I've included the address in the appendix. By joining the NTHP, you'll have access to helpful information and will support preservation efforts in your community. The second source I would recommend is *Victorian Homes* magazine. Aimed at owners of old houses who are working to restore them, this magazine is of interest even if you own a contemporary home, as I do, and want to adapt the Victorian style to your own. There's a lot of information on Victorian lifestyles, customs, architecture, and antiques.

Decorating—Victorian Style

If you think of a house, regardless of architectural style, as a container surrounding a series of smaller containers, you realize that within the limitations of the shapes and sizes of those containers are unlimited possibilities. Without actually making any structural changes, such as adding or removing walls or windows or putting on an addition, a house or apartment is something like a blank canvas. If you'd like to bring some actual Victorian detail into your home or simply make your home more romantic, there are some general tips to consider before looking at each room more closely for its particular function and character.

First, take a look at the ceilings. Are they high? Low? Textured? What do the existing light fixtures look like? Where are the windows and what are their basic shape? Are there any moldings? What style are they?

Sometimes it helps just to move everything out of a room and look at it as simple space without adornment. Without any major changes, through the use of wallpaper, stenciling, architectural details, gingerbread trim, moldings, window inserts, stained glass, and floor coverings, you can give a Victorian feel to any home. But what if you can't make even these physical changes?

Decide whether you want more of a country casual feel or a formal feel—both can be Victorian. The Victorian period encompasses so many styles—American Empire, Gothic Revival, Rococo, Eastlake, Renaissance Revival, Golden Oak, to name just a few—and many mix well with other decorating styles. I've given you a book list in the appendix so you can learn more about Victorian architecture and decorating styles. As you visit house museums you'll see that the Victorians mixed styles, too—Oriental, eighteenth century, and French Empire.

Invest in a few antique accessories—an old book, a vintage print, a piece of clothing, a shawl, some old sewing implements, antique glassware, or vintage valentines or calling cards. You can use your finds as they are or combine them in a display to make a new accessory. Use wall hangings and artwork to add historic touches. Period sheet music can be found in good condition and framed; so can postcards and old photographs. There are lots of reproductions of period art, and I've given you some mail-order sources for these in the appendix. In a modern house, the carefully assembled clutter that was so characteristic of Victorian decorating just doesn't work, but one piece becomes a showpiece when strategically placed.

If you're handy and crochet or embroider, look for Victorian-style patterns and make some period-looking accessories.

The Entrance Hall

In a typical Victorian one-family home, the entrance hall was an important theater for social interaction. Fixtures in what we now call the foyer were the hall tree for hats, coats, walking sticks, and umbrellas and the calling card receiver. Here a visitor could leave her calling card, carefully turning down the appropriate corner to communicate her intention (if she folded down the upper right corner, she came in person; if the upper left, she has left her congratulations; the lower right said good-bye; and the lower left offered her condolences). If staying the traditional half-hour (considered the appropriate length of time for a visit), a lady could deposit her belongings without cluttering the carefully arranged parlor.

Both antique and reproduction Victorian-style hall trees are available. Some have a bench for sitting and storing things, and most have a place to stand umbrellas and walking sticks, hooks for hats, and sometimes a mirror. You can even find these in unfinished furniture and finish it yourself. Even if all you have is a short hall opening into a larger room, this piece of furniture adds function as well as form.

You can add to its impact by hanging a vintage hat or frock coat on one of its hooks.

Antique calling card receivers are hard to find, but not impossible. Of course, customs have changed, but a lovely touch would be a receiver holding a handful of vintage calling cards.

The Parlor

The Victorian parlor was the main social area of the home and was designed to display a family's wealth, education, and culture. The Victorians believed that the objects they assembled and arranged around them produced a powerful "influence" and were, therefore, chosen very carefully.

The parlor was usually very cluttered, but the clutter was carefully chosen and arranged. This was the heart of the home, where visitors were received, where entertaining was done, and where members of the family spent their evenings reading by the fire, singing, or playing games.

Our living patterns today are quite different. The bath and bedroom have become centers of activity and relaxation. Kitchens are designed for entertaining and everyday family socializing, as well as efficiency. The parlor or drawing room is now divided into a living room (which, ironically, sees little "living" and is often reserved just for company) and a family room–den–recreation room. Try to think of one of these rooms as a parlor. Add bookshelves, a writing desk, perhaps a spinet or old upright piano (even if you don't play, someone visiting might or you could look into converting it to a player piano), small tables and shelves for curios, curio cabinets, and some antique or reproduction furniture.

You can uses tapestry fabrics, even if only for accent, and small touches like doilies and antimacassars (special crocheted pieces put on the backs and arms of upholstered furniture). You can drape a lace fringed shawl (I bought one in a discount store for eight dollars) over a small table and then assemble a collection of paperweights, shells, or old photographs and frames on top.

And speaking of collections, these are a fun way to decorate, easy to move from place to place and rearrange, and can be a way to learn about the Victorian era. When I first decided to write *Your Victorian Wedding* I began collecting wedding memorabilia. I have books of advice to young brides with old leather bindings and gilt-edged pages that I display in my office. I've started to collect turn-of-the-century wedding portraits, vintage postcards, and calling cards. None of these is expensive to collect (the wedding portraits were all around three dollars apiece) and when grouped together or assembled in a frame make an interesting accessory in any room.

The Dining Room

The dining room was a public room like the parlor and perhaps equal in its importance. It was the place where family eating rituals took place several times a day and household advice writers instructed young wives to make it cheerful, but easy to clean.

Most dining rooms had a sideboard and at least one serving table. There might be wainscoting and/or a chair rail and a large center light fixture over the table. Walls were painted rather than wallpapered and curtains were made of light and airy fabrics, not heavy ones, all in an effort to avoid collecting germs and dust, creating the dreaded "impure air."

It's easy to add a chair rail to enhance the look of your dining room. Home decorating stores have them unfinished and you can stain them to match the other wood in the room. I've given you several sources for lace panels and other curtains, as well as sources for period lighting fixtures, in the appendix.

Look for ways to use tablecloths and other linens such as runners, place mats, and doilies; furniture; china and flatware; curtains; light fixtures and candlesticks; and floor coverings to make your dining statement.

Whether you find wonderful reproductions or collect antiques, there are many ways to bring Victoriana into your everyday life. *Photo courtesy of Léron, New York, New York.*

The Kitchen

Usually a fairly large room, the Victorian kitchen was designed for work and organization. Some kitchens I've seen were pretty grim, although some home designers of the era were beginning to understand the value of pleasant surroundings to the accomplishment of hard work. Their spartan, practical decor was in keeping with the philosophy that if the room wasn't to be seen by outsiders, then it should be less adorned.

The kitchen was a no-nonsense place not only for preparing food but for preserving it as well. The Victorian homemaker needed places to store baking, canning, and other preserving equipment. There bread was baked, cheese and butter were made, and a lot of family living went on. If it was a rural farm kitchen, meals for farmhands were also a likely part of the daily routine.

Paint was usually the glossy enamel kind, which was easy to scrub and easy to spruce up with a new coat. There was often a separate pantry and open shelves that were painted, and some had glass-doored cupboards. There was a place for everything, and everything in its place.

Today we feel our private spaces are just as important as our more public ones. Our houses are often designed, in fact, so that guests can visit in the kitchen while the cook is preparing the meal, and some kitchens are combined with a dining or family room. Modern wall coverings and paints make it possible to decorate a kitchen much as we would any other room in the house.

Easy ways to add Victorian touches are through wall hangings, kitchen accessories, and fabrics. You might put lace or crocheted edgings on shelves and add bright floral or paisley curtains, or perhaps lace ones.

Put a rod inside a cupboard and add a lace valance to the top shelf, leave the doors open, and arrange your kitchen pottery and wooden ware. Add a display of fresh fruits and vegetables.

Again, just look at your kitchen as a blank space and rethink how you can work with its existing structure and character. Of course, you may be thinking of remodeling your kitchen. If you're starting from scratch, then you can make changes in cabinets, window size and shapes, flooring, wall coverings, and moldings.

Since Victorian is a popular style right now, there are lots of Victorian-look products out on the market, and these might be just what you want. But be aware that there's a difference between the actual products in Victorian homes and many of these products. As you learn more about period architecture and decorating, you'll begin to see the difference. You can choose to reproduce the old look using antiques or reproductions, decorate in a more "romantic" or adapted Victorian style, or integrate actual Victorian decorating elements into a more modern style.

The Bedroom

Bedrooms were generally plain, as they were private and rarely seen by outsiders. The basic pieces of furniture would

The bedroom is your own private world, a luxurious and comfortable retreat from a busy life. *Photo courtesy of Léron, New York, New York.*

probably have included a bed, bureau, washstand, small table, and several chairs, one of them a comfortable upholstered one. Another room subject to unsanitary dust and vapors, the bedroom had little clutter and furniture and was supposed to be easy to clean. Something I've noticed in most of the more elaborate house museums I've visited is that even in the houses of the wealthy, the bedrooms were quite spartan in appearance, although walls and ceilings might have been painted or otherwise adorned to add color and interest.

Today, an increasing percentage of the family home furnishings budget is being spent on the bedroom. As Americans seem to be moving back into their homes and spending more time and money pampering themselves, the selection of bedroom furnishings has grown tremendously.

There are so many ways to make a bedroom luxurious, romantic, and comfortable using Victorian touches! It can be formal or informal, strong and masculine, or more frilly and feminine. Just look through magazines and catalogs for ideas. Sometimes an interesting mixture of darker fabrics, such as a deep-shaded paisley or plaid, and darker furniture with light touches of white lace or wicker create a warm and subtly feminine environment. Consider ways to use artwork, sheets, and pillows. Look at wall coverings (including border papers), window treatments, and table coverings.

You might want to include a small writing desk, with antique-looking writing accessories and a small table for serving tea.

Accessories can include bed trays, a canopy (either as part of the bed or created from fabric and attached to the wall or ceiling), candlesticks and sconces (there's no such thing as a romantic bedroom without candles), personal grooming implements, and containers, mirrors, and potpourri baskets or containers.

Again, the bedroom is a place for a small collection or a few choice vintage items. On my vanity I have a small antique hand mirror and an old silver button hook. The vanity is built in and very modern, but those two pieces along with some etched glass containers, silk flowers, and perfume bottles works perfectly well.

There are so many new types of curtain hardware and new ways to do complicated-looking curtains with ease! The major pattern companies have craft patterns to help you do these yourself—from balloon shades to swags—and there are several good books out on the subject.

Add a dust ruffle to your bed. It turns a plain bed into a fancy one. Knit or crochet an afghan or buy a lap shawl for curling up. Make yourself a dressing table out of unfinished furniture and yards of chintz. Just add a glass top (you can put pressed flowers, old valentines, or Victorian scrap underneath) and you're all set.

Find an old trunk for blankets or keepsakes—you can buy one and restore it yourself. I've given you a source for supplies in the appendix. Use colorful boxes and baskets as containers in the closet, on shelves, or by the bed.

We have photographs of each of our kids and one black-and-white of each of us when we were children. Our bedroom is where we play, and we want to remind ourselves of the child within us that refuses to grow old. Perhaps you'd like to add a collection of old dolls or wooden toys to your bedroom!

The Bathroom

Bathrooms as we know them today weren't common until the late nineteenth century. Most personal care was done in the bedroom at the washstand; the bathtub was in a separate room and wasn't used every day and the toilet most likely wasn't in the house at all. If it was indoors, it was housed in a separate room, since the Victorians attributed all manner of disease and depravity to "vapors" and "impure air."

For us the bathroom is more than merely functional. It's a place to relax, to take care of our needs, and to pamper ourselves. Some modern baths even have spas or whirlpools, tanning beds, and lounge furniture.

The things that most easily transform a bathroom, I think, are art objects and prints. Even a small bathroom is enhanced by tiny framed prints or postcards, a pressed-flower picture, or a framed piece of music. I like things with fairly intricate designs and soothing colors to ponder, but you can choose anything from bold and bright to soft and tender. Try picking a theme (such as wildflowers or Gibson girls) and work along with that.

The bathroom is a retreat where we take care of ourselves. There should be supplies within easy reach for pampering the body and resting the soul. I've begun simplifying my personal care products and changing over to natural ones that are nonpolluting and produced without animal testing. There are simple soaps and other personal care products available at health food stores and most major supermarkets, and many of these have refreshing herbal or floral scents. I've even started experimenting with my own herbal concoctions (like some of those I listed in chapter 7).

The Perfect Gift

As with all things in a marriage, decorating a home is a joint venture and can best be accomplished with love and consideration. Consult each other before making a major change or buying something that will be displayed in the space you both share. Decide on a budget for each item and stick with it. Do sign up with a bridal registry for the items you need. People *want* to give you a gift you will truly enjoy. Just make sure that there's a selection of items in a wide price range, so no one feels pressured to spend more than he or she is able.

Because your wedding invitations and pre-wedding parties have probably made clear your interest in the Victorian period, some people may wish to give you a gift that is in keeping with your wedding theme but may not know how to go about it. One way might be to go in with several other people to purchase one fairly expensive item, such as a piece of furniture or an antique accessory.

The people most likely to be asked what the bridal couple needs or wants are the mother of the bride and the maid or matron of honor. Especially if the groom's family is from another town, the groom's mother might be another. You might give each of these people different suggestions, making it clear that these are to be offered only if

May the gods grant you all things which your heart desires, and may they give you a husband and a home and gracious concord, for there is nothing greater and better than this—when a husband and wife keep a household in oneness of mind, a great woe to their enemies and joy to their friends, and win high renown.

Homer

someone asks. Or you and your fiancé might want to put a deposit on an item in an antique store or furniture store and let people know that any contributions toward that item would be appreciated.

DEDICATION OF THE BRIDAL HOME

A custom that originated well before the Victorian era, but was widely practiced in the nineteenth century, is the dedication of the married couple's new home. Usually performed by a member of the clergy, the event included a blessing, sometimes mingled with some stern advice (as you can see from the excerpt included here). Pastor Thayer's advice includes ways of dedicating the home to "truth, virtue, religion, and to God" and points out the importance of making a good beginning. Keeping the Sabbath by attending church and avoiding "light, pernicious reading, magazines, newspapers, and novels" and "rides and walks for pleasure," according the Bible a prominent place, and making time for prayer would ensure a "prosperous and happy home."

"Let me reiterate, bridal pair, these needful counsels," ends Pastor Thayer. "Welcome Christ to your home. Let the gospel hallow it. Make it the centre of hope and joy. Live for it. Be content with the home that you now have, and not wait for one you may never possess. A hovel may be a happy home for those who truly love each other."

Today, our "housewarming" is an outgrowth of this custom. Because many couples live together before marriage, the custom has faded away. And yet, sentimental me, I think it's one that can be adapted to our modern ways.

Following our wedding reception, we invited anyone who could come back to the house for an informal party. Everyone was invited to change into casual clothes and they all chatted, sang songs around the grand piano, and sat visiting in the yard. It was a friendly ending to a wonderful day and was our way of dedicating our new home. At our guests' request, we opened our wedding presents and they were able to see just where their gifts were going to be used.

Remember, then, WEDDED PAIR, that you are to make a HOME,—a sweet bower of peace and joy in this desert world, where hope brightens, and love gathers its linked confiding circle;—a blissful retreat for jaded and weary hearts when the busy world drives on its votaries in the train of Mammon and pampered self;—a safe and alluring shelter for yourselves amid the vicissitudes of life, becoming more and more the abode of peace and love as the world grows dark without, and never more blessed and precious than when about to be exchanged for a brighter home hereafter. You are to make a HOME!

From "The Dedication of the Bridal Home, *Pastor's Wedding Gift* by William M. Thayer, 1858

The dedication of a new home can be a private ritual, if you like. Make a special meal; say a few words about how you each feel about the stage where life's drama will take place every day. Make a pledge that this home will be filled with honesty, love, and joy. Even the home you've been living in up until now takes on a new aspect once the wedding day is over. Pick a time and celebrate. Count your blessings and give thanks.

Flourishes

+ Buy some facsimiles of vintage catalogs (there are editions of old Sears, Montgomery Ward, and Bloomingdale's catalogs available by mail or in bookstores) and leave them out for browsing. If you can find some actual vintage catalogs or magazines, so much the better, but you'll have to be careful how you handle them. These are a great way to learn more about the objects Victorians used every day.

+ If you happen to have inherited a piece of vintage clothing or acquired one on your own, why not display it? Put up a hook in the bedroom and hang your find on a padded hanger. If it's very fragile and small enough to frame (like a child's christening dress or ladies' blouse) why not make a velvet backing, frame it, and hang it on the wall?

+ Use fresh flowers, fruits, and vegetables as part of your decorating scheme. A fruit basket in the bedroom looks lovely and encourages a healthy midnight snack!

+ Start a collection of old hats or trim new ones with antique silk flowers, ribbons, and lace. Hang them up on the bedroom wall, in your office, or maybe in the bathroom.

+ Take the wooden gingerbread trim normally used on Victorian home exteriors and think of interesting ways to use it indoors. How about as an interesting "valance" for a window or across a room opening? Larger pieces can be mounted on the wall. I've seen them used as a "cornice" above a bathtub with the shower curtain mounted behind it.

✤ Use lace or crocheted edging along the mantle. Add a collection of shells, candlesticks, or silver pieces to complete the look.

✤ Find or make a crazy quilt or traditional wedding quilt and hang it on the wall.

✤ Create cozy corners and "nooks," even if the space in your room isn't divided that way, by making small groupings of furniture and making use of screens and dividers. These encourage conversation and can make a large, open room much more inviting.

✤ Add a pressed-tin ceiling to your kitchen. These come in easy-to-install plates, and I've given you a list of sources in the appendix. Look at other, less traditional ways of using these as well.

✤ Consider the possibilities of plaster ceiling medallions and other interior architectural details available. Again, how could you use them in new ways? They might make an unusual wall decoration.

✤ Start an antique button collection and display it in an old glass jar. Leave a few choice buttons out on the table so people can look closely at them.

✤ Get out that old dollhouse and give it a place of honor. If you gave yours away, there are kits to make one just like a Victorian cottage or mansion. You can start decorating your house a little at a time and learn about nineteenth-century furnishings at the same time.

- If you have some vintage clothing accessories, such as a pair of crocheted gloves or high-button shoes, display them prominently in your bedroom, on a dressing table or on the floor near the bed.

- Hide small modern appliances such as a hand massager or a heating pad in a pretty basket or hatbox. Whenever possible, get rid of modern packaging (better yet, buy simple products in bulk with little packaging). We transfer the baking soda that we use in the bathroom for cleaning and brushing our teeth into a cut-glass jar with a lid.

- Hang pictures on ribbon hangers you can purchase or make yourself. The ribbon you can buy today with wire woven on either edge comes in antique-looking materials and makes wonderful bows.

- Use a beaded curtain in a doorway or partway across a room opening as a divider. You can find beautiful wooden or glass beads and string them yourself.

- If you have room, try using an unexpected piece of furniture in the bathroom. A wooden trunk can be placed along a wall and used to store linens and as a place to sit. A small table can hold a collection of bath accessories.

- Don't forget the whimsical! A serious sculptured bust could be a humorous hat stand. A cherub might appear smiling over the commode. Decorate with a sense of humor.

- Haunt old bookstores, flea markets, vintage clothing expositions, and garage sales. Here you might find memorabilia, old prints and postcards, advertising art, fashion plates, antique frames, clothing and accessories, and unusual books and magazines.

‑ Look for spots to create groupings of similar items, either on a flat surface or hanging on a wall. Start a collection of seashells, for example, and put them on a small bedroom table or shelf. Group a series of black-and-white prints from old books using a particular theme: Consider nature, children, Victorian-style buildings or houses, or landscapes.

‑ Find a special set of dishes just for two that you save for breakfast in bed or romantic midnight shacks. Add a special tray, an ice bucket, a pretty teapot, and a pair of lace or embroidered napkins.

‑ If you can possibly manage it, spend the extra money for 100-percent cotton sheets (with at least 200 thread count) and towels. They'll last longer, feel better against your skin, and make you feel pampered.

‑ Transfer personal care products into pretty containers. Pour shampoo and conditioner into glass bottles; put cotton balls and swabs in tins or jars.

‑ Put a candelabrum or several votives around the tub. Add some soft music, bubble bath, and some champagne—instant romance!

AFTERWORD

May your independence be equal, your dependence mutual, your obligations reciprocal.

Lucretia Mott

Thank you for letting me help you plan your Victorian wedding. I trust your day will be everything you both hoped for and more. In the years to come, I hope you'll continue to enjoy many Victorian anniversaries and a life full of celebrations, bringing along with you some of the customs you've just begun.

Perhaps the journal you started keeping during the hectic period leading up to your wedding will become an everyday ritual, and when your anniversary comes around, you may enjoy reading aloud some of the entries from the past year to your husband. Maybe your interest in herbs and flowers will have flourished and by this time next year your very own Victorian garden will be underway. Or you may have started a wonderful collection on your honeymoon trip that will soon take over an honored place on the mantle. Nothing could please me more!

I'd love to hear from you and hope you'll share your wedding stories with me. You can write to me at the following address: Georgene Lockwood, Your Victorian Wedding, P.O. Box 473, Newtown, Connecticut 06470–0473.

May you both live in enduring beauty and forever write your own modern Victorian romance!

APPENDIX

Unless indicated as "free," there's a cost for catalogs and brochures. Because these prices change periodically, it would be best to contact the source first and then send for a catalog. Some books listed are available in bookstores, others by mail order, and still others can be obtained through your local library. In the case of mail-order books, I have given you the source's address and, in some cases, phone number. Check on price and availability before ordering.

CHAPTER 1: Courtship, Proposal, and Engagement

BOOKS AND OTHER PUBLICATIONS

Elizabeth Barrett Browning. *Sonnets from the Portuguese: A Celebration of Love.* New York: St. Martin's Press, 1986.

Charles Fowkes, ed. *The Love Poems of John Donne.* New York: St. Martin's Press, 1982.

John Hadfield, ed. *Everyman's Book of English Love Poems.* London: Dent, 1980.

Lee Bennett Hopkins. *Love and Kisses: Poems.* Boston: Houghton Mifflin, 1983.

Helen Husted, ed. *Love Poems of Six Centuries.* Salem, MA: Books for Libraries Press, 1969.

Anne Morrow Lindbergh. *Dearly Beloved: A Theme and Variations.* New York: Harcourt Brace & World, 1962.

Peter McWilliams. *I Marry You Because . . . .* Los Angeles: Prelude Press, 1990.

Ara John Movsesian. *Pearls of Love: A Complete Handbook of Love Letters and Love Poems.* Fresno, CA: Electric Press, 1983.

Ellen K. Rothman. *Hands and Hearts: A History of Courtship in America.* Cambridge, MA: Harvard U. Press, 1987.

JEWELRY PUBLICATIONS

To order books from the Gemological Institute of America bookstore, call (800) 421–7250.

A helpful free publication about buying jewelry is available from the Federal Trade Commission. Request the June 1989 issue of their *Facts for Consumers* series of newsletters, "About Fine Jewelry." Write to: FTC Headquarters, Sixth and Pennsylvania, NW, Washington, DC 20580, (202) 326–2222.

Additional information on buying jewelry is available from:

JEWELERS VIGILANCE COMMITTEE
1185 Avenue of the Americas
New York, NY 10036

ORGANIZATIONS

ASSOCIATION OF BRIDAL
CONSULTANTS
200 Chestnutland Road
New Milford, CT 06776–2521
(203) 355–0464

Will give you a free list of wedding consultants in your area.

NATIONAL BRIDAL SERVICE
3122 West Cary Street
Richmond, VA 23221
(804) 355–6945

Also a source of referrals to bridal consultants.

THE VALENTINE COLLECTORS
ASSOCIATION
P.O. Box 1404
Santa Ana, CA 92702

Publishes quarterly newsletter filled with valentine lore and practices of old.

Scrapbooks

EXPOSURES
2800 Hoover Road
Stevens Point, WI 54481
(800) 222-4947

Old-fashioned scrapbooks, covered in hand-marbled paper and leather or simulated materials, with acid-free paper inserts. Catalog.

Stationery, Stickers, and Rubber Stamps

See complete listing for chapter 2.

Engagement and Wedding Jewelry

ABIGAIL'S HEIRLOOMS AT THE GOLDEN COVE
359–D Thames Street
Newport, RI 02840
(401) 847-0400

Exquisite and reasonable collection of never-before-worn Victorian jewelry, hidden away for over 100 years. Includes love-token jewelry, rings suitable for engagement, and wedding bands. Also has a reproduction of the "hidden heart" ring in a variety of stones.

THE BRIARS ANTIQUES
4121 Briars Road
Olney, MD 20832
(301) 774-3596

Owners Diane and Bill Grimes specialize in Victorian antique jewelry and are happy to work with customers on a mail order basis. Just tell them what you're looking for and they'll mail color photos with prices and dimensions. Transactions are complete after customer approval.

1,873 UNUSUAL WEDDING BANDS
National Jewelers Exchange
Booth 86
4 West Forty-seventh Street
New York, NY 10036
(212) 221-1873

Mostly new, although some antique, rings. Will make rings to customer's design.

SILVERSCAPE DESIGNS
264 North Pleasant Street
Amherst, MA 01002
(413) 253-3324

Ask for Denis Perlman. Has individually handmade wedding and engagement rings made from original Victorian dies, using nineteenth-century techniques. Will also make custom rings to your order. Available in 14K, 18K, 22K, or platinum and in antique finishes. Call for information.

WEDDING RINGS INC.
50 West Eighth Street
New York, NY 10011
(212) 533-2111

In business more than fifty years; carries some 500 different styles of bands.

YELLIN JEWELERS
215 Canal Street
New York, NY 10013
(212) 925-8854

Sells only wedding and engagement rings. Custom orders.

Your Trousseau

BRAVURA
555 De Haro Street, #332
San Francisco, CA 94107
(415) 626-7993

Denise Fiedler makes beautiful handmade woven ribbon lingerie cases, love letter bags, sachets, pillows, and more. Call or write for retail information.

COMO-SAN
P.O. Box 31141
Seattle, WA 98103
(206) 632-4402

Country-Victorian clothing by mail order, including nightgowns, camisoles, petticoats, bloomers, and other clothing and accessories. Catalog.

CUDDLEDOWN OF MAINE
312 Canco Road
Portland, ME 04103
(800) 323-6793

Source for camisoles and bloomers, 100-percent cotton trimmed with lace; also has quality bedding. Catalog.

FOLKWEAR PATTERNS

The Taunton Press
63 South Main Street
Newtown, CT 06470–5506

To make your own old-fashioned trousseau, Folkwear's pattern for Edwardian underthings (#203) includes patterns for a camisole, petticoat, and drawers with optional handmade crocheted lace (instructions provided), rows of tucks, and lace insertion. Cameos (#234) gives you two more camisoles to sew and one each to knit and crochet. See also the catalogs of other pattern companies listed for chapter 3.

LÉRON

750 Madison Avenue
New York, NY 10021
(212) 753–6700

Nothing but the best in lingerie and linens, from a French company founded at the turn of the century that has a boutique in Manhattan. Brochure.

MARCELA CREATIONS

1515 West Kennedy Boulevard
Tampa, FL 33606
(813) 253–0556

Indescribably gorgeous boxes, sachets, ornaments, bridal accessories, frames, and albums. Call or write for retail information and a store location near you.

TRUNK REPAIR AND RESTORATION

CHARLOTTE FORD TRUNKS

Box 536
Spearman, TX 79081
(806) 659–3027

Tools, supplies, and step-by-step instructions for restoring an old trunk to keep your trousseau in.

HOPE CHESTS

LANE COMPANY, INC.

Department Q090
Altavista, VA 24517–0151

Cedar chests in more than 100 styles. Brochure.

MAB WOODWORKS

39 Virginia Avenue
Poughkeepsie, NY 12601
(914) 454–8234

Ask about their entirely handcrafted "Forever and Thensome Hope Chest."

CHAPTER 2: Say It in Writing

BOOKS AND PUBLICATIONS

Beverly Clark. *Planning a Wedding to Remember*. Los Angeles: Wilshire Publications, 1986. Available from the Beverly Clark Collection, 6385 B Rose Lane, Carpinteria, CA 93013; Wilshire Publications, Suite 208, 12021 Wilshire Boulevard, West Los Angeles, CA 90025; or bookstores. This wedding planning workbook is one of the best around and becomes a treasured keepsake, documenting the entire wedding planning process.

The Millinery Institute Staff. *The Art and Craft of Ribbon Work*, ed. Sandra Nager. St. Helena, CA: Body Blueprints, 1986. Order from: Body Blueprints, 1734 Scott Street, St. Helena, CA 94574. In two volumes, this is a reissue of an old pattern book. It will show you how to make ribbon roses.

Sheila Pickles. *A Bridal Bouquet: Penhaligon's Scented Treasury of Verse and Prose*. New York: Harmony, 1991.

Alexandra Stoddard. *Gift of a Letter*. New York: Doubleday, 1990.

The Art of Ribboncraft Video Workshop (with Susan Sirkis) is available from:
Concept Associates
Suite 1214
7910 Woodmont Avenue
Bethesda, MD 20814
(800) 333–8252

For a catalog of clip art books, borders, and typographic illustrations, all copyright free, contact:
Dover Publications, Inc.
31 East Second Street
Mineola, NY 11501

STATIONERY AND INVITATIONS

BRONWEN ROSS
Morning Star Publishers
P.O. Box 6388
Destin, FL 32541

Original designs for stationery; invitations with matching reception, RSVP, note, and place cards; calling cards. Catalog.

CREATIONS BY ELAINE
6253 West Seventy-fourth Street
Box 2001
Bedford Park, IL 60499–2001
(800) 323–1208

Call for catalog and samples; traditional panels and Victorian era fine-art invitations.

THE GIFTED LINE
999 Canal Boulevard
Port Richmond, CA 94804
(800) 5-GIFTED

Using authentic images from Victorian scrap art, this line of stationery, paper baskets, bags, boxes, cards, and office accessories is available in most fine stationery and gift shops. Call or write for a location near you.

HUDSON STREET PAPERS
581 Hudson Street
New York, NY 10014

There's also a location at 234 Third Avenue.

IMAGEM
BrideBouquet
P.O. Box 57901
Salt Lake City, UT 84157
(800) 748–4898; (801) 263–9090

Real pressed-flower wedding invitation ensembles. Call for brochure and samples.

POSTIQUE GREETINGS
501 East Peach
Bozeman, MT 59715
(800) 442–1800; (406) 587–0937

Gift cards containing original antique postcards.

PAULA G. RUBINSTEIN
2615 South Belvoir Boulevard
Cleveland, OH 44118
(216) 932–1007

Heirloom lace drawings reproduced as stationery items.

VICTORIAN PAPERS
Box 411332
Kansas City, MO 64141
(800) 800–6647

Everything from extra frilly valentines to stationery, stickers, gift cards, and even an antique replica pen to write with. Catalog.

WISTERIA PRESS
231 Lawrenceville Road
Lawrenceville, NJ 08648

Some lovely invitation ensembles, including matching napkin rings and place cards. Brochure.

RUBBER STAMPS

ARCHITECTURAL ORIGINALS
P.O. Box 8023
Newport Beach, CA 92658

Wonderful Victorian house stamps; also stationery, calendars, books, and gifts.

INKADINKADO
105 South Street
Boston, MA 02111

Victorian Romance Set can be used for announcements, place cards, or correspondence. Company plans to expand Victorian lines. Available both in shops and by mail. Catalog.

PERSONAL STAMP EXCHANGE
345 South McDowell Boulevard, Suite 324
Petaluma, CA 94954
(707) 763–8058

Wide range of rubber stamps and supplies. Available in stores or through mail order. Catalog and how-to ideas.

STICKERS

DOVER PUBLICATIONS, INC.
See listing for chapter under "Books and Publications." Publishes books of pressure-sensitive stickers taken from authentic Victorian sources. Also postcards and gift wrap from the advertising and fine art of the period. Free catalog.

CALLIGRAPHERS

PENDRAGON, INK
27 Prospect Street
Whitinsville, MA 01588

Complete set of wedding stationery, first hand-lettered, then printed, and finally hand-painted with an array of roses, lady-slippers, and violets. Includes place cards, invitations, programs, menus, informals, and marriage scrolls.

If you want to work to with a calligrapher in your area and can't find one through the phone book or a local printer, contact the following organizations for the address of your regional organization. From there you should be able to find a professional calligrapher close to home:

SOCIETY FOR CALLIGRAPHY
P.O. Box 64174
Los Angeles, CA 90064
(213) 380–5957

THE SOCIETY OF SCRIBES AND ILLUMINATORS
P.O. Box 933
New York, NY 10150

WASHINGTON CALLIGRAPHERS GUILD
P.O. Box 3688
Merrifield, VA 22116–3688
(301) 897–8637

MARRIAGE CERTIFICATES

THE SCRIBE & SCROLL
P.O. Box 470789
Tulsa, OK 74147
(800) 274–2669

Reproduction of a 1903 wedding certificate, inscribed by calligrapher and framed. Call for order form. Calligrapher Anita Robertson also does place cards, invitations, and envelopes.

VICTORIAN HOUSE AND CARPENTER & COMPANY
1203 Columbus Circle, Room 222
Janesville, WI 53545
(608) 754–2635

Antique reproduction certificates and greeting cards. Brochures.

WEDDING GUEST BOOKS

LILLIAN ROSE COLLECTIONS
P.O. Box 182
Mukwonago, WI 53149
(800) 521–8760; (414) 363–5286

Guest books shaped like fans or hearts. Catalog.

CHAPTER 3: Her Best Dress

BOOKS AND PUBLICATIONS

From Hobby House Press Inc., 900 Frederick Street, Cumberland, MD 21502, (301) 759–3770; fax (301) 759–4940:

Donna Felger. *Bridal Fashions: Victorian Era.* Cumberland, MD: Hobby House, 1986. Includes trousseaus and fashions for the wedding party; also has doll pattern for an 1889 bridal gown.

Terry McCormick. *Consumer's Guide to Vintage Clothing.* New York: Dembner Books, 1987. Includes tips on finding, buying, cleaning, and storing vintage clothing.

Hazel Ulseth and Helen Shannon. *Victorian Fashions 1880–1890,* Vol. 1. Hobby House, 1988.

Hasel Ulseth and Helen Shannon. *Victorian Fashions 1890–1905,* Vol. 2. Cumberland, MD: Hobby House, 1989.

From Ayer Company Publishers, Inc., P.O. Box 958, Salem, NH 03079, (603) 898–1200:

Jay Anderson. *The Living History Source Book*. Lists organizations and suppliers. The association is a private organization that provides grants and specialized information for local museums.

Jay Anderson. *Time Machines—The World of Living History*. About interpreters, experimenters, and reenactors of "living history" who do this for the public.

Elizabeth McClellan. *Historic Dress in America*, Vol. 2. Salem, NH: Ayer Publishing, 1977. Covers 1800 to 1870; expensive, but thorough.

From the American Association for State and Local History, Suite 102, 172 Second Avenue, Nashville, TN 37201:

A Lady. *The Workwoman's Guide*. Guilford, CT: Opus, 1986. Facsimile from 1838 on needlework of all kinds.

Linda Otto Lipsett. *To Love and to Cherish: Brides Remembered*. Gualala, CA: Quilt Digest Press, 1989. To order, write or call: Quilt Digest Press, P.O. Box 1331, Gualala, CA 95445, (707) 884–4100.

Other titles:

Janet Arnold. *Patterns of Fashion: Eighteen Sixty to Nineteen Forty*. New York: Drama Books, 1977. Includes patterns and instructions; historical patterns adapted to fit the modern figure.

François Boucher. *20,000 Years of Fashion: The History of Costume and Personal Adornment*. New York: Harry N. Abrams, 1967.

Wolfgang Bruhn. *A Pictorial History of Costume*. New York: Crown, 1988.

Millia Davenport. *The Book of Costume*. New York: Crown, 1964. Goes up to 1867; includes wonderful photographs of clothing and accessories from museum collections. 3,000 illustrations.

Therese de Dillmont. *Encyclopedia of Victorian Needlework*. New York: Crescent Books, 1987.

Denise Dreher. *From the Neck Up: An Illustrated Guide to Hatmaking*. Minneapolis, MN: Madhatter Press, 1981. Available from Madhatter Press, P.O. Box 7480, Minneapolis, MN 55407, (612) 822–1102.

Alison Gernsheim. *Victorian and Edwardian Fashion: A Photographic Survey*. Mineola, NY: Dover, 1963.

The Ladies' Self Instructor in Millinery & Mantua Making,

Embroidery & Appliqué, Canvas-work, Knitting, Netting and Crochet-work. Mendocino, CA: R. L. Shep, 1988. This 1853 reprint reflects the dressmaking and needlework techniques of the less well-to-do.

Margot Lister. *Costume: An Illustrated Survey from Ancient Times to the 20th Century*. Plays, Inc., 1968.

Eileen MacIntosh. *Sewing and Collecting Vintage Fashions*. Radnor, PA: Chilton, 1988. Includes entire chapter on buying wearable vintage fashions.

These titles may be available from your local library. Some are available for purchase from the following sources:

AMAZON DRYGOODS
2218 East Eleventh Street
Davenport, IA 52803
(319) 322–6800; fax (309) 786–3504

DOVER PUBLICATIONS, INC.
31 East Second Street
Mineola, NY 11501

R. L. SHEP
Box 668
Mendocino, CA 95460

Another important source for reprints of Victorian and Edwardian tailoring, costume, and needle arts books. Free brochure.

WOODEN PORCH BOOKS
Box 262
Middlebourne, WV 26149

Out-of-print books books and magazines relating to fashion and fiber arts. Catalog.

Magazines and Newsletters

CUTTERS' RESEARCH JOURNAL
c/o Krannert Center for the Performing Arts
University of Illinois at Urbana-Champaign
500 South Goodwin Avenue
Urbana, IL 61801

Quarterly publication with information on patterning, construction, etc. Comes with annual membership.

THREADS

The Taunton Press
63 South Main Street
P.O. Box 5506
Newtown, CT 06470–5506
(203) 426–8171

A beautifully photographed, informative magazine on all aspects of fiber arts and fashion.

VINTAGE CLOTHING NEWSLETTER

P.O. Box 1422
Corvallis, OR 97339

Six issues a year cover all aspects of vintage clothing.

VINTAGE FASHIONS

Hobby House Press Inc.
900 Frederick Street
Cumberland, MD 21502
(301) 759–4940; fax (301) 759–4940

Magazine covering all aspects of vintage clothing, from re-creating to collecting; lots of how-to articles.

For a booklet from the Sewing Fashion Council on how to design your own gown, with fabric selection and sewing tips, write to:

THE SEWING FASHION COUNCIL

"Wedding Belles"
P.O. Box 431M
Madison Square Station
New York, NY 10010

PATTERNS

AMAZON DRYGOODS

See address and phone information under "Books and Publications"; carries most of the pattern companies listed here in one comprehensive catalog. Request the "Pattern Catalog," because their "General Catalog" is separate.

BRIDAL ELEGANCE

408 South Rock Boulevard
Sparks, NV 89431
(702) 359–1110

Create your own wedding gown from separate patterns for bodices, skirts, sleeves, etc. Brochure.

CAMPBELL'S

R.D. 1, Box 1444
Herndon, PA 17830
(717) 425–2045

Carries Past Patterns and Old World Enterprises, as well as books and stationery. Catalog.

FAIR WINDS PATTERN COMPANY

819 North June Street
Hollywood, CA 90038

1900 to 1945; all drafted from actual historical garments. Catalog.

FOLKWEAR PATTERNS

The Taunton Press
63 South Main Street
P.O. Box 5506
Newtown, CT 06470–5506
(203) 426–8171

These wonderful patterns were recently saved from extinction by the Taunton Press, also publisher of Threads magazine. Adapted to modern figures and use. Catalog.

LACIS

2982 Adeline Street
Berkeley, CA 94703
(415) 843–7178

Uses the Block Pattern System; has complete catalog of needlework tools and books, lace, and lacemaking supplies.

OLD WORLD ENTERPRISES

29036 Kepler Court
Cold Spring, MN 56320

"Original creations that faithfully represent the prevalent fashion trends of each 19th Century period." Each pattern includes complete sewing instructions, from construction techniques to detailing; suggestions for proper fabric and color selection; and informative background on period fashion trends.

PAST PATTERNS

P.O. Box 7587
Grand Rapids, MI 49510
(616) 245–9456

Request the catalog specifically for 1830–1939. The owner, Sandra, can answer your questions relating to historical costume. Catalog includes wedding gowns from 1885 and 1907, and a 1900 princess gown that could easily be used for a wedding. Has undergarment patterns, corsets, and corset kits.

PATTERNS OF HISTORY

State Historical Society of Wisconsin
816 State Street
Madison, WI 53706

Authentic nineteenth-century patterns from 1835 to 1896, including a wedding dress from 1865 and several dresses that could be adapted from other decades.

PRAIRIE CLOTHING CO.

3732 Tanager Drive NE
Cedar Rapids, IA 52402
(319) 378–0125

Catalog.

FABRIC

AMAZON DRYGOODS

See listing under "Books and Publications."

DONNA LEE'S SEWING CENTER

25234 Pacific Highway South
Kent, WA 98032
(206) 941–9466
Order line: (800) 87–DONNA

Swiss batiste, imperial batiste, China silk, silk charmeuse, French val laces, English laces, ribbons, and trims. Specializes in imported fabrics and laces for heirloom dresses; also source for books on French handsewing, smocking, and doll clothing. Catalog.

GLADSTONE FABRICS

P.O. Box 566
Orchard Hill Road
Harriman, NY 10926–0566
(914) 783–1900

Source for theatrical, novelty, and costume fabrics and antique trims and beading. Catalog and retail.

HOMESPUN FABRICS AND DRAPERIES

P.O. Box 3223
Ventura, CA 93006
(805) 642–8111

Mail order only; 100-percent cotton fabrics. Good source for liners for vintage clothing.

LACIS

See listing under "Patterns."

KATHLEEN B. SMITH

Textile Reproductions
P.O. Box 48
West Chesterfield, MA 01084

Provide historically accurate textile to museums, needleworkers, and historic clothiers. Mostly eighteenth century, but has some fabrics useful to nineteenth-century re-creation. Catalog available.

SOUTHERN FABRICS

1210 Galleria Mall
Houston, TX 77056
(713) 626–5511

Imported velvets and silks, bengaline faille, moire faille, taffeta, polyester satin and shantique, silk face satin, silk taffeta, and silk doupioni in white and ivory. Catalog and retail.

ACCESSORIES AND UNDERGARMENTS

MARY ELLEN & COMPANY

29400 Rankert Road
North Liberty, IN 46554
(800) 669–1860; (219) 656–3000

Sewing tools, hats, fans, shoes, gloves, and parasols.

RAIMENTS

3345 East Miraloma
Suite 134
Anaheim, CA 92806

Corset kits, hoops, bustles, hat-making patterns, and supplies; distributes patterns from other companies. Catalog.

VICTORIAN DAINTIES

Box 492162
Redding, CA 96049

Camisoles, French drawers, chemises, petticoats, and night-gowns. Write for free catalog.

See also Amazon Drygoods, under "Books and Publications."

PEOPLE WHO MAKE REPRODUCTION CLOTHING

LINDA L. ASHFORD

91 Page Road
Bow, NH 03304
(603) 224–8485

"A Victorian seamstress," Linda also does consulting and sells patterns. Brochure.

HARRIET A. ENGLER

P.O. Box 1363
Winchester, VA 22601
(703) 667–2541

Tailoring and custom sewing by a highly recommended pro. Costumes, uniforms, authentic reproductions, even rentals. Catalog.

KATRINA OJHA

67 Moriches Drive
Mastic Beach, NY 11951
(516) 395–1880

Custom-designed handmade wedding gowns, bridesmaids' dresses, and headpieces. Works with customers from out of town using a detailed measurement sheet and by making a mock-up of the dress in cotton, which is then fitted and used to make the final version.

RAIMENTS

See listing under "Accessories and Undergarments."

Mela of Raiments has made many Victorian dresses, including a $6,000 beaded ballgown with accessories. She says the average reproduction wedding dress runs about $2,000.

VINTAGE GOWNS FOR SALE OR RENT

THE AMHERST MUSEUM

Colony Park
3755 Tonawanda Creek Road
East Amherst, NY 14051

A unique collection of heirloom bridal gowns circa 1860–1960 available for rental. Consultant and/or restoration service available to brides interested in wearing vintage ensembles. For appointment, call (716) 689–1440 or fax (716) 689–1409.

BIRD-N'-HAND ANTIQUES

221 West Grandview Parkway
Northport, MI 49670
(616) 386–7104

Vintage clothing and accessories. Will work by mail or phone.

DESIGNER'S ARMOIRE

49 Union Street
Newton Centre, MA 02159
(617) 244–7737

Restored antique gowns and dresses and custom-designed headpieces. Will send items by mail for approval.

NANCY GUZZETTA

Antiques at Trader's Cove
230 Trader's Cove
Port Jefferson, NY 11777
(516) 331–2261

Antique and reproduction props and clothing for rent; consulting; has outfitted entire wedding parties.

READY-MADE GOWNS AND REPRODUCTIONS

ELAINE'S

513 Lafayette Street
Cape May, NJ 08204
(609) 884–1199

Full-service bridal salon specializing in Victorian styles from top manufacturers, enhanced by custom-made headpieces, hats, shoes, and other accessories. Also will restore vintage dresses, arrange receptions, and make dried floral bouquets and arrangements. Bridal consultants and millinery available.

JESSICA McCLINTOCK BRIDAL

1400 Sixteenth Street
San Francisco, CA 94103
(800) 888–3801 or (415) 495–3030

Write or call for a catalog and a list of stores near you that carry this romantic bridal line.

MICHELLE'S

3 Salem Street
Nantucket, MA 02554
(508) 228–4409
and
58 Depot Road
Box 314
Hollis, NY 03049
(603) 465–3286

Exquisite one-of-a-kind wedding and special-occasion dresses made from antique laces. The Nantucket store is open during summer only.

SUSAN LANE'S COUNTY ELEGANCE

7353 Greenbush Avenue
North Hollywood, CA 91605
New York showroom: (212) 302–5906

Victorian- and Edwardian-inspired gowns and dresses. Consult bridal magazines for locations nearest you or write for brochure and nearest store carrying the Country Elegance line.

SWEET MATERIAL THINGS

P.O. Box 689
Wallkill, NY 12589
(914) 895–2519

Heirloom-quality fabrics made into Victorian, Edwardian, and 1920s wedding gowns that are elegant and affordable. Owner Karyn Sanders also includes in her catalog headpieces, hats, cake toppers, lingerie, wedding albums, parasols, and silver-plated items perfect for attendant gifts. Also has tussy mussies and reproductions of antique wedding and birth certificates.

VERA WANG BRIDAL HOUSE

991 Madison Avenue
New York, NY 10021
(212) 628–3400

WESTMINSTER LACE

(800) 262–LACE

Call for the location of a shop near you. Lovely Victorian cotton and lace blouses that could be coupled with a vintage or reproduction skirt for a simple wedding look.

CONSERVATION SUPPLIES

CHERISH

P.O. Box 941
New York, NY 10024–0941

Does preventative conservation for heirloom textiles and clothing. Send for free brochures.

TALAS

213 West Thirty-fifth Street
New York, NY 10001
(212) 736–7744

Source for conservation supplies and advice.

TECHSTYLES

Suite 654
2210 Wilshire Boulevard
Santa Monica, CA 90403–5784

Has a one-hour video to help you repair and restore vintage garments. Professional seamstress Mary Kinsley will show you how to select, repair, alter, clean, and refurbish garments.

RE-CREATION GROUPS

ASSOCIATION FOR LIVING HISTORICAL FARMS AND AGRICULTURAL MUSEUMS (ALHFAM)

Smithsonian Institution
Washington, DC 20650

Offers regional workshops in living history interpretation; not only agriculturally oriented. Has standing committees on historic clothing, foodways, and interpretation.

THE NORTH-SOUTH SKIRMISH
ASSOCIATION
9700 Royerton Drive
Richmond, VA 23228
(804) 266-0898

Civil War; a group devoted to period firearms, but also authentic period costume, especially military.

SINGLE ACTION SHOOTING SOCIETY
6865 Airport Drive
Riverside, CA 92504

Although a Western shooting group, its period is technically Victorian and some members sew their own costumes, including women's dresses.

THE SOCIETY FOR CREATIVE
ANACHRONISM
P.O. Box 743
Milpitas, CA 95035

Medieval re-creation group; ask for the name of your local contact. Local "baronies" and "cantons" will be the most helpful. Members can often refer you to skilled garment makers or help with sources.

GENERAL ORGANIZATIONS

THE COSTUME SOCIETY OF AMERICA
55 Edgewater Drive
P.O. Box 73
Earleville, MD 21919
(301) 275-2329

Collects and disseminates information on the preservation, interpretation, and exhibition of costume. Provides referrals for the identification and conservation of individual pieces. Publishes a quarterly newsletter and Dress, an annual scholarly journal.

THE VICTORIAN SOCIETY IN AMERICA
219 South Sixth Street
Philadelphia, PA 19106
(215) 627-4252

Holds symposiums, meeting, tours; also has summer schools and publications. A companion organization to the Victorian Society in Great Britain.

CHAPTER 4: Members and Guests

BOOKS AND PUBLICATIONS

Many of the costume and sewing books (as well as other sources) already listed for chapter 3 will help you with clothing for the men in your wedding, your other attendants, and guests. These are some additional books:

Janet Burgess. *Clothing Guidelines for the Civil War Era.* (Available from Amazon Drygoods; see listing for chapter 3, under "Books and Publications.")

Louis Devere. *The Handbook of Practical Cutting on the Centre Point System (1866).* Mendocino, CA: R. L. Shep, 1986. On tailoring men's garments, all types, some ladies' and boys', and some military garments; 350 model patterns and diagrams.

Men's Fashion Illustrations from the Turn of the Century (available from Dover Publications; see listing for chapter 3).

Norah Waugh. *The Cut of Men's Clothes, 1600–1900.* New York: Theatre Arts Books, 1964.

ACCESSORIES

High-laced men's and boy's shoes and spats, as well as period hats, available from Amazon Drygoods (see listing for chapter 3).

For women's accessories, see sources for chapter 3, under "Accessories and Undergarments."

PATTERNS

See sources for chapter 3, under "Patterns"; most of the catalogs have patterns for men's clothing.

VINTAGE CLOTHING

ANTIQUES AT TRADER'S COVE
(See listing under chapter 3, "Vintage and Reproduction Gowns for Loan, Sale, or Rent.")

Ready-Made Clothing

AMAZON DRYGOODS

(See listing under chapter 3.) Offers readymade men's shirts and vests.

THE MILLINERY SHOP

Kari Geiger
P.O. Box 135
Grand Island, NE 68802
(308) 382–2229

A Civil War reenactor and "sutler," Kari sells patterns, finished garments, fabrics, laces, men's and women's hats, jewelry, sewing notions, gloves, feathers, linens, shoes, and some items for restoring old shuttle sewing machines. A unique service she provides is to help customers put together men's garb from used tuxedos and accessories.

NEW COLUMBIA

P.O. Box 524
Charleston, IL 61920
(217) 348–5927

Custom-fitted Civil War military uniforms. Uses authentic patterns drafted from originals. Catalog.

VICTORIAN DREAM

222 Gentry
Spring, TX 77373
(713) 350–8518

Child's Cluny lace and moire jumper and Battenburg lace blouse; in adult sizes also. Call for information.

See also sources for bridal dresses in chapter 3 of the appendix. Many have clothing appropriate for the rest of the bridal party.

Attendant Gifts

ANNA GRABER ORIGINALS, LTD.

182 Warwick Avenue
Staten Island, NY 10314–4312
(718) 698–0087

Sachet pillows, heirloom photo albums, satin hangers, and other lacy personal gifts.

ANTIOCH BOOKPLATES

(800) 543–2397

Bookplates and bookmarks. Call for the location nearest you.

THE ENCHANTED VICTORIAN

Attn: Bob Heimanson
11460 Christy Avenue
Lakeview Terrace, CA 91342

Antique-style silver-plated comb, brush, and mirror sets. Brochure of Victorian giftware.

EX LIBRIS

(800) 637–8728

Bookplates. Catalog.

G. E. WILSON DESIGNS

6412 Orbit Way
Ft. Collins, CO 80525
(303) 226–22339

Antiqued, solid brass charm jewelry. Brochure.

THE HEIRLOOM COLLECTION

P.O. Box 147
Plainfield, NJ 07060
(201) 561–1286

Victorian-inspired jewelry and accessories, reasonably priced. Catalog.

HENRIETTA'S BEADING SUPPLY CO., INC.

19 Indiancreek Road
Matawan, NJ 07747
(908) 566–3952

If you'd like to string your own beaded jewelry as gifts for your attendants, this is the source; owner Henrietta Virchick has produced a clear and informative video and a book, provides an impressive array of beads and supplies, and will consult with brides about wedding jewelry and gifts. Catalog.

MARCELA CREATIONS

See listing for chapter 1 under "Your Trousseau." Source for attendant gifts such as boxes, sachets, frames, and albums.

ON ANGEL'S WINGS

59 Swaggertown Road
Scotia, NY 12302
(518) 372–5601

Jewelry, accessories, decorations, and keepsakes. Catalog.

PAYNE COLLECTION OF HAND-
CRAFTED FURNITURE
P.O. Box 2058
Clarksville, IN 47131
(800) 688–9198

Rose-embellished lap desks perfect for filling with stationery and supplies. Free brochure.

For stationery sources, see listings for chapter 2, "Stationery and Invitations."

Period games and toys for children can be ordered from Amazon Drygoods; see listing for chapter 3, under "Books and Publications."

For stationery and rubber stamp sources for gift baskets, see listings for chapter 2.

The following books make good attendant gifts:

National Trust and the West Country Tourist Board. *Book of Afternoon Tea*, ed. Marika Hanbury Tenison. New York: David & Charles, 1987. Order from David & Charles Inc. at (800) 423-4525. Add this to a basket you've prepared for your attendants filled with English tea, cups and saucers, and scones or crumpets.

Barbara Milo Ohrbach. "A Token of Friendship." Clarkson Potter, 1987. Add this to baskets you've made up for your attendants.

PHOTO RESTORATION AND DISPLAY

ELBINGER LABORATORIES, INC.
220 Albert Street
East Lansing, MI 48823
(517) 332-1430

Museum-quality "archival" reproductions and restorations of your heirloom photographs. Brochure.

EXPOSURES
2800 Hoover Road
Stevenspoint, WI 54481
(800) 222–4947

Unusual frames, albums, and photo filing systems. Catalog.

CHAPTER 5: A Place to Wed

BOOKS AND OTHER PUBLICATIONS

Allison Kyle Leopold. *Cherished Objects: Living with and Collecting Victoriana*. New York: Clarkson Potter, 1991.

Barbara Norfleet. *Wedding*. New York: Fireside, 1979.

Elizabeth Pomada and Michael Larsen. *Painted Ladies: San Francisco's Resplendent Victorians*, 1978; *Daughters of Painted Ladies: America's Resplendent Victorians*, 1987; and *The Painted Ladies Revisited: San Francisco's Resplendent Victorians Inside and Out*, 1989.

PLACES
Tenth House Enterprises, Inc.
Caller Box 810
Gracie Station
New York, NY 10028

"A Directory of Public Places for Private Events & Private Places for Public Functions"; updated regularly.

GAMES AND ENTERTAINMENTS

Cornelius Agrippa. *The Ladies' Oracle*. Farrar, Straus and Giroux, 1933. English edition published in 1857. An oracle consulted on matters of love and life as a popular parlor fortune-telling game.

Vernon Bartlett. *The Past of Pastimes*. Hamden, CT: Archon Books, 1969.

Jack Botermans et al. *The World of Games: Their Origin and History*. New York: Facts on File, 1989.

US GAMES SYSTEMS INC.
179 Ludlow Street
Stamford, CT 06902

Victorian-design playing cards.

Chapter 6: Romantic Repasts

Books and Publications

Adrian Bailey. *Mrs. Bridges' Upstairs, Downstairs Cookery Book*. New York: Simon & Schuster, 1974.

Mrs. Isabella Beeton, ed. *Beeton's Book of Household Management*. London: S.O. Beeton, 1861.

Isabella Beeton. *Mrs. Beeton's Victorian Cookbook*. Edited by Simon Rigge. Topsfield, MA: Salem House, 1988.

Elizabeth David. *An Omelette and a Glass of Wine*. New York: Viking, 1985.

Janet Halliday Ervin, ed. *The White House Cookbook*. Chicago: Follett Publishing, 1964.

John Crosby Freeman. *Victorian Entertaining*. Philadelphia: Running Press/Friedman Group, 1989.

Iris Ihde Frey. *Crumpets and Scones*. New York: St. Martin's Press, 1982.

Marilyn Hansen. *Entertaining in the Victorian Style*. New York: E.P. Dutton, 1990. Includes recipes adapted to modern ingredients and methods plus information on decor and table settings.

Angela Hynes. *The Pleasures of Afternoon Tea*. New York: HP Books, 1987.

Joanna Isles. *A Proper Tea*. New York: St. Martin's Press, 1987.

Edita Lausanne. *The Great Book of Wine*. New York: Galahad Books, 1970.

National Trust and West Country Tourist Board. *Book of Afternoon Tea*, edited by Marika Hanbury Tenison. David & Charles, 1980. To order, call David & Charles, Inc. at (800) 423–4525.

Sandra Oddo. *Home Made*. New York: Atheneum, 1972.

Irma S. Rombauer and Marion Rombauer Becker. *The Joy of Cooking*. New York: Bobbs-Merrill, 1931. Regularly updated.

Oscar Tschirky. *The Cook Book by "Oscar" of the Waldorf*. Chicago: Saalfield Publishing, 1896.

Susan Williams. *Savory Suppers and Fashionable Feasts: Dining in Victorian America*. New York: Pantheon Books, in association with the Strong Museum, 1985.

Linda Wolfe. *The Literary Gourmet: Menus from Masterpieces*. New York: Harmony Books, 1985.

Edible Flowers

FOX HILL FARMS
444 West Michigan Avenue, Box 9
Parma, MI 49269
(517) 531–3179
Fresh roses untreated with preservatives for cooking.

GOOD SCENTS HERB & FLOWER CO.
253 Elser Hill Road
Lititz, PA 17543
(717) 627–3578 *or* 626–5219
Will ship pesticide- and chemical-free flowers overnight, from spring to early fall.

Fresh Herbs, Herb Seeds, Etc.

HERB GATHERING INC.
5742 Kenwood Avenue
Kansas City, MO 64110
(816) 523–2653
Minimum purchases required for orders shipped overnight.

NICHOLS GARDEN NURSERY
1190 North Pacific Highway
Albany, OR 97321
(503) 928–9280; fax: (503) 967–8406
Common and unusual herb and vegetable seeds, bulbs, and plants. Books, flower-pressing equipment, potpourri-making kits, garden implements, and winemaking supplies.

Wedding Cakes

Here are some people who still make elaborate sculptured Victorian wedding cakes:

CILE BELLEFLEUR BURBIDGE
12 Stafford Road
Danvers, MA 01923
(508) 774–3514

JAN KISH
La Petite Fleur
P.O. Box 872
Worthington, OH
(614) 841–9794 or 444–6766

Jan Kish's custom-made cakes are works of art. Ships by airline all over the country; featured in national bridal and food magazines. She is also available for travel if work needs to be done on location.

LE ROYALE ICING
329 South Ridgeland Avenue
Oak Park, IL 60302
(708) 386–4175 (by appointment only)

Brochure.

Cake Toppers

LILLIAN ROSE COLLECTIONS
See listing for chapter 2, under "Wedding Guest Books."

THE PINK ROSE PASTRY SHOP
630 South Fourth Street
Philadelphia, PA 19147
(215) 592–0565

SWEET MATERIAL THINGS
Line of antique reproduction cake toppers; see listing for chapter 3, under "Ready-Made Gowns."

Foods and Beverages

BEST FRIENDS COCOA
P.O. Box 157
Newtown Highlands, MA 02161
(617) 969–5240

Wonderful instant cocoa in a variety of flavors: amaretto, raspberry truffle, mint, mocha, spice, and traditional.

THE ROSEMARY HOUSE, INC.
120 South Market Street
Mechanicsburg, PA 17055
(717) 697–5111

Mint molds, extracts, and wreath and other herbal crafts supplies. Catalog.

ROSE TREE COTTAGE
824 East California Boulevard
Pasadena, CA 91106
(818) 793–3337

Tea and accessories; scones and other baked goods. Catalog.

A TASTE OF BRITAIN
P.O. Box 1044-V
Norcross, GA 30091
(800) 735–3751, ext. 102

Marmalades, biscuits, teas, pickles, soups, puddings, meat pies, candies, and more. Gift items, including food hampers. Catalog.

Chapter 7: Flowers That Speak of Love

Books and Publications

Penny Black. *The Book of Potpourri*, 1989; and *The Book of Pressed Flowers*, 1988. New York: Simon & Schuster.

Roberta Moffitt. *Step-by-Step Book of Preserving Flowers* and *Step-by-Step Book of Dried Bouquets*. Ordering address: P.O. Box 3597, Wilmington, DE 19807.

Jane Newdick. *The Five-Minute Flower Arranger*. New York: Crown, 1989.

Barbara Milo Orbach. *A Bouquet of Flowers*. New York: Clarkson Potter, 1991.

Sheila Pickles, ed. *The Language of Flowers*, 1990; and *A Victorian Posy*, 1987. New York: Harmony Books.

Bertha Reppert. *The Bride's Herbal*. Mechanicsburg, PA: Remembrance Press, 1989. Available from Remembrance Press, 120 South Market Street, Mechanicsburg, PA 17055, (717) 697–5111.

Jeri Schwartz. *Tussie Mussies: Victorian Posey Holders*. Order from Tussie Mussies, Box 271, Hartsdale, NY 10530.

Mrs. William Dana Starr. *How to Know the Wild Flowers*. Boston: Houghton Mifflin, 1989. First published in 1893, it is full of quotes from writers and poets of the age, along with details of the author's adventures in tracking down American wildflowers.

The Herb Quarterly
P.O. Box 548
Boiling Springs, PA 17007
Magazine devoted exclusively to herbs: growing and using them, plus lots of herb lore and history.

Potpourri Party-Line
Dody Lyness, Editor
Berry Hill Press
7336 Berry Hill
Palos Verdes Peninsula, CA 90274
(213) 377-7040
Quarterly newsletter on floral and herb arranging and crafts. Year's subscription and back issues available. Dody's book Potpourri . . . Easy as One, Two, Three! *is a clear, simple guide for making potpourri.*

HERBS AND SPICES

OAK TREE HERB FARM
RR 1, Box 135-B
Rising Sun, IN 47040
(812) 438-3742

SAN FRANCISCO HERB COMPANY
250 Fourteenth Street
San Francisco, CA 94103
(800) 227-4530, outside California; (800) 622-0768, California only

Spices, herbs, and potpourri supplies. If you request their price list, you'll get free recipes for potpourri, simmering potpourri, herbal blends and extracts, and sachets.

TUSSY MUSSIES

PAINTING WITH FLOWERS
298 Main Street
Port Washington, NY 11050

Store proprietor Gail Silver offers silver-plate and sterling posey holders with or without dried flowers, as well as other Victorian floral accessories and gifts.

TUSSIE MUSSIES
Box 395
Silverado, CA 92676
(714) 649-2144

Both hand-held and lapel versions. Also sells potpourri, sachets, and other gifts. Catalog.

PRESSED FLOWER SPECIALISTS

GOLD LEAF DESIGNS
15 Elaine Drive
Moodus, CT 06469
(203) 873-8290

Provides a styrofoam container and freeze-ahead ice pack for mailing your bouquet overnight.

FREEZE-DRIED FLOWER SPECIALISTS

JEANETTE CZERWINSKI
PRESERVE THE MEMORIES
P.O. Box 351
Marion, CT 06444
(203) 620-0477

MELANY MOORE
SHANEL'S SPRING
266 East Campbell Avenue
Campbell, CA 95008
(408) 378-8096

To find a freeze-dried flower specialist near you, contact the International Freeze-Dry Floral Association, P.O. Box 71272, Clive, IA 50325, (515) 226-9225.

PRESERVED FLORAL ARRANGEMENTS

SURA KAYLA
484 Broome Street
New York, NY 10013
(212) 941-8757

Well-known floral designer, featured regularly in magazines; Sura's shop is a delight.

A VICTORIAN GARDEN
P.O. Box 673
366 Hebron Avenue
Glastonbury, CT 06033
(203) 657–4933

Ships your wedding flowers overnight and has them made into a wreath, swag, or arrangement; best drying techniques are used for each flower and herb. Brochure.

SHADOW BOXES

MEMORIES TO HEIRLOOMS
1310A Los Robles Boulevard
Sacramento, CA 95838

Also portrait lights and Victorian picture hangers. Brochure.

CHAPTER 8: Music and Entertainment

BOOKS AND PUBLICATIONS

Gerald Abraham. *A Hundred Years of Music.* London: Duckworth, 1938.

John Tasker Howard and George Kent Bellows. *A Short History of Music in America.* New York: Crowell, 1957.

Arthur Hutchings. *Church Music in the Nineteenth Century.* New York: Oxford University Press, 1967.

VINTAGE DANCE SOCIETIES & SCHOOLS

COMMONWEALTH VINTAGE DANCERS
39 Capen Streeet
Medford, MA 02155
(617) 396-2870

Consults on vintage balls nationwide.

WALTER AND NANCYANNA DILL
Suite 168
2442 Northwest Market Street
Seattle, WA 98107
(206) 781–1238

Instructors, specializing in early nineteenth-century dance.

ELM CITY VINTAGE DANCERS
c/o 114 Layton Street
West Hartford, CT 06110

Offer workshops, demonstrations, and instructions at events. Victorian costume.

FLYING CLOUD ACADEMY
3623 Herschel Avenue
Cincinnati, OH 45208
(513) 321–4878

Vintage dance school run by dance researcher and historian Richard Powers; one week of intensive study, then a grand soiree.

ROBERT MORRIS AND KATHERINE TERZI
86 East Stewart Avenue
Lansdowne, PA 19050
(215) 259–1642

Dance teachers and historians. Offer instruction, demonstration, and workshops; will create balls or dances with musicians and period garb.

THE VINTAGE DANCE SOCIETY
P.O. Box 832
Bloomfield, CT 06002
(203) 286–9191

Will coordinate, arrange, or provide information on period music, dance, costumes, and ballroom etiquette; holds performances, workshops, and seminars. Will travel. Has brochure. For consulting, call Marc Casslar, director.

PLAYER PIANOS

RAGTIME AUTOMATED MUSIC OF VERMONT
P.O. Box 138
Poultney, VT 05764
(802) 287-5717

Sells and restores antique player pianos, music boxes, and nickelodeons; also has rentals. Has a complete selection of player piano music on cassette. Owner John Ashback will refer you to a company near you that offers similar services if you call or write him.

Chapter 9: A Month of Sweetness

Bridal Tour

Alice Cromie. *A Tour Guide to the Civil War* and *A Tour Guide to the Old West*. Nashville, TN: Rutledge Hill Press, both updated in 1990.

Seaside Resorts

CORONADO CHAMBER OF COMMERCE
1090 Seventh Street
Coronado, CA 92118-2112
(800) 622–8300 *or* (619) 437–8788

HOTEL DEL CORONADO
1500 Orange Avenue
Coronado, CA 92118
(800) 522–3088

Victorian Costume Holiday

MOHONK MOUNTAIN HOUSE
Lake Mohonk
New Paltz, NY 12561
(914) 255–4500

Ask about their Victorian Holiday weekend.

Cozy Bed-and-Breakfasts

Suzanne Dane and Barbara Sturni. *Feather Beds and Flapjacks: A Preservationist's Guide to Historic Bed and Breakfasts, Inns and Small Hotels.* The Preservation Press, National Trust for Historic Preservation, 1785 Massachusetts Avenue, NW, Washington, DC 20036.

AMERICAN BED & BREAKFAST ASSOCIATION AND THE GLOBE PEQUOT PRESS
138 West Main Street
Chester, CT 06412

THE CHATEAU TIVOLI
1057 Steiner Street
San Francisco, CA 94115
(800) 228–1647 *or* (415) 776–5462

THE CHAUTAUQUA INSTITUTION
Chautauqua, NY 14722
(800) 836–ARTS

A call will get you the latest Accommodations Directory, the Chautauqua Summer School schedule, calendars of events, and a vacation brochure. For information about the surrounding area, request a Chautauqua-Allegheny Travel Guide by calling (800) 242–4569.

THE JULIAN HOTEL
P.O. Box 856
Julian, CA 92036
(714) 765–0201

A small, charming B & B hotel from gold-rush days in the California hills, with a separate honeymoon cottage.

NORUMBEGA
61 High Street
Camden, ME 04843
(207) 236–4646

Grand Hotels

THE ADELPHI HOTEL
365 Broadway
Saratoga Springs, NY 12866
(518) 587–4688

GRAND HOTEL
Mackinac Island, MI 49757
(906) 847-3347
In Winter:
31181 Kendall Drive
Fraser, MI 48026
(313) 293-0600

GREATER SARATOGA CHAMBER OF
COMMERCE
494 Broadway
Saratoga Springs, NY 12866
(518) 584-3255

MACKINAC ISLAND CHAMBER OF
COMMERCE
P.O. Box 451
Mackinac Island, MI 49757

View From the Veranda: History and Architecture of
the Summer Cottages on Mackinac Island *is available
from the Mackinac Island State Park Commission, Dept.
A, Mackinac Island, Michigan 49757.*

MISSISSIPPI RIVERBOAT HOLIDAY

THE DELTA QUEEN STEAMBOAT
COMPANY
Robin Street Wharf
New Orleans, LA 70130-1890
(508) 586-0631
*To book, contact your travel agent or call (800) 543-1949.
Free brochure.*

ST. LAWRENCE CRUISE LINES, INC.
253 Ontario Street
Kingston, Ontario
Canada K7L2Z4
(800) 267-7868
Call or write for free brochure or contact your travel agent.

CHAPTER 10: A Home for the Two of You

BOOKS AND PUBLICATIONS

Harvey Green. *The Light of the Home: An Intimate View of
the Lives of Women in Victorian America.* New York: Pantheon, 1983.

Allison Kyle Leopold. *Victorian Splendor, Recreating
America's 19th Century Interiors.* Stewart, Tabori &
Chang, 1986; and *Cherished Objects: Living with and Collecting Victoriana.* Clarkson Potter, 1991.

Peg B. Sinclair. *Victorious Victorians.* New York: Holt,
1985.

Samuel Sloan. *Sloane's Victorian Buildings.* New York:
Dover, 1980.

Country Victorian Accents
P.O. Box 471
Mt. Morris, IL 61054-7924
*Quarterly magazine covering "decorating ideas, kitchens,
baths, windows, walls, romance, nostalgia, antiques,
food, gardening, inns."*

Traditional Home
1716 Locust Street
P.O. Box 11445
Des Moines, IA 50380-1445
*This monthly magazine covers traditional style, including
Victorian.*

Victoria
P.O. Box 7150
Red Oak, IA 51591
Monthly magazine devoted to the "Return to Loveliness."

Victorian Homes
8900 Renovator's Old Mill
Millers Falls, MA 01349
*Monthly magazine aimed at those restoring Victorian-era
homes.*

Victorian Sampler
P.O. Box 344
Mount Morris, IL 61054-0344
Quarterly magazine on Victorian-style decorating, collectibles, restoration, gardening, and crafts.

LACE CURTAINS AND ACCESSORIES

The following sources offer catalogs.

LINEN LADY
5360 H Street
Sacramento, CA 95819
(916) 457-6718

LONDON LACE
167 Newbury Street
Boston, MA 02116
(617) 267–3506

RUE DE FRANCE
78 Thames Street
Newport, RI 02840
(800) 777–0998

WOVEN WATERS
HC-73 Box 193E
Cincinnatus Lake
Route 41
Willet, NY 13863
(607) 656–8672

Home Furnishings and Accessories

CARTER CANOPIES
P.O. Box 808
Troutman, NC 28166
(704) 528-4071

Six designs of custom-made canopies. Also coverlets, bedspreads, and dust ruffles. Brochure.

LAURA ASHLEY HOME
Laura Ashley, Inc.
1300 MacArthur Boulevard
Mahwah, NJ 07430
(800) 223-6917

Furniture, fabric, curtains, bedcoverings, furniture, housewares, and accessories. Bridal registry. Catalog.

LAVENDER & LACE
656 North Larchmont Boulevard
Los Angeles, CA 90004
(213) 856–4846

Bedding and accessories. Catalog.

PAPER WHITE, LTD.
P.O. Box 956
Fairfax, CA 94978
(415) 457–7673

Linens and lace.

WINTERTHUR MUSEUM AND GARDENS
Winterthur, DE 19735

Antique reproductions from famous collection. Catalog.

Decorative Ceilings and Ornaments

CHELSEA DECORATIVE METAL COMPANY
9603 Moonlight Street
Houston, TX 77096
(713) 721–9200

Metal ceilings. Has brochure.

CUMBERLAND WOODCRAFT COMPANY, INC.
P.O. Drawer 609
Carlisle, PA 17013
(717) 243–0063

Millwork, architectural trim, and carvings. Catalog.

HICKSVILLE WOODWORKS COMPANY
265 Jerusalem Avenue
Hicksville, NY 11801
(800) 526–6398

Brackets, moldings, roof trim, finials, and porch parts for interior and exterior use. Catalog and newsletter.

LATTICE AND LACE
8235 Northeast Beech Street
Portland, OR 97220

Pickets, knoll posts, and arbors. Catalog.

VINTAGE WOOD WORKS
513 South Adams, #2048
Fredricksburg, TX 78624

Turnings, brackets, and spandrels. Catalog.

J. P. WEAVER & COMPANY
2301 West Victory Boulevard
Burbank, CA 01506
(818) 841–5700

Ornaments. Has brochure and instruction videos.

Folding Screens

VINTAGE FOLDING SCREENS
P.O. Box 2236
Ventura, CA 93001
(805) 652–0292

Frame and wood panels or frame for fabric or lace panels. Brochure.

Stencils

EPOCH DESIGNS
P.O. Box 33
Elwyn, PA 19063

Precut reproductions of original Victorian designs. Catalog.

Hardware

BATHROOM MACHINERIES
Box 1020-X
Murphys, CA 95247
(209) 728–2031

Victorian door and cabinet hardware, towel bars, and stair rods. Catalog.

RENOVATOR'S SUPPLY
5061 Renovator's Old Mill
Millers Falls, MA 01349

Lighting fixtures, hardware, etc. Catalog.

Artwork Reproductions

AROUND THE CORNER
5135 Pheasant Ridge Road
Fairfax, VA 22030
(703) 631–3227

Art reproductions and canvas replicas imported from England. Color catalog.

SCHRADER'S VICTORIAN PRINTS
230 South Abbe Road
Fairview, MI 48621

Brochure.

Miscellaneous

NATIONAL TRUST FOR HISTORIC PRESERVATION (NTHP)
1785 Massachusetts Avenue NW
Washington, DC 20036

For trunk restoration supplies, see listing under chapter 1.

CREDITS

Cover: pressed flower picture courtesy of Gold Leaf Designs, 15 Elaine Drive, Moodus, Connecticut. All other cover photos appear elsewhere in text.

Pages viii–1, 122: sterling silver brush and mirror and cameo courtesy of Jana Starr, Jean Hoffman Antiques; headpiece courtesy of Chapeau Carine, 47 Irving Place, New York City, 212-529-4238

Pages 44–45: wedding gown courtesy of Jana Starr, Jean Hoffman Antiques

Page 55: hat pins courtesy of Chapeau Carine, 47 Irving Place, New York City, 212-529-4238

Pages 94–95, 126: cake platter courtesy of Wolfman Gold and Good Company (Bridal Registry, 212-431-1888); tea service and forks courtesy of Claire Eisner Antiques, 870 Lexington Avenue, New York City; other platters courtesy of Imported French Faience From Segries At Solanee, 866 Lexington Avenue, New York City; tablecloth and napkins courtesy of Anichini, 745 Fifth Avenue, 800-553-5309

Page 114: armchair, candle holder, and mirror courtesy of Claire Eisner Antiques, 870 Lexington Avenue, New York City

Page 136: silver tray, napkins and holders, cheese board, pig platters, silver servers, and crudité basket courtesy of Wolfman Gold and Good Company (Bridal Registry, 212-431-1888); knives courtesy of Claire Eisner Antiques, 870 Lexington Avenue, New York City; platters and linen cloth courtesy of Imported French Faience From Segries At Solanee, 866 Lexington Avenue, New York City

Page 144: teacups and plates courtesy of Claire Eisner Antiques, 870 Lexington Avenue, New York City; cake platter courtesy of Wolfman Gold and Good Company (Bridal Registry, 212-431-1888); tablecloth and napkins courtesy of Anichini, 745 Fifth Avenue, 800-553-5309

Page 159: bronze hands courtesy of Jana Starr, Jean Hoffman Antiques

Page 169: armchair and tassels courtesy of Claire Eisner Antiques, 870 Lexington Avenue, New York City

Page 173: preserved flower dome courtesy of Preserve the Memories, P.O. Box 351, Marion, Connecticut

Pages 204–205: bed linens, silk throw, and tapestry courtesy of Anichini, 745 Fifth Avenue, 800-553-5309; breakfast tray setting from Claire Eisner Antiques, 870 Lexington Avenue, New York City

Page 219: all pieces on tray courtesy of Claire Eisner Antiques, 870 Lexington Avenue, New York City

Index

263